Corporate Financial Strategy
and
Decision Making to Increase
Shareholder Value

Harold Bierman Jr.
The Nicholas H. Noyes Professor of Business Administration
Johnson Graduate School of Management
Cornell University

Published by Frank J. Fabozzi Associates

Cover design by Scott C. Riether

ISBN: 1-883249-67-8

Printed in the United States of America

Table of Contents

Preface

In the past 50 years there has been a knowledge explosion in the areas of managerial finance and investment decision making. The literature on business decision making has shifted from a more or less intuitive qualitative approach to one that is much more analytical. Equally important, we can now better define those policies that can be expected to increase a firm's value and those policies which are not likely to increase value.

An analytical approach to financial decisions is useful for two important reasons:

1. The use of analysis (including a mathematical model) may give a specific optimum answer.
2. The use of the model may lead to a better understanding of the decision process, which in turn may lead to a better decision, even where it is not possible to apply the model in an exact fashion and obtain a specific answer.

Analytical models of financial decisions do not replace judgment, but rather they apply the judgment and experience of the decision maker more effectively to the problem studied. Many of the situations with which we deal are decisions made under uncertainty; thus the decision indicated by the model may, after the event has occurred, turn out to be a less desirable alternative than others that were available. This is, of course, a characteristic of decision making under uncertainty. When there is uncertainty there is generally a probability that an event may occur for which there is a better action than the action chosen.

An attempt has been made in this book to interpret financial models and make clear their uses and limitations. Some algebra is used. However, all that is required to understand this book is a little patience with basic mathematics. No understanding of advanced mathematics is required. The financial models generally have been translated into words and supplemented by numerical examples to ensure that the basic principles are understood.

Simplifying assumptions have been made in many places. The reader must evaluate the extent of damage done to the usefulness of each model by the assumptions that are the basis of the model. All model building involves abstracting from the complexities of the real world.

Imagine what would happen if managers tried to incorporate all the consequences of each of their decisions every time they make decisions. Generally, managers focus on the more immediate and apparent consequences of their actions, rather than those which are far removed and difficult to determine. If this book is successful, the reader will continue the search for better ways of analyzing financial decisions. It is a characteristic of written material in the area of finance that it becomes obsolete shortly after publication. This is a price we willingly pay for progress.

Harold Bierman Jr.
Ithaca, New York

v

Chapter 1

Corporate Financial Planning and Strategy

Consider the following three questions that apply to corporate financial planning:

1. What kind of capital financing is desirable and when?
2. How and when should funds be returned to investors?
3. What corporate strategy should be followed relative to growth through product diversification, mergers, and acquisitions?

There are no simple answers to any of the questions, but we can develop some generalizations that will lead to improved financial decision making. There are some situations for which the alternatives may be listed, and we can conclude that one alternative is the best. In other situations, it is necessary to make simplifying assumptions, and we are less sure that the solution resulting from these assumptions holds for real world conditions. One of the most famous and respected finance articles ever published proved that under given conditions the value of a firm was not affected by its capital structure.[1] From that article has flowed an avalanche of useful insights, but the primary conclusion of the paper had to be adjusted for the facts that there are corporate income taxes and investor taxes. With income taxes (or with market imperfections) capital structure decisions do affect the value of a firm. Nevertheless, studying the no tax situation was extremely important because it helped finance scholars to isolate the relevant and nonrelevant factors.

The term "corporate financial planning" correctly implies that future consequences are considered in making decisions today. Improvements in financial decision making will lead to opportunities for improving the wealth position of stockholders. Answers to the three questions are offered. Unfortunately, many of the answers require qualification. The person who requires well-defined exact answers to all questions should not be making decisions in the area of corporate financial planning.

Corporate financial planning also implies that an objective or goal has been set. Throughout the book the appropriateness of different goals is evaluated. There are a variety of objectives for a firm, such as maximization of:

Sales
Share of market

---

[1] Franco Modigliani and Merton H. Miller, "The Cost of Capital, Corporate Finance and the Theory of Investment," *American Economic Review* (June 1958).

Profits or earnings per share
Return on investment
Growth
Stock price
Stockholders' well being

Unfortunately, each of these objectives is deficient in some sense as a guide for managerial action. Although increased sales are good if they lead to increased profits, increased sales (or market share) are not desirable if the sales are "bought" by decreasing the present value of profits. Increased profits are good, but not if the amount of investment necessary to accomplish the increase could have been put to better use by the investor, or if the effect on immediate earnings per share growth is positive, but in the long run would result in a lower growth rate of earnings and a negative net present value. Maintaining a high return on investment (ROI) may be desirable, but not if it is accomplished by rejecting desirable investments that will raise total net income; more on this later. Although "maximization of the stockholders' well being" is somewhat ambiguous and requires further explanation, it comes closest to being the appropriate guide for managerial action.

DECISION MAKING AND FINANCIAL DECISIONS

It comes as no surprise that managers make decisions and that many financial executives make good decisions. Why study the subject of financial decision making? You should remember that long ago there was an ancestor of yours, with a native intelligence that matched yours, who did not know of the wheel. That which is a brilliant innovation, a result of rare genius, becomes available to great numbers of people though the interpretative medium of books. Hopefully by studying financial decision making we can increase the likelihood of making "good" decisions. We can improve decision making by improving our general understanding and approach to the decision process and by improving our techniques for approaching specific decisions.

We want to have a decision process that is "most effective" and likely to lead to decisions that are consistent with the goals of the organization. Why do we not choose *the* correct decision? Given a suitably powerful forecasting device (always correct in its prognostications), we could make many more correct decisions. Unfortunately, our ability to forecast the future of economic affairs is very limited.

This book is oriented to business firms organized to make profits. However, to describe the primary goal of any business corporation as the maximization of profits is to simplify excessively. The measure of profits presented to the managers and stockholders is generally a very inadequate measure of the change in well-being of the corporation, and if the goal is to maximize this measure the stockholders are apt to be short-changed. For example, the conventional account-ing measure of income omits the opportunity cost of the funds utilized in an investment. The measure of profits might be increasing through time and the stockholders' position improving, but their position might increase even more if the earnings were distributed to them and they were able to invest the funds out-side the firm.

Financial accountants are scorekeepers. They report on where the firm is now and how it has performed through time. In a manner similar to that of athletic games, the method of scoring a firm's operations affects how the business game is played. To understand why decisions are made, it is necessary to understand how a decision will affect the well-being of the decision maker. If a desirable decision from the stockholders' viewpoint will adversely affect income as measured by the accountant, a factor has been introduced that amounts to a conflict of interest. Although such devices as stock option plans and incentive bonuses have been used to minimize this conflict, it still exists in many instances.

Businessmen and women have been putting numbers together for the purposes of decision making for centuries. Although we can agree that quantita-tive approaches to decision making are not a recent discovery, it is also true that several developments have accelerated the rate of usage of quantitative methods. For example, consider the advent of the computer and the entry of mathematically trained technicians into business decision making.

Decisions may be classified in numerous ways. First let us consider the frequency of the decision, and divide decisions into two classifications:

1. A unique one-time decision.
2. A repetitive decision with either reasonably constant or randomly spaced time between decisions.

Most unique one-shot decisions are convertible into randomly spaced decisions; however, it is still true that there are many decisions that are unique. They may be repeated, but there is likely to be a large space of time between decisions. A firm may choose a plant site or a new executive vice-president. Those are important decisions, and despite the fact that the firm may make the decisions only once for this particular plant and vice-presidency, it may choose to spend considerable time and effort in making the decisions because of their importance.

Many decisions are repetitive, and the store of information gathered for making the previous decisions may be carried forward and applied to future deci-sions. Complex decisions become routine through familiarity. A New Yorker of average intelligence can choose the correct subway in New York City; visitors of superior intelligence are apt to head off in the wrong direction. The computation of the net present value of an investment and the application of a simple accept or reject decision rule is a complex task for managers the first time they approach the problem. After the fiftieth computation an adventuresome clerk is likely to com-plain of the routine work load.

It is very helpful when we can move a decision from the unique classification to the repetitive classification, for then there is a possibility that we can effectively use information accumulated for similar decisions made in the past. Hopefully we can routinize the decision. However, not all repetitive decisions can be made routine. Repetitive decisions may be classified as to whether or not each decision is unique in some manner. We can imagine a continuous spectrum measuring the different degrees of uniqueness of decisions. The subway decision for the New Yorker going to work is an example of a relatively homogeneous set of repetitive decisions (assuming no special trips requiring special travel plans). A financial executive establishing decision rules for issuing bonds is faced with this same type of repetitive decision.

On the other hand, there are many decisions that although repetitive, are each a little (or greatly) different from previous decisions. The hiring of personnel for managerial jobs or promoting individuals are examples of repetitive but different decisions.

Decisions may also be classified as to the degree of importance of the outcome. If the future existence of the firm hinges on the outcome of a decision, this decision will receive a different degree of consideration than if the decision is apt to affect the level of profit by some small amount. Fortunately for our mental health, most decisions we make are not of crucial importance; that is, no matter how the decisions turn out, the organization will survive and the decision maker will survive also.

Placing the decision in perspective is extremely important. Taking a broad point of view, how important is the decision? Is it worthy of the effort being devoted to its resolution? In technical language, what is the value of additional information and how does the value compare with the cost of obtaining the information?

There are other important characteristics of decision making. We may make an incorrect decision and have it turn out to be correct, that is, we can make a correct decision for the wrong reasons. Because of random events, a well-made and well-researched decision may turn out to be incorrect, or an "incorrect" decision may turn out to be correct. Whenever we deal with decision making under uncertainty, we face the possibility of a "bad" outcome in spite of a correct *a priori* decision.

In evaluating a business plan (a course of action or a set of decisions that have long-run implications where these implications have been considered) before the plan has been implemented, we want to determine whether or not the plan has considered all factors and has effectively brought them into the analysis. After the plans have been executed and we are attempting to evaluate management's performance, it is important to consider the information available to management at the time of setting the plan rather than the information currently available. A mediocre management is likely to be critical in retrospect of others who failed to anticipate the obvious (after the fact). But the crucial question will always be, what do we do now, where we do not yet know what is going to happen in the future?

In the following chapters, we apply basic decision techniques to financial decisions. We see that defining the elements of decision making enables us to grasp better the critical factors that distinguish the consequences of one action compared to another.

Financial Planning

Financial planning is frequently defined as forecasting the amount of cash that will be needed, or will be generated, in the coming time periods. More sophisticated planning systems develop a complete set of financial reports for each set of decisions considered. This type of pro forma accounting is important to a finance officer, but is not the topic of discussion of this book. We assume that if the consequences of a decision can be forecasted, a set of financial statements can be prepared (by hand or by computer) that reflects the consequences of the decision.

The focus of this book is the formulation of financial policy and plans so that the results, based on the given set of assumptions, will tend to maximize the well-being of the investors. We are concerned with establishing financial strategies so that there are guidelines for future decisions.

ELEMENTS OF STRATEGIC PLANNING

We shall consider five elements of the strategic planning. The number one element in developing a strategy is the identification of the problems and opportunities that exist. A successful firm will have a fertile idea-generating environment. Problem and opportunity identification is one of the more important outputs resulting from good strategic planning. You cannot solve a problem or seize an opportunity unless you know it exists.

The second element is to set goals (objectives). Goal setting is not independent of the identification of opportunities. If the goal is to achieve growth in sales of 15% per year, it will be necessary to spend more resources generating ideas than if the goal is to avoid growth. Some would argue that top management should stop with the setting of the goals and leave everything else to the operating managers. For example, top management might set the goals to earn at least a 25% return on investment (ROI), to maintain a 15% growth rate per year, and to corner 20% of the total market as the firm's operating goals. Operating management would then establish the details as to how the goals would be achieved. The results are important, not the method of getting to the results. Performance measurement is substituted for detailed supervision. Thus goal setting becomes a crucially important element in the strategic planning.

We now have problems and goals defined. The third step is to have a procedure to describing possible solutions, or "paths" the firm can follow.

The fourth element of strategic planning is to choose the best solution, given possible solutions and the firm's objectives. The goal might be to maximize the well-being of the stockholders. This is easy to state, but which method should be chosen? It might be decided to choose the path with the largest net present value. But then risk considerations should enter analysis. Choosing the best solution, even with well-defined goals established, is a difficult job.

The fifth and final element of strategic planning is to have some type of review procedures to check how the best solution has actually performed. How this review function is executed will depend on the preferences and style of management.

The above five elements of strategic planning do not reveal anything about the style in which they (and the resulting plans) will be implemented. They are broad enough to encompass a wide range of financial decisions. For example, if the goal is to have reasonable growth but little risk, the amount of risk that is acceptable to the owners of the corporation (or in most large corporations to the board of directors) will greatly affect the amount of debt that is used to finance the corporation.

A major planning question not yet answered is to what extent the interests of the organization come ahead of the interests of the different groups of employees. If you were a college president, would you fire your football coach on Christmas eve? What sort of performance measures will be used, and what happens when goals are not met? Will excuses (explanations) be listened to, or will there be an insistence on performance? A "no excuse" policy is easy to understand. Managerial style will circle back and affect things like idea generation.

An Important Assumption

Throughout this book profit maximization (where profit is defined in terms of risk-adjusted present value and thus includes the cost of the capital used) is deemed to be the primary objective of the firm. More is better. You can assume that the profit maximization objective includes the information cost and cost of search. The assumption is that decisions should be made from the point of view of improving the well-being of the stockholders.

No manager submits an investment or other decision proposal without carefully considering the impact of the decision being reviewed on his or her well-being. The board of directors will consider the well-being of managers if for no other reason than to retain their services. Employees must be considered, since an obvious and continuous disregard of their interests will cause them to protect their interests. Customers also gain their right to be considered by the economic power they wield, not in the board room directly, but indirectly via the right of a consumer to avoid buying a corporation's product.

The first question to be asked about a strategy plan that has been prepared is whether it is understood by the managers who have to implement it. The second question is to determine whether the plan is consistent with the firm's resources (e.g., money and managerial talent) and consistent with the objectives of the firm. Recognize that the objectives can range from profit maximization (and there are many ways of measuring profits) to survival. The final step in the evaluation of the strategy is to determine whether any crucial information or consideration has been omitted. For example, is the action legal?

It is easy to fall into the trap of too simple generalizations. Assume a glass fiber factory has excess capacity and the plant manager is using the plant to process cotton textiles. This additional activity generates incremental business and incremental profit. Should top management terminate the contract to process textiles since the corporation is in the glass fiber business and does not want to dilute the specialization and expertise that is its competitive advantage? Or should top management recognize that marginal revenue exceeds marginal cost and accept the textile business as long as there is excess capacity? One position is that the firm is in the "processing business" and it does not make any difference what it is processing as long as it makes profits and the product is legal.

In a real case like the above situation, the plant manager was told to cease the activity. The textile business was thought to be inconsistent with the broad corporate strategy. The plant manager, whose salary was affected by the amount of profits made by the firm, was extremely upset by the loss of profits that resulted.

Two Styles of Planning

Let us consider two different styles of planning.

For *style 1*, the first step is to set a growth goal. The second step is to inventory the tools that will enable you to reach the growth goal. Will the present set of products and markets do the job? If so, the plan is simple: ride the growth curves of the present products. If more growth is needed, the second possibility is to expand the technologies and markets of the firm. Again, if this satisfies the growth objective, the search is stopped; if not, we proceed to the next step. This final way to achieve the growth objective is to find new products not closely related to present products and technologies.

Style 2 differs from style 1 by first inventorying the profitable investment and marketing opportunities. Only after this is done is an expected growth rate computed consistent with the optimum set of decisions. The resulting expected growth rate may be more or less than some target growth rate that is in the mind of the chief executive. If the expected growth rate is not satisfactory, there is a review of the administration and budget of the research and development efforts.

The two styles differ greatly. With style 1 a growth rate is set, and then the ways of achieving that goal are found. We can expect there to be a forcing of numbers in the forecasts in order to meet the preestablished goals. With the second style of planning the focus is on all profitable opportunities. A zero growth rate is acceptable if that is consistent with the present opportunities. But a zero growth rate might also give rise to new research efforts that will mean that in the future the likelihood of having profitable growth opportunities will be increased.

There is an implication with the first style that good opportunities will be placed on the back burner if the target growth can be achieved without them. Equally bad is the fact that the expected profitability of bad investments may be made to look good so that the expected growth is equal to the target growth. Style 2 planning eliminates these two objections but introduces one of its own, an implied willingness to live with a low expected growth rate if that is what is indicated by the available opportunities. The answer to this objection is an acceptance of a low growth rate consistent with the fact that all alternatives presently available have been investigated and the firm has no alternatives that will lead to profitable growth. Profit (net present value) is a necessary condition for a prospect to be accepted. Without profit, growth is not desirable. Having found an expected zero growth, if growth is desired, the next step is to spend resources to develop profitable opportunities. Zero expected growth does result in changes in resource allocation if growth is desired.

CONCLUSION

Consider a division of the states of the world into high and low relative market shares and high and low real market growths. One would prefer a high relative market share in a market that is growing in real terms. It is a fact that a high market share in a growing market is better than the other alternatives, all things being equal. But this fact is not a decision. It is a description of a preference (wanting more compared with less). Business decisions are of the type "Given this relative share of the market, where we forecast that the market is going to grow at $X\%$, then we should do..." The decision involves determining the amount of expenditures to affect market share.

We shall define some of the financial policy paths a corporation may take and point out the advantages and disadvantages of the different paths. Frequently we shall find that we know how to analyze the situation, but we will not necessarily know which specific decision is the correct decision. For one thing, that conclusion is going to depend on the objectives of the firm, and to a large extent on the subjective preferences of the decision makers who have sufficient power or influence to set the financial policies.

Chapter 2

Common Stock

The residual ownership of a corporation lies with the common stockholders. In the event of financial difficulty the debt and the preferred stock are paid first, and the common stockholders have claim to what is left. Because the common stockholders of a firm are in a more risky position compared to the debt and preferred stock, it is reasonable to expect that they would require a higher expected return than the other capital contributors.

From the viewpoint of the corporation (and its managers) the use of common stock is a very attractive way in which to raise capital. The primary advantage of common stock as a form of capital is that there is no legal obligation for the corporation to pay cash dividends in a given year. The declaration of dividends is a discretionary act on the part of the firm's board of directors. If it is deemed desirable to cease paying a dividend, there is no threat of bankruptcy. There is no maturity date for the common stock; thus management does not have to be concerned with meeting at a given date a balloon payment as with some forms of debt. The common stock capital is a buffer. When operations are not going well, it is the common stockholders who act as the shock absorbers. They bear the brunt of downturns in the economic well-being of the corporation.

The crucial questions for an investor in common stock is: What is going to happen to an investment made now in common stock? Is it better to buy now or to wait for prices to go lower? These are difficult questions for either a financial adviser or an investor to answer. The corporate financial officer has an equivalent question to answer. Is it better to issue common stock now, or is it better to wait until the price per share goes up?

There are interesting psychological traps awaiting the financial manager. One is the "trend trap." If the stock has been increasing in value, it is easy to fall into the trap of thinking that the price tomorrow will be higher so we should not issue the shares today.

The second trap is the "looking back" trap. If the price yesterday was higher than today's price, the stock today is assumed to be undervalued. It is incorrectly concluded that the firm should wait until the stock returns to its historical high; otherwise the stock will be issued at a depressed price, harming the interests of the present stockholders.

If these two traps reflect the actual thinking of management (or more exactly the board of directors), then the firm will tend not to issue common stock in any year. Either the price is increasing and we should wait for it to go higher, or it is depressed and we should wait for it to increase. A financial theorist may say the market is efficient and at any moment in time reflects all the information that is available. In addition, the short-run changes in the stock price from the current

9

price will be random. The current price is an accurate reflection of the firm's value at the present time unless the market does not have significant information that is available to management. Thus the board of directors thinking of issuing common stock should not worry about whether the stock is going to go up or down in the future, as long as the investors have all the relevant information. Any day is as good as any other day to issue the stock.

It is true that in some cases the development of events will indicate that a wrong decision was made, but there is no way today to forecast the results of such a decision made today.

THE VALUE OF COMMON STOCK

In theory a share of common stock has value either because of the intrinsic value of the firm in which it represents ownership or because we expect the market to behave in a nonrational manner and to attribute value when there is none. We discard this latter approach to value, which requires that a "greater fool" exist who is waiting to pay more for a security than it is worth. We assume that a share of common stock has value because of the future dividends (or other cash flows) that will be paid, and price increases in common stock reflect increased expectations about the future of the company.

The investor of a publicly held firm benefits in two ways from holding common stock. There are the possibilities of receiving cash dividends and obtaining increments in value (price appreciation). The remainder of the chapter is concerned with describing the required return of common stockholders and stock valuation relationships.

We want to define the value of a share of common stock in terms of the future benefits that the common stock will earn for its owner.

Let

P_t = the market price per share at time t (P is the price now)
k = the time discount rate applied by stockholders
g = the growth rate in earnings and dividends
E_t = the earnings per share at time t
b = the retention rate and $(1-b)$ be the dividend payout rate
D_t = the dividend at time t where $D_t = (1-b)E_t = D_1(1+g)^{t-1}$

We can describe the price now of a share of common stock P in terms of the next dividend to be received (assume the dividend is to be received one year from today, and we can use D_1 to designate this dividend) plus the price of the common stock one time period in the future P_1 discounted back to the present by dividing by $1 + k$.

$$P = \frac{D_1 + P_1}{1 + k} \qquad (1)$$

This equation states the well-known fact that the value today is equal to the present value of the next dividend plus the discounted value of the future price. We can now write P_1 in terms of the dividend and the price at time 2.

$$P_1 = \frac{D_2 + P_2}{1 + k} \tag{2}$$

Substituting $(D_2 + P_2)/(1 + k)$ for P_1 in equation (2) we have

$$P = \frac{D_1}{1 + k} + \frac{D_2}{(1 + k)^2} + \frac{P_2}{(1 + k)^2} \tag{3}$$

Continuing this process of substitution, we obtain an infinite series of dividends discounted back to the present.

If we assume that dividends grow at a constant rate g so that $D_t = D_1(1+g)^{t-1}$ and if g is less than k this infinite series can be summed to obtain the very important stock valuation relationship:

$$P = \frac{D}{k - g} \tag{4}$$

This relationship is more important for understanding the factors affecting value (the value of $k-g$) than in determining the value of a specific stock (equation (4) is difficult to apply because we do not know the value of $k-g$).

Solving equation (4) for k we obtain

$$k = \frac{D}{P} + g \tag{5}$$

We can define k to be the *cost of common stock equity*. Although k is defined in terms of future dividends, it should be noted that the growth in dividends (g) that is forecasted cannot be independent of the forecasted future incomes. In practice, a forecast of future dividends is apt, to some extent, to be based on past incomes and past dividends.

Note also that the above derivation of k in terms of (D, P, g) assumes that transforming the future price per share (or dividends) back to the present can be accomplished by using a constant k each time period and compounding the term 1 plus k for the number of time periods. With an assumption of a constant interest rate and certainty, this procedure would be completely acceptable. Relaxing this certainty assumption, it is not clear that investors do, or should, behave in this manner. Nevertheless, the normal interpretation of the required return of common stockholders is consistent with the interpretation implicit in the derivation.

An important conclusion resulting from the above formulation is that the cost of stock equity is not generally equal to earnings divided by price, or the dividends divided by price. For example, if the dividends are $2, stock price $100, and the growth rate 0.14, we obtain:

$$\text{Cost of stock equity} = \frac{\$2}{\$100} + 0.14 = 0.16$$

To use the dividend yield of 0.02 to estimate the cost of equity would be an error. The cost of equity is actually 0.16 if we accept the model and the given facts.

The use of dividends in the relationship just given is confusing to some. They would prefer to see earnings used. Letting E be earnings, b the proportion of the earnings retained, then dividends are $(1-b)E$, and substituting $(1-b)E$ for D in equation (4):

$$P = \frac{(1-b)E}{k-g} \tag{6}$$

In equation (6) the stock price P is expressed in terms of the earnings and the growth in the earnings as well as the dividend policy that is consistent with the assumed growth rate. It makes no difference if we use dividends or earnings as long as we do not ignore the growth factor and do adjust the earnings for the retention factor.

A DIFFERENT APPROACH: THE CAPM

In the above section the formulation for the cost of stock equity was based on a definition of the cost of equity as the rate of interest that equates the present value of all future dividends to the stock price.

There is a different approach which can be used based on a theory called the "capital asset pricing model." Essentially the model adds to the default-free government borrowing rate, a factor reflecting the risks of the firm. The firm's risk that is relevant for this model is based on the degree to which the affairs of the corporation are linked to the return earned by investing in the overall market (more exactly the risk is measured using the correlation of the stock's return with the market's return). It is argued that this correlation is the only risk for which the market demands compensation (all other risks can be diversified away).

Theoretically the cost of equity obtained using the capital asset pricing model will be equal to the cost of equity obtained using the dividend valuation model. Problems of estimation will cause differences to result, but this does not mean that the two models are inconsistent.

THE COST OF EQUITY:
THE OPPORTUNITY COST METHOD

Assume that investors are taxed at a rate of t_s on common stock returns and that they can earn r_0 after the investor tax on alternative investments. Thus the after tax opportunity cost is r_0. Assume that r_0 is 0.06 and t_s is 0.20. To invest new capital in common stock the firm must earn (after corporate tax) k_e where

$$(1-t_s)k_e = r_0 \tag{7}$$

or

$$k_e = \frac{r_0}{1 - t_s} = \frac{0.06}{1 - 0.2} = 0.075$$

For example, if a $1,000 stock investment earns $75, the tax is 0.2(75) = $15 and the investor nets $60. The same amount could have been earned by investing the $1,000 in the alternative security that yields 0.06 after investor tax. Thus the opportunity cost establishes a 0.075 cost of new equity capital.

But now assume the firm must decide on whether or not to retain earnings. Now the firm only has to earn $r_0 = 0.06$. For example, assume $1,000 is retained, earns 0.06, so that at the end of a year $1,060 is taxed to that investor. The tax is 0.2(1,060) = $210 and the net is $848.

If the $1,000 had been paid to the investor at time zero the investor nets $800 after paying $200 of taxes and earning 0.06 (after tax) the investor again has $848 at the end of the year. There is indifference between retaining and earning 0.06 or paying the $1,000 to investors who then earn 0.06 after tax.

Because of taxes there is a significant difference in the cost of retained earnings (r_0) and the cost of new capital

$$\left(\frac{r_0}{1 - t_s} \right)$$

The tax rate, t_s, needs additional explanation. Above, it was assumed that all types of stock returns are taxed at t_s. Conceptually t_s is a combination of:

the tax rate on dividends
the tax rate on realized capital gains
the tax rate on unrealized capital gains (this can be zero)

Operationally we cannot be sure of the exact value of t_s, but it is likely to be greater than zero and less than the tax rate on ordinary income.

If instead of assuming that returns on stock are taxed at a rate of t_s we could assume dividends are taxed at t_p and realized capital gains are taxed at a rate of t_g. The formulations would be more complex than illustrated above, but the results would be consistent with the above analysis.

STOCK VALUATION

Let us consider the stock valuation model of equation (4). Although we would hesitate to use this specific model in practice (it unrealistically assumes a given growth rate of g that goes on forever), it does supply interesting insights.

The price of a share of stock is defined in terms of the current dividend (D), the required return (k), and the growth rate in dividends (g). A change in any of these amounts will change the value (P) of the share of stock.

For example, let us assume that a share of stock is paying $2 of cash dividends, the stockholders want a 0.15 return, and the expected growth rate in dividends is 0.05. The value of a share is $20:

$$P = \frac{\$2}{0.15 - 0.05} = \$20$$

If the growth rate were to increase to 0.14, the stock value would increase to $200:

$$P = \frac{\$2}{0.15 - 0.14} = \$200$$

A situation in which the company is actually going to shrink (the dividends have a decay rate) at a rate of 0.10, the value of a share would be:

$$P = \frac{\$2}{0.15 - (-0.10)} = \frac{\$2}{0.25} = \$8$$

The next step in the stock valuation analysis would be to assume a growth rate for a period of time and then a shift to a different growth rate after a given number of years. Alternatively, a whole series of growth rates can be assumed.

Despite the unrealism of the stock valuation model of equation (4), we can expect it to be used in the future as in the past because of its simplicity and the insights it provides.

A Change in Interest Rates

Consider the situation where the stock value is $200 and the growth rate is 0.14, but assume the cost of equity capital increases from 0.15 to 0.16. The stock price falls from $200 to $100.

$$P = \frac{\$2}{0.16 - 0.14} = \$100$$

The managers who see their firm's stock price decrease from $200 to $100 are going to find it difficult to believe there is not a faulty evaluation taking place if the operations of the firm are just as profitable and growing this year at the same rate as in the past. However, an increase in the cost of money can cause the value to decrease.

While special information available only to the board of directors might well lead to a decision to defer the issuance of common stock, given the price decrease, there is an important reason for arguing that the stock should be issued. Assume the expected value of the use of the cash to be received is positive. In this case even if the common stock were to be somewhat undervalued in the market, this underevaluation could be compensated by the increase in the net value resulting from the use of the cash receipts made possible by the stock issue.

Some corporations will raise interim capital using short-term debt while they wait for the common stock price to increase. This strategy would be reasonable if there are real reasons for thinking the common stock is undervalued. A second strategy is to issue long-term debt as a substitute for the expensive common stock.

Present Value of Growth (PVGO)

Analysts frequently divide the value of a stock into two components, the value of a constant stream and the value of the growth increment (PVGO). The value of the constant stream of E is

$$\frac{E}{k}$$

The PVGO is:

$$PVGO = \frac{(1-b)E}{k-g} - \frac{E}{k} \tag{8}$$

For the example where $k = 0.15$ and $g = 0.14$, assume that $b = \frac{2}{3}$ and $E = \$6$.

$$PVGO = \frac{\$2}{0.15 - 0.14} - \frac{\$6}{0.15} = \$200 - \$40 = \$160$$

The growth component has a value of $160.

The same type of calculation can be done for a finite-lived investment. The first step is to compute the total present value with growth and then subtract the value of an annuity assuming no new net investment.

For example, suppose the discount rate is 0.15 and assume the following facts:

Year	Earnings	Residual Value and Dividends	Investment
1	100	40.0	60.0
2	130	52.0	78.0
3	169	67.6	101.4
3		239.4[1]	

The present value of constant earnings of $100:

$$PV = \frac{\$100}{1.15} + \frac{\$100}{1.15^2} + \frac{\$100}{1.15^3} = \$228.32$$

The value of the growth increment is:

$$PVGO = \$275.96 - \$228.32 = \$47.64$$

The total present value is $228.32 + $47.64 = $275.96.

---

[1] This is the value of the investment at time 3 and equal to $60 + $78 + $101.40. Other assumptions can be made that would be as reasonable.

The present value of the cash flows is:

$$PV = \frac{\$40}{1.15} + \frac{\$52}{1.15^2} + \frac{\$307}{1.15^3} = \$275.96$$

A Stock Valuation Model

Previously we used the relationship

$$\text{Stock price} = \frac{\text{Annual dividend}}{\text{Cost of equity} - \text{Growth rate}} = \frac{D}{k - g}$$

to illustrate the effect of increasing interest rates on stock prices. The relationship is obtained from summing an infinite series of dividends where the dividends of each year have the same growth rate and all cash flows are discounted at a rate of discount called the cost of equity capital. It is necessary that the growth rate used be less than the rate of discount; otherwise the formulation is not valid. Also, the model assumes a constant growth rate (thus increasing investment through time). If it is desired to use changing growth rates through time, we could have a much more complex model. Also, if the current dividend is equal to zero, the model in the form presented cannot be used. But the basic formulation using the present value of *future* dividends can be used, even if the resulting formulation is more complex than that presented.

Some observers object to the use of the dividend valuation model, since they know that investors buy common stock not only because of dividends but also because of the prospect of capital gains. This complexity is easily resolved. If the future price is based on value, the dividend valuation model completely and correctly incorporates the price appreciation. If it is expected that the stock price will be higher than the value based on future dividends, we again would have to shift from the model presented. But for the model not to be valid for this reason, the future price would have to be based on "the greater fool theory." Someone next period will have to pay more than the dividend-based value because another fool is around the corner. Basing business decisions on the assumption that the market is not rational and will continue not to be rational in the future is not an attractive strategy.

The Price-Earnings Multiplier

The price of a share of common stock divided by the earnings per share is defined to be the P/E ratio of the stock. One company earns a $1.20 per share, and its stock sells at a price of $6 (a P/E of 5). A second company earns exactly the same, and its stock sells at $24 per share (a P/E of 20). Why does this "unfair" state of the world exist?

There are rational reasons why one company will have a P/E of 5, and at the same moment in time a second company will have a P/E of 20 (there are also irrational reasons). To explain P/E ratios, we apply the stock valuation model of equation (6). The model assumes a constant growth rate through time, which is a drastically simplified version of the real world. Despite this limitation (which can be modified), the model is very useful for explaining the basic factors affecting the P/E ratio of a company in a rational stock market.

Dividing both sides of equation (6) by E, we obtain the ratio of price to earnings:

$$P/E = \frac{(1 - b)}{k - g} \tag{9}$$

Equation (9) shows that the target price-earnings ratio is equal to the dividend payout rate $(1 - b)$ divided by $(k - g)$. The larger the growth rate g, the larger the value of P/E ratio that will be justified for the stock. Although we can use equation (9) to compute a target ratio of price to earnings that is consistent with the expected growth rate, required return, and dividend policy, the actual price-earnings multiplier will be observed in the market.

Illustration

Assume that a firm is retaining 0.4 of its earnings, the investors in common stock require a 0.10 return, and the firm is growing at a rate of 0.07 per year. Substituting in equation (9), we obtain:

$$P/E = \frac{1-b}{k-g} = \frac{1-0.4}{0.10-0.07} = 20$$

A P/E of 20 is justified if the growth of 0.07 is expected to continue forever into the future. Now assume that the earnings are expected to decrease to a decay rate of 0.02 in the future (g is negative). We now have a P/E of 5.

$$P/E = \frac{1-b}{k-g} = \frac{1-0.4}{0.10-(-0.02)} = \frac{0.6}{0.12} = 5$$

By changing the assumed growth rate, we are able to explain the two P/E's previously described. Growth rate assumptions make a great deal of difference in setting what a company's ratio of price to earnings should be.

In the real world we can expect the value of k to change through time, reflecting such things as changes in the rate of inflation or the riskiness of a specific firm. For example, consider the situation in which

$$b = 0.4, k = 0.10, g = 0.07, \text{ and } P/E = 20$$

Now assume that k changes from 0.10 to 0.19 because of a high rate of inflation and an increase in alternative earning opportunities. Investors now require a 0.19 return per year. Then,

$$P/E = \frac{(1-b)}{k-g} = \frac{1-0.4}{0.19-0.07} = \frac{0.6}{0.12} = 5$$

If the market believes the model and acts accordingly, the corporate president will see the P/E shrink from 20 to 5 because of an increase in the average return required by investors. The firm's stock price decreases despite the fact that the firm has never been more profitable.

A change in b (b is a decision variable because it is determined by the board of directors) may also affect the P/E multiplier. Assume that b (the retention rate) and r (the average reinvestment rate) are linked together so that the more that is reinvested the lower the average return, and that $g = rb$ (the relationship is more complex if the firm uses debt). Then,

b	r	$g = rb$
0.4	0.175	0.070
0.7	0.140	0.098

If b is raised from 0.4 to 0.7, r will be 0.14 and $g = rb = 0.14(0.7) = 0.098$. With $k = 0.10$, we can expect a P/E of:

$$\text{P/E} = \frac{(1-b)}{k-g} = \frac{1-0.7}{0.10-0.098} = \frac{0.3}{0.002} = 150$$

When g is very close to k, the P/E will be very sensitive to small changes in g or k. Before accepting a P/E of 150, we must be willing to accept the assumption that the firm will be able to maintain a growth rate of 0.098. Growth rates of this magnitude are difficult to maintain for long periods of time by very large firms (a 10% growth rate implies doubling in size every seven to eight years). It is important to keep in mind the implicit assumptions of the model.

Growth Rate Expectations

There are many reasons for the earnings of a company to grow. The reasons can include raising (or lowering) prices, increased efficiency, improved business conditions, new products, etc. But after all of these factors are implemented, the next improvement in growth must come from new investments. If debt is equal to zero, then we obtain the following relationship:

$$\text{Growth = return on investment} \times \text{retention rate} = rb \tag{10}$$

The relevant return on investment is the return expected on the new investment. For example, assume a firm is currently earning $100 and retaining 0.40, or $40. If the firm can earn 0.25 on new investment, the expected growth rate is:

$$\text{Growth} = 0.40 \times 0.25 = 0.10$$

The $40 of investment will earn 0.25, or $10. The $10 new earnings added to the basic $100 of earnings is $110, which is a growth rate of 0.10. The dividends will also increase 0.10 from $60 to 0.6 of $110, or $66.

If the firm is using debt, the expected growth rate is more complex than that given. Growth then becomes a function of the retention rate, the expected return of new investment, the amount of leverage, and the cost of debt.

The types of models presented in this section move the estimate of growth from a purely subjective "wish" of management to an estimate based on such decisions as retention rate and amount of leverage, as well as such other variables as the earning opportunities available to the firm and the cost of debt.

If the president of an already efficient, well-managed firm forecasts a 0.20 growth rate when the firm is retaining 0.40 of the earnings, with zero debt the president is implicitly assuming a return on new investment of 0.50:

0.20 = 0.40 (Return on investment)
Return on investment = 0.50

If the president does not think new investments will earn an average return of 0.50, the estimated growth rate should be changed, or alternatively the retention rate should be changed. Following the logic of this section, estimated growth rates result from basic estimates of the economics of new investments. We derive growth rates from information and analysis. They are the end result of analysis, not the starting point.

The growth rate calculation would be further complicated by a share repurchase program, a dividend reinvestment plan, or the raising of new capital in the market.

Cost of Common Stock

The cost of common stock with zero debt is equal to the weighted average cost of capital (common stock is the only security outstanding). As the amount of leverage increases, the cost of equity increases. The stockholders require larger expected returns as the amount of leverage increases. The *actual* return might decrease, but the *required expected* return increases.

When we discuss the cost of debt we will find the cost of debt curve is everywhere below the cost of stock equity. This occurs because debt is senior to common stock, meaning that the debtholders are ahead of common stockholders on "payday." Since debt has less risk than common stock, we can expect the holders of common stock to require a higher expected return than with debt (the tax laws could require a modification in this generalization).

COMMON STOCK ISSUANCE: BASIC STRATEGY

We want to consider the basic strategy considerations entering into a decision to issue more common stock. A prime consideration is control. If the issuance of more shares will increase the likelihood of loss of control by the stockholders presently controlling the corporation, you can expect a high reluctance to issue those shares. Since the only way to insure control of a corporation is to own more than 50% of the shares, the holders of 50% of the shares are not likely to want shares issued that will reduce their ownership to less than 50%, if they have alternatives.

The second consideration is the direct economic effects. We could determine the economic consequences by a conventional capital budgeting analysis, but for purposes of illustrating the effects on the common stock, we will take a different approach.

Assume a situation where a firm has 1 million shares of common stock outstanding and the stock has a market price of $40 per share. Management has information that leads it to think that the intrinsic value of the shares is $50 per share. The company is thinking of issuing 500,000 shares at a price of $40 to finance an investment. Should it do so, given that the shares are undervalued?

One strategy would be to issue debt until such time as the market recognized the intrinsic value of the stock. We will bypass this alternative, in the interest of simplicity, though it is worthy of consideration. Assume that there are good reasons why the firm cannot issue debt.

While there is a real incentive not to issue the common stock given the depressed stock price (a value of $50 and a market price of $40), there is need for additional information before a decision can be made. Assume the $20 million of capital raised with the issuance of 500,000 shares will lead to an increment in value (real and perceived) of $30 million. Each new share of common stock will add $60 of value. Since the current intrinsic value per share is $50, there will be an increase in the intrinsic value of the currently outstanding shares, and the issuance of the new shares is desirable. The total stock value would be $80 million, or with 1.5 million shares outstanding, $53 per share.

While the above explanation is sufficient to justify the stock issue, we can give other calculations. The $30 million of new value added to the present market value of $40 million gives a total value of $70 million for 1.5 million shares, or $46.67 per share. This is larger than the present market price of $40 per share; thus the shares should be issued. Comparable calculations could be done using the present intrinsic value per share, and the same conclusion would be reached.

If the value resulting from the issue of the new shares is $22.5 million or $45 per share, the decision is less clear-cut. The $45 is less than the $50 per share of intrinsic value; thus the value per share will be diluted. The total value per share after issue will be reduced from $50 per share. On the other hand, the $45 is larger than the $40 market price. If the market believes the value added is truly $22.5 million, we can expect the market price to increase from $40 to $41.67 (the $64.5 million of total value divided by 1.5 million shares). Thus if the value per share added to the firm is greater than the market price but less than the intrinsic value, the correct decision is not obvious.

If one is willing to assume an efficient market, where it is assumed that the market has access to the same information as management, then the $50 measure can be assumed not to be relevant. The shares should be issued as long as the new value per share is larger than the current market price.

We have assumed that the market will be able to measure the change in value arising from the new investment and that the market's measure is exactly equal to the value measurements of management. If there are wide differences, we may again not be able to arrive at a definite conclusion that the issue of common stock is desirable.

STOCK RIGHTS

The use of stock rights varies among the companies of different countries. But the topic is also important because the method of analysis applies whenever shares are issued for a price (or a value) that differs from the current market value.

Consider a stock that is currently selling at a price of $50. For every four shares of stock a new share can be purchased at a price of $40 (each outstanding share receives a right to buy ¼ of a new share at a price of $40). The stock price after the rights are separated from the shares is:

$$\text{New Stock Price} = \frac{4(\$50) + \$40}{4 + 1} = \frac{\$240}{5} = \$48$$

where the numerator is the total value for a unit of four shares and the denominator is the new number of shares.

Since it takes four rights to pay $40 for a share to be worth $48, each right (for ¼ of a share) has a value of $2.

If not all the rights are exercised, the final price will be larger than $48 and each right that is exercised will have a value somewhat larger than $2. If during the period the rights can be exercised, the stock price drops below $40, at time of exercise the price is below $40 the rights would have zero value.

THE EARNINGS-PRICE RATIO

Some executives use the reciprocal of the P/E ratio as an estimator of the firm's cost of equity capital k is E/P. The numerator is this year's earnings, and the denominator is the current common stock price. The expression fails to consider reinvested funds and the return they will earn. It fails to consider the growth the investors expect from the firm investing in activities that yield better than normal returns.

The ratio can be used as a reasonable estimator of the cost of equity capital, if certain conditions are satisfied (e.g. zero growth or the firm only earns its cost of capital). If the stock price (P) is affected by expectations of future earnings growth, the ratio of E/P may be a poor estimator of the cost of equity.

CONVERTIBLE SECURITIES

Convertible preferred stock and convertible bonds have increased in popularity in recent years, especially as securities issued to facilitate mergers and acquisitions. Preferred stock and bonds have the virtue of defining a return and a priority of payment. This is reassuring to an investor who desires more security than is available to common stockholders. However, both the preferred stock dividend provision and the contractual interest rate of debt set upside maximums that are undesirable from the point of view of an investor. Since these investors share in difficulties if the financial affairs of the firm get bad enough, it is not unreasonable for them to want to share in the benefits if the rosy expectations are realized.

A feature allowing conversion into common stock offers the possibilities of large gains to the investors in convertible preferred stock and debt, enhancing the desirability of such debt and preferred stock to the investing community. From the point of view of the corporation, a conversion feature reduces the necessary dividend payout with preferred stock and contractual interest payment with debt, and thus may be attractive to the corporation. The drawback of the conversion feature is that it dilutes the ownership of the current stockholders by enabling fixed-income capital contributors to participate in the upside gains that might develop.

Buying a convertible bond may be viewed as the same as buying a bond with an option to acquire common stock (by converting the debt) or buying common stock with downside protection, since the bond value acts as a type of minimum value. It is, by its nature, a complex security and one that is difficult to value, since it incorporates both bond valuations and common stock valuation. The adding of a conversion feature is an excellent device for muddying up the waters of valuation. A bond that might not have seemed to be desirable because of the risk-return situation, might become desirable by incorporating the right to convert to common stock.

In addition to convertible bonds, there are bonds with warrants attached. The advantage of such a security to the investor is that the host bond is retained when the common stock is acquired, since the stock is issued in return for the warrant and some additional cash. The advantage to the corporation of a detachable warrant is that the corporation receives cash at the time of exercise (if the warrant is exercised). The disadvantage compared to a convertible bond is that the bond is still outstanding after the warrant is exercised, whereas with conversion the bond has been replaced with common stock. Thus some warrants have provisions that make it desirable and feasible to use the bonds to satisfy the exercise price to acquire the common stock.

CONCLUSIONS

The P/E multiplier is an easily computed number that gives a prospective purchaser of a firm's common stock an idea of the relationship between earnings and price of the stock. However, each P/E multiplier implicitly assumes something about the future retention rates, earning opportunities, use of debt, and the required return of stockholders. If these assumptions applied by the market are not realistic, the stock price may be too high or too low.

The value of the required return and the value the market places on future earnings opportunities are not controllable by management, assuming a reasonable level of market efficiency. However, management can change the amount of leverage, the amount of funds retained, and by seeking out profitable investments can affect the actual return on investment. In addition, management can generally affect the effectiveness with which the assets are employed. Thus management, in a variety of real ways, can affect a firm's P/E multiplier.

Making decisions based solely on P/E factors is a dangerous type of analysis, because it bypasses all the assumptions that are implicit in a P/E measure (such as the level of risk, earning opportunities, retention rate, etc.). It is important to keep in mind the assumptions implicit in the derivation of the model before making decisions based on the model.

There is nothing easy about analyzing decisions involving common stock. While the cost of debt is merely a matter of calculation once we have the contractual terms and the market price, with common stock there are no contractual terms. All we have are estimates of market expectations. It is difficult to determine exactly the cost of equity capital.

It will be shown that debt has obvious tax advantages (the interest is tax deductible), but the advantages of common stock are more subtle. Common stock's retention of earnings delays the payment of taxes by investors, and offers the possibility that the gain resulting from retention will be taxed as a capital gain in the future.

The primary justification for issuing common stock is that the presence of the common stock and the cash received with its issuance tend to be risk reducing for the present investors. The amount of benefit associated with the risk reduction is difficult to quantify in terms of dollars. Thus justifying the issuance of common stock rather than some type of debt alternative is apt to be a difficult task. Nevertheless, when the going gets rough, management will greatly appreciate the fact that common stock was used rather than debt (to the extent it was used). Common stock capital is truly a cushion protecting the corporation against the disruptions of bankruptcy and the costs of financial distress.

Chapter 3

The Use of Preferred Stock

The issuance of preferred stock is a method of financing that, from the short-run point of view of the stockholders of an issuing corporation, has less risk than bonds and more risk than common stock. It is a form of equity, and the dividend is well-defined, but is optional (the board of directors may decide not to pay the dividend). While without taxes one would expect the yield on preferred stock to be higher than on bonds to compensate investors for increased risk, because of peculiarities in the tax code the before tax yield of preferred to investors is frequently less than that of bonds issued by the same firm, even though the bonds have less risk.

When corporate tax rates were low, preferred stock was a popular method of raising capital. In recent years the use of preferred stock, with some exceptions, has been limited to corporations not paying taxes, public utilities and firms engaged in mergers and acquisitions. There is a good reason for the decrease in its use. Preferred stock dividend payments are not deductible for income tax purposes, whereas debt interest is deductible. This tends to make preferred stock a high-cost (after-tax) method of raising capital compared to debt. However, preferred stock may be useful as a substitute for common stock.

Preferred stock is somewhat like debt (a contractual commitment by the corporation to pay a dollar amount of dividends) and somewhat like common stock (the amount to be paid is not a fixed legal commitment; although the amount of the dividend is defined by contract, it does not have to be paid by the corporation). Thus preferred stock falls between debt and common stock on the capital structure spectrum.

It should not be assumed that all preferred stocks are equal. They may differ in respect to conversion into common stock, be cumulative, be callable, be participating, and may be of finite or infinite life. The dividend may be a fixed amount or a floating (variable) amount.

COMPARING DEBT AND PREFERRED STOCK

Preferred stock is similar to debt but a dividend rather than interest is specified. The company's legal obligation to pay interest on debt is much stronger than its obligation to pay the preferred stock dividend. Failure to pay interest can lead to bankruptcy, but failure to pay dividends does not; thus debt is said to be more risky than preferred stock from the viewpoint of the issuing firm.

All bonds currently being issued by U.S. corporations have maturity dates, and some bonds have sinking funds. Preferred stock may or may not have maturity dates and/or sinking funds. Obviously the inclusion of these characteristics moves the preferred stock in the direction of being more like debt than like common stock. There have been issues of preferred stock with provision for repurchase each year for a sinking fund or with provision for mandatory redemption.

A maturity date is considered by the tax courts to be a necessary condition for the security to be classified as debt (though there is no essential reason for this requirement). A maturity date imposes more risk on the borrower of being unable to pay. If the firm does not have the funds for repayment at the maturity date, it may be forced into receivership. Preferred stock has no such risk since even where the preferred stock has a maturity date, the preferred shareholder cannot force the issuing firm into bankruptcy if it chooses not to pay.

The investor holding a debt instrument in a given corporation is subject to less risk than someone having an equal dollar investment in preferred stock of the same corporation, since the debtholders have prior claims to assets in case of liquidation and have first claim to earnings. The counterpart of this is that the stockholders of a corporation issuing debt have more risk at the time of issue than the stockholders of an otherwise identical firm issuing preferred stock. The statement requires two explanatory qualifications. First, the average life or duration of the two securities may be different. Secondly, while the issuance of debt results in more risk to the corporation's stockholders as long as it is outstanding, the after-tax cost of debt is likely to be lower than the after-tax cost of preferred stock, since dividends are not generally deductible for taxes.

The Dividend Received Deduction

The existence of a "dividend received deduction" increases the after-tax return on preferred stock to a *corporate* investor. But the existence of the dividend-received deduction does not necessarily imply that debt does not have a tax advantage compared with preferred stock. It is sometimes incorrectly concluded that the dividend-received deduction makes it desirable for corporations to issue preferred stock rather than debt. The deduction makes it easier to sell (issue) preferred stock, but normally for a tax-paying competitive firm the deduction does not overcome the tax deductibility of the debt interest.

Example

Assume a firm has $100 of net revenue (before tax). There is a 0.70 dividend received deduction. The corporate tax rate is 0.35. The following analysis compares the net returns to a corporate investor if $1,000 of bonds were issued to yield 0.10 with those from $1,000 of preferred stock to yield 0.065.

	Calculation for:	
	Preferred Stock	Bonds
Net revenue	$100.000	$100
Tax	35.000	0
Dividend (interest)	65.000	100
Amount taxable to investing corporation (0.30): 19.50		100
Tax (0.35 rate)	6.825	35
Net return	58.175	65

Assuming the issuing corporation earns $100 before tax, the bonds lead to a larger conservation of cash for the joint affairs of the issuer and investor than the preferred stock. Note that only 0.30 of the preferred stock dividend ($19.50) is subject to the 0.35 corporate tax paid by the corporate investor.

The Cost of Preferred Stock

Assuming that the life of the preferred stock is infinite, the cost of the preferred stock is:

$$\text{Cost of preferred stock} = \frac{\text{Annual dividend}}{\text{Price}}$$

For example, a stock being issued for $50 and promising to pay $3.25 a year dividend would have a cost of 0.065, that is:

$$\text{Cost of preferred stock} = \frac{\text{Annual dividend}}{\text{Price}} = \frac{\$3.25}{\$50} = 0.065$$

Note that the par value of the stock does not affect the cost, but the market price and the amount of the promised dividend do affect the cost.

If the company currently has the preferred stock outstanding and the stock can be repurchased at a cost of $50, the cost of the outstanding preferred stock is again 0.065, where the 0.065 is an opportunity cost. By buying a share the company can save $3.25 of dividends per year.

Now assume that the corporation has a tax rate of 0.35. The before-tax cost to the corporation of the 0.065 preferred stock is 0.10. For example, if the corporation raised $50 and earned $5, before tax, the corporate tax would be $1.75 and the after-tax earnings would be $3.25, just enough to meet the 0.065 dividend requirement.

If the $50 had been raised by issuing debt paying 0.065, the firm could pay the $3.25 interest by earning just $3.25, since the entire $3.25 is tax shielded. With a 0.35 tax rate, the after-tax cost of 0.065 debt is 0.065(1 − 0.35) or 0.04225. In order to pay the $3.25 preferred stock dividend the issuer has to earn $5 before tax whereas to pay the 0.065 debt the firm only has to earn $3.25. Thus the 0.065 debt had lower after-tax costs than the 0.065 preferred stock, and the firm raising capital has an incentive to issue debt rather than preferred stock. This is reflected in the fact that there is many more times as much debt as preferred stock issued by competitive firms.

Considering the issuer, debt has a clear tax advantage compared to preferred stock. However, the analysis is complicated by the fact that the investor also has tax considerations that affect the return required by investors. This factor helps explain why corporate investors will buy lower yielding, riskier preferred stock rather than only investing in debt.

Comparing Bond Risk and Preferred Stock Risk

A given amount of debt imposes more risk on the stockholders of a corporation than an equal amount of preferred stock at a particular moment in time (time of issue). Preferred stock dividends may be omitted by a corporation with much less severe consequences than the omission of bond interest. Despite this fact, the question of whether preferred stock or bonds impose more risk on stockholders of the issuing corporation is not clear-cut. A complicating factor arises because the two securities issued at the same time may not be outstanding for the same period of time. To compare the relative desirability of issuing debt and preferred stock assume that the difference between the bond interest and preferred stock dividends (both on an after-tax basis) are used to retire the bonds. In this situation, assuming the yields required by investors of the two securities are reasonably close, and that the after-tax interest cost is less than the after-tax preferred stock dividend cost, in a finite number of years the bond can be completely retired using only these tax savings to accomplish the retirements.

As the tax laws currently stand, preferred stock is inferior to bonds as a means of raising capital by a corporation paying taxes. A change in the tax laws would change the analysis and the conclusions. For example, if the preferred stock dividend were tax deductible by the issuing corporation, this would make preferred stock more than competitive with debt from the point of view of the issuing corporation. A larger dividend received deduction would also enhance the competitive position of preferred stock.

Despite the tax advantage of debt, it can be argued that debt is more risky to the issuing corporation because of the fixed legal commitment to pay interest that is not present with preferred stock. There is an important limitation of the risk argument. First, and most important, the difference between the after-tax cost of interest and preferred stock dividends can be used to retire the debt and thus reduce the total risk of the debt. In fact, in a surprisingly short period of time a large percentage of the debt issue can be retired with such savings.

If we equate the present value of the annual cash flow savings to the present value of the debt using the after-tax borrowing rate, we find the length of time required to use the savings from the debt to retire the entire amount of debt.

Example

Assume that $10 million of debt costs 0.10, and an equal amount of preferred stock costs 0.09. The corporate tax rate is 0.40. How long would it take to pay off the debt using the after-tax difference in cash outlays?

The after-tax cash outlay of the interest is $1,000,000(1 - 0.4) = $600,000, and for the preferred stock dividends the outlay is $900,000. The firm can save $300,000 each year in outlays necessary to service the $10 million of capital assuming debt is issued and the firm has taxable income.

Let $B(n,r)$ be the present value of a dollar a period for n periods. We want to equate the present value of $300,000 of savings a year to the present value of $10 million using the after-tax borrowing rate of 0.06:

$$\$300,000\, B(n,0.06) = \$10,000,000(1.06)^{-n}$$

Solving for n: $n = 18.84$ years

In approximately 19 years, the company issuing debt, by reinvesting the savings (or buying the debt) can retire the entire debt issue. Thus we cannot say absolutely that the debt is more risky than preferred stock. If one considers a long-time horizon, initially the debt is more risky, but as debt is retired, the small amount of debt becomes less risky than a large amount of preferred stock, until finally it becomes obvious that debt is less risky (e.g., there is no debt outstanding).

The important advantage of preferred stock compared with debt in a risk comparison is that if a preferred stock dividend is omitted, the company is not in default as it would be if an interest payment is omitted. While bonds have a clear-cut tax advantage over preferred stock, it can be argued that if the corporation has reached its limit of debt issuance, preferred stock may be the only feasible alternative. But if preferred stock is issued, the corporation wants to have the right to call the preferred.

PREFERRED STOCK VERSUS COMMON STOCK

Even if preferred stock is less risky than debt, there still remains the issue of whether preferred stock or common stock should be issued. It can be argued that common stock has tax advantages compared to preferred stock. Common stock may lead to capital gains based on superior performance of the corporation. Preferred stock may lead to a capital gain because the discount rates used by the market have fallen, but superior performance by the firm is not apt to affect significantly the market price of the preferred stock because the cash dividend is set by the terms of the preferred stock.

There is one strategy that enhances the desirability of issuing preferred stock. Assume common stockholders are given the choice between holding common stock or exchanging the common stock for an equal or greater value of preferred stock. The company announces the common stock dividend will be zero after the exchange, The company saves the difference between the total common stock dividend and the preferred stock dividend.

The equity investor who chooses the preferred rather than common gains the following advantages:

1. a larger initial dividend (the same or larger present value)
2. less risk

However, the above is gained at the expense of:

1. loss of voting rights
2. loss of upside potential
3. loss of expected larger dividends

To get the common stockholder to exchange, the value of the offer might have to exceed somewhat the current stock price.

The special tax treatment afforded capital gains gives common stock an institutional advantage compared to preferred stock. If it were not for the tax consequences, assuming market forces worked rationally, a firm would not expect to gain an advantage or suffer a disadvantage by issuing preferred stock.

There are several ways the indifference between preferred stock and common stock without taxes can be shown, but only one technique is illustrated below.

Example

Assume a firm with $10 million of assets is expected to earn $1 million. There are zero taxes. If the firm is financed by common stock, the investors will expect to earn 0.10. If $4 million of preferred stock can be issued at a cost of 0.08, and substituted for $4 million of common stock, the expected return to common stockholders investing $6 million will be:

$$\frac{\$1,000,000 - \$320,000}{\$6,000,000} = \frac{\$680,000}{\$6,000,000} = 0.11\tfrac{1}{3} = \frac{0.34}{3}$$

Although the return on investment of the common stockholders has increased from 0.10 to 0.11⅓, their investment is subject to more risk than if no preferred stock had been issued (the preferred stock investors have prior claim to earnings, although the claim may not be effective).

The investors can adopt a strategy to neutralize the use of preferred stock by the issuer if they *invest in both common stock and preferred stock* in the following proportions:

$$\text{Percentage investment in common stock} = \frac{\text{Common Stock}}{\text{Total Capital of Firm}} = \frac{6}{10}$$

$$\text{Percentage investment in preferred stock} = \frac{\text{Preferred Stock}}{\text{Total Capital of Firm}} = \frac{4}{10}$$

The expected return of the investors is:

$$\frac{0.34}{3}\left(\frac{6}{10}\right) + 0.08\left(\frac{4}{10}\right) = 0.068 + 0.032 = 0.10$$

This is exactly the same expected return they would earn if the firm had been financed completely with common stock.

With the described investment strategy the investor will earn the same return with the given investment mix as would have been earned with all common stock financing for any corporate earnings. For example, if the firm earns $2 million and if it is financed completely by common stock, the stockholders will earn 0.20. If preferred stock is used, the investor following the above strategy for investing in both preferred and common stock will earn:

$$\frac{\$2,000,000 - \$320,000}{\$6,000,000}\left(\frac{6}{10}\right) + 0.08\left(\frac{4}{10}\right) = 0.168 + 0.032 = 0.20$$

Effectively this means that with zero taxes a firm's securities cannot sell at a discount because it is using preferred stock, compared to an identical company using just common stock. If it is selling at a discount, the knowledgeable investor can switch from the common stock firm to a mixture of the securities of the preferred stock firm. With taxes, the indifference situation is eliminated because common stock offers tax deferral advantages to the investor.

It can also be shown that the preferred stock issuing firm cannot sell at a premium.

Since the return to preferred stock is reasonably well defined and since the preferred stockholders precede the common stockholders (the preferred dividends are paid before the common dividends), preferred stock is a popular type of security for mergers and acquisitions where the sellers want a well-defined return each year. The seller of a firm wants to avoid the taxes that are imposed if cash or debt is received as payment but wants more safety than is offered by common stock. Dividends of both common and preferred stock are taxed as ordinary income, but since the common stock offers better likelihood of capital gains, there are tax advantages associated with the common stock not available to the preferred stock. This advantage can be exploited even more by shifting to earnings retention for common stock rather than cash dividends. The prospect of the capital gains treatment adds to the relative advantage of common stock compared to preferred stock for high-tax-paying investors.

OTHER REASONS FOR ISSUING PREFERRED STOCK

Preferred stock might appear to have a lower cost than common stock. Consider a situation where the common stock is selling at a P/E of 6 and preferred stock can be issued to yield 0.10. There are managers who will take the reciprocal of the P/E and conclude that the cost of stock equity is 0.167. Since preferred stock can be issued to yield 0.10, it would appear that preferred stock is cheaper than common stock. It should be remembered that issuance of preferred stock at 0.10 will result in a higher cost to the common stock, since there will be another party having claims ahead of the common stockholders on payday. This "cost" is implicit and thus difficult to measure exactly, but it does exist. Secondly, if the 0.167 is the result of the market expecting a decline in earnings to the common stock, the discount rate required by the stockholders (the cost of stock equity) may actually be less than the ratio of earnings to price (the expected growth rate affects the interpretation of the E/P ratio).

Public utilities find it useful to issue preferred stock for two reasons. First, insurance companies, given the 70% dividend-received deduction, like to buy it. Secondly, since the dividend cost is explicit, state regulatory commissions find it easy to accept the preferred stock cost measure. With common stock there are no objective measures of the cost of common stock equity.

From the point of view of an issuing corporation's common stockholders, preferred stock offers the opportunity to introduce a form of leverage (the preferred stockholders receive a maximum dividend return) that can benefit the common stockholders if the corporation does well in the future. The preferred stockholders do not participate in any bonanza that might occur, if their dividend rate is fixed.

It is not at all obvious that a tax-paying firm's common stockholders benefit from the issuance of preferred stock (this is not to imply that they are harmed), unless the issuer uses the preferred stock as a substitute for dividend paying common stock. It is obvious that the holders of preferred stock have a different risk situation than the holders of common stock. However, by the buying of mixtures of different types of stock and by the use of personal borrowing, the same types of risks and returns can generally be obtained as are obtained by the purchase of preferred stock. Market forces will tend to limit severely the advantages of capital structure manipulation unless there are tax advantages for one type of capital compared with another.

If the types of risks offered by the common stock and preferred stock purchased individually (not a mixture) are what the market desires and if the risks and returns cannot be exactly duplicated in any other way, then it is possible for a firm issuing preferred stock to sell at a premium. On a theoretical basis, it is unlikely that investors need the preferred stock to accomplish their investment objectives, but the existence of preferred stock in the capital structures of many firms suggest that the theoretical model is incomplete. Investors find having a broad spectrum of securities useful.

When we compare preferred stock with common stock, we find that preferred stock offers a type of leverage but that the investors by purchasing a mixture of securities can wipe out the leverage effect if they wish. If they desire the leverage and if the leverage of this type cannot be obtained in any other way, then at worst the preferred stock is akin to common stock and at best it might enhance somewhat the total value of the firm by offering the investors the form of investment that is desired.

TYPES OF PREFERRED STOCK

Convertible Exchangeable Preferred Stock

Assume that a corporation is operating at a level that leads to zero taxes. There are no current tax benefits associated with the issuance of debt. If exchangeable (into debt at the option of the issuing firm) preferred stock can be issued by a corporation not paying taxes at a lower before-tax yield than debt and it will have a lower cost than debt.

But what if the corporation starts earning sufficient income to start paying taxes? The corporation would then prefer to have outstanding debt rather than preferred stock. The "exchangeable" feature of the security allows the corporation to force the investors to accept debt for the preferred stock. If both the preferred stock and debt cost 0.10 before tax, with a 0.35 tax rate, the after-tax cost of debt becomes 0.065. This is a significant saving compared with the 0.10 cost of the preferred stock.

The corporate investor that purchased the preferred stock with its dividend received deduction will not be pleased with the forced exchange into a debenture. The corporate investor can sell, convert into common stock, or merely accept the exchange. The interest rate on the bond is likely to be at least as large as the preferred stock dividend, and will be somewhat safer. Zero-taxed investors, such as pension funds, are likely to find the debentures of more value than will a corporation taxed at a marginal rate of 0.35.

The fact that the security is exchangeable at the option of the issuing corporation reduces the expected overall cost to that corporation, but it does decrease the attractiveness of the security to the normally taxed corporate investor that prefers the preferred stock and the dividend received deduction.

The individual investor or the zero-taxed institutional investor would welcome the exchange, since the bond interest is safer than the preferred stock dividend. The investor cannot initiate the exchange and thus has to wait until the corporate issuer finds it advantageous to force the exchange.

The conversion feature is valuable to the investor since the investor can convert into common stock at any time. If the conversion value is $1,900 at the time of maturity of the exchangeable debenture, and the maturity value is $1,000, the value of the conversion right at that time will have a value above the maturity value of approximately $900.

The investor is not likely to opt for conversion prior to call or maturity unless the common stock dividend exceeds the preferred stock dividend or the debenture interest (the relative safety to the debenture interest and principal should also be considered), and even then there are strong reasons (risk avoidance) for not converting. The corporation is likely to call the convertible security if it can call and if the conversion value exceeds the call price.

The corporation can move the security from being preferred stock to being a debenture (desirable if the corporation changes from having zero taxable income to needing tax deductions). It can also call the security if the conversion value is larger than the call price and change the security into common stock.

The convertible exchangeable preferred stock is a sensible security. We would expect the corporate and personal tax laws as written to encourage further flexibility in the definition of securities. As long as the tax law distinguishes between securities, we can expect corporate financial officers to exploit this fact.

Convertible Money Market Preferred

A *convertible money market preferred stock* is an interesting security. The issuer adjusts the dividend to maintain the market value equal to the security's face value.

Assume the face value is $100 and the stock is convertible into four shares of common stock (not paying a dividend). A non-convertible preferred of comparable risk is yielding 0.07.

If the common is selling at $50, the dividend on the convertible would be set at zero. The market price would be approximately equal to the $200 conversion value.

If the common is selling at $5, the dividend on the convertible would be approximately $7 (the same yield as the non-convertible preferred) since the conversion value is worth very little.

Preference Equity Redemption Cumulative Stock

A *preference equity redemption cumulative stock* (PERCS) is a convertible preferred stock with the following characteristics.

1. preferred stock issued at the common stock price (for ease of comparison). The preferred pays a larger dividend than the common.
2. is convertible into common stock.
3. declining call price.
4. at maturity the preferred stock converts to common; the conversion value is capped.

Since there is a cap on the gain, the issuer likes the security. The investor receives a higher dividend than is being paid on the common.

The following facts apply to a 1992 issue of PERCS by Westinghouse.

Westinghouse PERCS (June 3, 1992)

	PERCS	Common Stock
Market Price	$17.00	417.00
Dividend	1.53*	0.72
Yield	0.09	0.042

* 0.3825 per quarter.

Mandatory Conversion Date: September 1, 1995. PERCS tend to have a 3-year life (investment bankers like this security).

Callable at any time.

> Initial Call Price = $26.23
> Call price after Q days
> Call price = $26.23 - 0.002095\ Q$
> > Equal to $23.93 on July 1, 1995
> > Equal to $23.80 from July 1 – September 1, 1995

On conversion the shares to be received are (Call Price/Market Price) but not more than one share. The investor cannot initiate conversion, but the issuer can call and force conversion. Since the call price is reduced through time, the number of shares to be received may also be reduced through time.

Each year the PERCS pays $0.81 more in dividends than the common. Thus if the stock price does not increase (say it remains at $17) at maturity, the buyer of the PERCS has the extra amount of cash dividend and one share of common after conversion. Thus the PERCS was a better investment than the common.

However, if the common stock price goes up significantly, say to $30, the common will beat the PERCS. For simplicity assume the investor buys the PERCS for $17, holds it for 3 years, and the discount rate is 0.09. At maturity the investor receives the $23.80 maturity value. If the stock price at maturity is less than $23.80, the investor receives one share of common. Assume the stock price is equal to $23.80 at maturity. Then

$$\text{Present value of PERCS} = \$1.53\ B(3,\ 0.09) + \$23.80(1.09)^{-3}$$
$$= \$3.87 + \$18.38 = \$22.25$$

With a PERCS if the stock price is larger than the Call Price the investor receives (Call Price/Market Price) shares with a value of "Call Price." With a $23.80 call price and a $30 market price (or any price larger than $23.80), the PERCS investor has $23.80 of value.

With a $30 stock price at maturity the value of the investment in common at time of purchase is:

$$\text{Present value of common} = \$0.72\ B(3,\ 0.09) + \$30.00(1.09)^{-3}$$
$$= \$1.82 + \$23.17 = \$24.99$$

The investment in the common is better than the PERCS if the stock price is $30. Reduce the stock price and the PERCS improves relative to the common.

Buying a PERCS is equivalent to:

1. Buying a share of common.
2. Writing (sell) a call option on the common.
3. Investing proceeds from writing the call.
4. Selling a call to the company for the PERCS.

The PERCS allows the investor to earn a larger dividend than the common stock investor. Of course, the investor is giving up a call option on the stock, but this may be considered to be of little value by the investor ("the stock will go up, but not that much"). The proof that investors think this way is that investors like PERCS or their variants.

There are other securities that are similar to PERCS. These include DECS, ACES, PRIDES, SAILS, and PEPS. It is necessary to read the prospectus to determine the nature of the security.

Monthly Income Preferred Shares

Monthly income preferred shares (MIPS) are equity (preferred) shares, but they result in a tax deduction for interest. All the characteristics are subject to modification.

A parent (U.S. firm) establishes subsidiaries (partnerships) offshore. The subsidiaries issue preferred stock to investors and use the cash to buy the debt of the parent. The interest on the debt is equal to the dividends paid on the preferred. The dividends and the interest can be deferred for up to five years.

Some of the rating agencies and analysts consider the MIPS to be equity. To date, the Internal Revenue Service has treated the payments by the parent to be interest, thus tax deductible, but MIPS (or the equivalents) are likely to be challenged by the U.S. Department of the Treasury.

CORPORATE INVESTING IN PREFERRED STOCK

A corporation has a tax incentive to use borrowed funds to invest in preferred stock. Because risk exists it is not a "money machine," but it is close. The company exercising this strategy has to have other taxable income so that the tax saving from the debt interest can be realized. To see this, assume a 0.70 dividend received deduction and a 0.35 corporate tax rate. Assume also a corporation invests in preferred stock paying $800 dividends. The firm has $1,000 of other before-tax income ($650 after tax) and pays $800 interest on the debt to finance the stock. Then,

Tax Calculation		*Income Calculation*		
Other income	$1,000	Other income		$1,000
Preferred dividends,		Preferred dividends		+ 800
800 × 0.30	+ 240			
Total Income	1,240	Total Income		1,800
		Deductions:		
Interest expense	− 800	Interest	800	
Taxable income	440			
		Tax	154	− 954
Tax rate	× 0.35			
Tax	154	Net Income		846

The net was increased from $650 to $846 as a result of receiving $800 dividends and paying $800 interest. Of course, the risk to the firm following this strategy has been increased.

This example implies that short-lived preferred stock could be an interesting investment for a corporation with idle cash (or the opportunity to borrow) and taxable income to protect.

PREFERRED STOCK AND INDIVIDUAL RETAIL INVESTOR

Is preferred stock a good investment for the individual retail investor? A zero-tax or low-tax investor might find a high-yielding preferred stock to be attractive compared with low-yielding common stock, but probably the investor would be better off with an equally high-yielding corporate bond if the rates are being set by corporate investors.

While straight preferred stock yielding less than safe debt is useful to corporate investors, it is difficult to see its advantages for individual retail investors because the dividends are taxed at ordinary rates. Corporations should not expect to sell large amounts of preferred stock to such investors. A few investors might be attracted by high yields, but the primary market for preferred stock is likely to be corporate investors.

If there was a large increase in preferred stock issues so that the yields were set by individual retail investors rather than by corporate investors, the yields might increase sufficiently so that they would be attractive to individuals.

There is a preferred stock paradox. Preferred stock is inferior to debt because the use of debt leads to a tax deduction for interest. Preferred stock is inferior to common stock because common stock leads to potential capital gains but preferred stock dividends are taxed at ordinary rates. Since high quality preferred stock tends to yield (before tax) less than comparable risk debt, it is purchased by corporations eligible for the 70% dividend received deduction.

The paradox is that if more preferred stock were issued (in excess of corporate demand) so that it was purchased by individuals it would yield more than debt since it has more risk. A corporation could use preferred stock to pay cash dividends and use common stock to retain earnings. Such a strategy could result in a significant enhancement of value for common shareholders.

ACCOUNTING FOR PREFERRED STOCK

It is not clear exactly what purpose the amount "preferred stock" shown on a balance sheet actually serves. Currently the measure alerts the reader to the fact that some preferred stock is outstanding. The number shown — for example, par — is likely to be of little use to an analyst.

There are several other reporting (at least disclosure) possibilities that would be improvements over present practice. These include using:

1. Market value (either at time of issue or the current market price).
2. The present value of the preferred stock dividends, using an independently determined rate of discount.
3. Liquidation value of the preferred stock.
4. Call price of the preferred stock.

MERGERS AND ACQUISITIONS

Preferred stock has been a popular security in mergers and acquisitions when the acquiring firm has felt that it could not issue more debt because of risk consider-ations, and when the stockholders selling out wanted a somewhat more certain return than could be obtained from common stock (which might be paying a low dividend or not paying a dividend at all). Add a conversion feature to further enhance the pre-ferred stock (the new investors have a chance to share in the benefits if the firm per-forms in a superior fashion), and common stockholders accepting the preferred stock in exchange have a chance to participate in any large gains that might occur.

It is in connection with mergers and acquisitions that the use of preferred stock by a competitive firm can be explained. But, it is still difficult to overcome the tax advantages of debt and common stock.

PREFERRED STOCK AND SHORT-TERM INVESTMENT

Most preferred stock is issued without a maturity date (however, the stock may be callable by the issuing corporation). This infinite life causes the price of the security to be more sensitive to changes in the market discount rate than shorter-lived securities.

If a preferred stock has a maturity date, the short-lived preferred is an interesting security for a corporate treasurer investing short-term funds because of the 70% dividend received deduction (although it might still be hard to beat debt with tax-deductible interest). However, as long as preferred stock has an infinite life, a corporate treasurer who likes to sleep at night will tend not to invest short-term money in preferred stock with a fixed dividend rate. Small changes in interest rates can cause large changes in value. This risk has led firms to issue preferred stock with a floating dividend rate so that the value remains close to face value.

PREFERRED STOCK AND
CORPORATE FINANCIAL PLANNING

Real-world situations tend to differ from each other, and it is difficult to reach iron-clad generalizations. The logic of this chapter leads to the conclusion that tax-paying corporations should rarely issue plain vanilla preferred stock. A change in the tax law or other institutional factors (such as a law requiring insurance companies to hold preferred stock) could alter this conclusion, as could a group of investors insisting on receiving preferred stock in a merger or acquisition.

The right to issue preferred stock gives the corporate financial officer more flexibility in choosing financing alternatives. This flexibility in choosing financing alternatives has value because it might enable the firm to move rapidly in a situation in which preferred stock is the only feasible alternative. Although the long-range financial plan might not include preferred stock, at any moment in time it might be appropriate for a corporation to use preferred stock, because of special circumstances. It is wise for a corporation issuing preferred stock to have that preferred stock callable at the option of the firm. Preferred stock issued today can be very expensive tomorrow if interest rates and required dividend yields were to decrease dramatically.

How often should preferred stock pay dividends? Let us assume that a $100 preferred stock purchased at $100 is paying $10 a year in dividends. On the day before the dividend payment the stock will sell for $110, assuming that it will sell for $100 *ex dividend* and assuming the group of investors setting the price pay no taxes. Now assume a second group of investors who pay 0.396 tax on ordinary income and 0.20 on capital gains presently hold the stock. The investor holding the security and receiving the dividend will have the security worth $100 plus $6.04 after tax on the $10 dividend. The investor selling the day before the dividend will pay a $2 capital gains tax and will have $108.00 of cash. With zero transaction costs this investor can then buy a preferred share of a comparable firm after the dividend payment for $100 and have $8.00 of cash left over. This is $1.96 more than the $6.04 that would result from receiving the cash dividend.

To justify a $110 price the day before the dividend, we have to assume the price is set by investors with a zero tax rate. A zero-tax investor would be willing to pay close to $110 for the share immediately before the dividend.

The conclusion is that there is a transaction cost advantage to the investing community in having a preferred stock that pays a cash dividend relatively infrequently. Imagine a preferred stock that paid cash dividends annually or biannually or even every fifth year. This stock would facilitate interesting investment strategies for investors wanting capital gains. The proposed plan requires tax rate differentials among the investors and approval by the tax authorities. Also, the tax authorities define the number of days the stock must be owned for the firm to qualify for the dividend received deduction.

PREFERENCE SHARES

Preference shares are similar to preferred stock except that they are likely to be junior to preferred stock (they will generally be rated by rating agencies one letter grade below preferred stock).

CONCLUSIONS

The use of preferred stock should always be evaluated but preferred stock should only be used in special situations. Until the tax laws are changed, preferred stock tends to be inferior to debt and common stock. However, if a firm does not need the tax shields of the interest, the gap between the issuance of preferred stock and debt is greatly narrowed, especially when the preferred stock is viewed as strengthening the capital structure. Also, preferred stock is a popular vehicle for achieving acquisitions. With the 70% dividend-received deduction we can expect preferred stock to be considered an attractive security by public utilities that want to fill the desires of insurance companies for this type of security. Finally, specially structured preferred securities such as PERCS and MIPS have greatly enhanced the attractiveness of using preferred stocks.

If the firm combines a preferred stock issue with a change in common stock dividend policy (changing the common stock to zero), this offers the possibility of tax savings at the investor level, and is a strategy worthy of consideration.

Chapter 4

The Nature of Debt

W hy have corporations in the post World War II period tended to use debt rather than newly issued common stock? The primary reason is closely tied to the level of taxation (high) and the tax structure, which gives a tax advantage to debt. The interest paid to debt holders is a tax deduction to the corporate issuer; thus the interest expense acts as a tax shield. With a tax rate of 0.35, the effective cost of debt capital to a profitable (tax-paying firm) is normally reduced by 35%. A second reason for the use of debt is that debt introduces a leverage effect that is attractive to aggressive managers willing to accept a high level of risk in return for high expected returns. Thus the use of debt is called *leverage* or *gearing*.

DEBT AND RISK

Imagine a situation where a firm with $50 million of common stock can have the following two earnings outcomes:

	Probabilities	Common Stock Earnings	Return on Stock Equity
Good business conditions	0.6	$10,000,000	0.20
Bad business conditions	0.4	$2,000,000	0.04

While considering only two outcomes is artificially simplified, the example could be extended to a continuous spectrum of outcomes with no change in the basic method of analysis or conclusions.

Note that in this example even with bad business conditions the firm has positive earnings. An investor in the common stock will always earn something. Now let us substitute $30 million of 0.10 debt for $30 million of common stock. The debt pays $3 million interest. Continuing the above example but now subtracting the interest, the following outcomes can occur:

	Probabilities	Common Stock Earnings	Return on Stock Equity
Good business conditions	0.6	$7,000,000	0.35
Bad business conditions	0.4	−$1,000,000	loss

The good return on stock equity increases from 0.20 to 0.35, but the bad return to the stockholders is now negative. Negative returns in one or more years imply there is a risk of bankruptcy.

Of course, normally there is the possibility of a firm having negative incomes even if there is zero debt. But that does not change the fact that the addition of debt tends to increase the probability of the earnings to the common stockholders being negative.

A small increase in debt might leave the probability of negative earnings relatively unchanged (in the above example $2 million of debt paying $200,000 of interest would not change the probability of loss) and in fact might decrease the probability of loss if the funds obtained were invested in profitable real assets with little or no risk. But in most realistic situations where debt is substituted for common stock we can expect an increase in the probability of loss.

While debt increases risk, we also need to stress the positive leverage aspect. The good outcomes are amplified in such a way that debt can appear to be very desirable. In the example, the return on investment was increased from 0.20 to 0.35 for the good event. If the probability of this event were 0.99 instead of 0.60, we would have a very strong case from the viewpoint of common stockholders for the substitution of $30 million debt for the common stock in this situation.

Frequently the variance of the outcomes is used as a measure of risk for an undiversified investor. Variance is a measure of spread or dispersion. The more spread out the outcomes, the more risk there is. We can use the example to illustrate the way that debt affects the variance of the outcomes. Without debt there was either a 0.20 return or a 0.04 return. With debt there was either a 0.35 return or a loss. The debt increased the range of the returns on investment. We could make comparable calculations using earnings per share and find the same type of increase in variance (the variance can be defined exactly mathematically, but the notion of spread is adequate for this discussion).

Debt is most attractive when the analysis assumes there is one highly desirable highly probable outcome. For the current example, we assume the earnings before interest are $10 million, and the substitution in turn of $30 million and $40 million of debt causes substantial changes in the return on stock equity investment. Moving from $30 million to $40 million of debt increases the return on equity (ROE) from 0.35 to 0.60. This process of using debt to increase the ROE is called "trading on the equity." The example illustrates well the way that debt can be presented as an attractive means of financing.

	Zero Debt	Debt of $30 million	Debt of $40 million
Earnings before interest	$10,000,000	$10,000,000	$10,000,000
Interest	0	3,000,000	4,000,000
Earnings to stockholders	10,000,000	7,000,000	6,000,000
Stock Equity	50,000,000	20,000,000	10,000,000
Return on equity (ROE)	0.20	0.35	0.60

Assume that initially (zero debt) there are 10 million shares of common stock earning $1 per share. The $30 million of new debt is used to retire 60% of the shares, so that after the debt issuance there are only 4 million shares outstanding and the earnings per share become $1.75. With debt of $40 million there are 2 million shares outstanding, and the earnings per share are now $3 per share. Again, as long as we assume only one desirable event is possible, the arguments are very strong that debt should be used. Even when it is well known that more than one event is possible, corporate financial analysts sometimes prepare reports and reach conclusions as if there were only one possible event.

The use of debt should be considered by all firms, but the decision as to the optimum amount of debt is not easy.

THE COST OF DEBT

Debt has a lower explicit cost than common stock, generally has a fixed maturity, and since the debt holders are senior to stockholders, the issue of debt adds to the risk of the stockholders. The tax deductibility of interest cost tends to further reduce the explicit cost of debt.

With zero taxes we define the cost of debt to be the rate of interest that equates all future contractual payments of interest and principal to the holders of the debt. Thus if the debt promises to pay $100 a year interest for 20 years and $1,000 at maturity, and the bonds are issued at $1,000, we conclude that the cost of the debt is 0.10. If the bonds were issued at a price of $851, we assume that the cost of debt is 0.12, because that is the discount rate that equates the sum of the present value of all future payments to $851:

	Contractual Dollar Amounts	Present Value Factors (0.12)	Present Values (using 0.12)
Principal	$1,000	0.1037	$104
Interest per year	100	7.4694	747
			$851

If interest is deductible for taxes in the situation in which the 0.10 bonds are issued at par, and if the corporate tax rate is 0.35, the after-tax cost of the debt is 0.065. This assumes the presence of taxable income; thus the tax deduction can be used. If the tax deduction cannot be used, the before-tax cost of 0.10 becomes the after-tax cost.

The definition of cost used here is not exact. If we considered uncertainty explicitly, we would recognize that the payment of interest and principal are not certain, that the expected values to be collected are likely to be less than the contractual amounts, and that the investors will not be making their decisions using expected monetary values if there is risk aversion. Also, if the debt has been outstanding and can be retired at a cost different than the par value, the cost of the debt is based on the after-tax outlay required to retire the debt. The cost is the internal rate of return of the after-tax debt cash flows.

The cost of debt is generally defined as the internal rate of return of the debt cash flow stream. A bond paying $100 interest per year for 50 years and

$1,000 at maturity issued at a price of $1,000 has a cost of 0.10. If we discount all the cash flows using 0.10, the net present value of all the debt flows including the initial cash receipts of $1,000 is equal to zero.

Despite the seeming simplicity of defining the cost of debt, there are some interesting complexities. For example, assume a firm has $300 million of 0.06 debt outstanding, and if it issues additional debt, the cost will be 0.14. What is the cost of debt? The 0.06 is not relevant to the decision making of a manager of a firm engaged in normal business activity unless there is a possibility of retiring the debt. If a firm has cash and there is 0.06 debt outstanding and if the next best use of funds to the firm is 0.04, then it might be desirable to retire the 0.06 outstanding debt. The 0.06 becomes a form of opportunity cost, and this opportunity cost is relevant to a decision to retire the debt at its face value.

But if the firm has no cash and investment opportunities yielding 0.07, the 0.06 cost of the outstanding debt is not of any relevance in deciding whether or not to undertake those investments since new capital is needed. If external capital is needed, one would not want to borrow at 0.14 to invest in projects yielding 0.07. The 0.14 becomes a minimum necessary return for new investment. Unless the investment yields more than 0.14, it must be rejected (this is inexact, since the risk characteristics of the investment might lead to its acceptance, but the conclusion is correct with no uncertainty and no taxes). The average cost of debt, including the embedded cost, does not affect the investment decision.

In the above discussion we ignored taxes and the fact that debt interest offers a tax shield. With a 0.35 corporate tax rate and a borrowing rate of 0.14, the after-tax cost of debt is:

$$(1 - 0.35)\,0.14 = 0.091$$

If the firm found that it could not use its tax shield to reduce taxes (say that its losses were so large that it was not paying taxes and did not expect to pay taxes in the future), the cost of debt would then return to 0.14. So a firm borrowing at a cost of 0.14 could expect its after-tax cost of debt to be between 0.091 and 0.14 depending on its tax status. The introduction of the 0.20 alternative minimum tax means that the after-tax cost could be $(1 - 0.2)0.14 = 0.112$ or something else. A prospective change in tax rate would be another factor causing a complexity in computing the after-tax borrowing rate. The after-tax cost of debt issued at face value can be defined as:

$$\frac{\text{Interest Cost} - \text{Tax Savings from Use of Debt}}{\text{Present Value of Debt}}$$

Subordination and the Cost of Debt

Assume that a firm has assets that have been financed with common stock, and now it is considering substituting debt for common stock. Furthermore, the firm may wish to issue additional debt in the future. This additional debt may or may not be identical to the original debt with respect to its priority in case of bankruptcy. The primary question we consider is how the cost of present and future issues of debt is influenced by the number of different categories of debt used, and by the protection that may or may not be given the holders of a particular category against the possibility that additional debt of an equal or higher priority may be issued in the future.

In this chapter, a debt category is defined to be senior to a second debt category (the subordinate debt) if all the claims of the senior debt's contract must be fully satisfied before any assets can be applied to satisfy the claims in (the subordinate debt) contract. A bond category is said to be protected against equal or senior issues if, during the life of the given category, the firm cannot have outstanding a larger quantity of equal or senior debt than was outstanding at the time the given category was issued. If a bond category is protected against both senior and equal issues, the category is described as fully protected. A bond category is said to have limited protection against senior (equal) categories if the firm is allowed to issue a specified amount of additional senior (equal) debt.

Given the assumptions we are making about the possible types of relative priority, in theory there is no logical reason for the potential purchaser of a given category of debt to be concerned about the amount of subordinate debt that is currently outstanding or that may be issued in the future. In the real world, the presence of subordinate debt may cause transaction costs by triggering bankruptcy, thus it is relevant.

A firm has a number of options available to it. First, it must decide the number of debt categories (one or more) to issue simultaneously. Second, it must decide, for each category, whether the category is to be given full protection or only limited protection, and if the latter, how large the limits should be. These decisions influence the current cost of borrowing and the cost of future borrowing.

Costs of Sequential Issues of Protected Subordinated Debt

Suppose that the firm first issued $10 million of fully protected bonds at a cost of 0.05 and then decided to issue an additional amount of debt. Since the first $10 million of debt is fully protected, the second category of debt must necessarily be subordinate to the first. The first category is the senior debt and the second category the junior or subordinate debt.

Conceivably some financial analysts might feel that the assets of this company are relatively secure, the risk of default is slight, and that the fact that the second block of debt is subordinated to the first is of minor importance. They might be willing to recommend purchase of this block of junior debt if it were priced to yield slightly more than 0.05. It would, however, be inconsistent with the assumption of a probability of default to suggest that with no change in the market interest rates the junior debt could be priced to yield an amount equal to 0.05, since in this case the second block of $10 million is subordinate. If we assume that the average cost of a single $20 million issue of fully protected senior debt would be 0.06 then the incremental cost of the second $10 million would be 0.07. We would expect many financial analysts to be apprehensive about risk, and thus be concerned about the fact that the debt is subordinated. They would be unwilling to recommend purchase unless the junior debt were priced at or above 0.07.

It might be argued that if the firm set out to raise $20 million by debt, two separate issues of $10 million each (one subordinated to the other) might be more or less expensive than one $20 million issue of equally protected debt. The one large issue would be more or less expensive, depending on whether the subordinated $10 million issue would require a quoted yield of more or less than 0.07.

In a perfect market the cost to the firm will tend to be the same regardless of which choice it makes. In essence, the argument, as it applies to the present problem, is that if the firm issued two blocks of bonds, one subordinate to the other, and both fully protected, an investor could buy a proportion of both blocks of bonds and have the same risk as if the firm had issued one block of debt with equal rights, and the investor had invested the same total amount in that block. Assuming that there are some potential investors willing to switch, and that bonds of the same risk class are available as substitutes elsewhere, we expect the average return on the two blocks taken together to be equal to the average return on the large block.

Now assume that potential investors, because of preferences or legal restrictions, are unable to switch from one type of debt to another. The conclusion may still hold that a large issue of nonsubordinated debt will cost the firm the same amount as two separate issues, one senior to the other. Suppose the conclusion were not true, and two separate issues, one subordinate to the other, cost the firm less than a single large issue. Other firms would observe the lower cost and would also issue new debt in the form of separate categories. The firm would refund old debt (in the form of more expensive large blocks) into the less expensive separate issues with different seniorities. Over time the supply of the relatively expensive debt would decrease, and the supply of relatively inexpensive types of debt would increase. This shift would continue until the alternatives of one large issue or several smaller issues (with the different issues having different priorities) were equally expensive.

We conclude that the firm, considering the costs of servicing the debt, should be indifferent as to whether it raises a given amount of debt by making one large issue or several smaller issues, of unequal priority.

Debt Cost and Leverage

The cost of debt is a function of the amount of leverage. We define the amount of leverage as the amount of debt (B) divided by the amount of stock (S) plus amount of debt (B). The cost of debt curve goes up as the amount of debt increases. For example, if with zero debt the cost is 0.08, with 0.5 debt the cost is 0.10, and with 100% debt the cost is 0.12, then the cost curve would be linear (a straight line).

The debt cost of a 100% debt firm is equal to the cost of stock equity for a zero debt firm (the debt is essentially common stock). At 100% debt the cost of debt is equal to the weighted average cost of capital.

The contractual interest cost does not represent the total cost of debt. The issuance of debt increases the cost of common stock (as well as the cost of other more subordinated debt) and thus has a cost in excess of the explicit contractual interest cost.

Consider a situation where with zero debt the addition of $1 of debt costs 0.08 and the addition of $1 of common stock costs 0.12. Capital (all equity) is costing 0.12 but it would appear that debt costs less than common stock and should be substituted for common stock. However, assume that the issuance of debt leading to a capital structure of 0.5 debt results in a cost of debt of 0.10 and a cost of common stock of 0.14. With a capital structure of either zero debt or 0.5 debt, the weighted average cost of capital is 0.12.

We know that both the cost of debt and the cost of common stock increase as the amount of leverage increases. For decision making purposes it is inaccurate to state that the yield of a debt issue represents the cost of the debt, since the cost of common stock and the cost of other debt are affected by the issuance of the debt.

INCOME BONDS

Finance officers are constantly seeking cheaper sources of capital. An income bond is a form of security that has not been used to a large extent, but a discussion of income bonds is particularly useful as a learning device because it helps open our imagination to the possibility of new types of securities. On the spectrum of securities ranked according to riskiness to investors, income bonds would be between subordinated debentures and preferred stock.

Income bonds are not easy to define because they come in a variety of forms. They have many characteristics found in regular bonds or preferred stock and thus may be said to be merely variations on bonds or preferred stock. However, if income bonds have essentially the qualities of preferred stock, they would seem to warrant consideration by prospective issuers of securities as a way to avoid income tax; however, if income bonds had the same characteristics as preferred stock there would be no reason to expect special treatment under the tax code as compared to preferred stock. It is necessary that income bonds be enough like debt so that the deduction of interest on income bonds is included in the government's definition of interest on debt.

Income bonds have a set rate of interest, but the interest must be paid only if earned. The interest may be cumulative to give the investor more security. The interest features of income bonds are different from the dividend features of preferred stock. The most significant difference is that the payment of dividends on preferred stock is more discretionary; it is usually mandatory to pay interest on income bonds if income is earned. The interest payment on an income bond is substantially different from that on straight bonds, since there is no obligation on the part of the corporation to pay interest when it has not earned an amount equal to the interest. Consequently, income bondholders cannot force a corporation, which has a loss period, into receivership.

Income bonds may give their holders a position preferred to that of general business credits in the hierarchy of creditor's rights, but below other bondholders. Preferred stockholders are placed below the general business credits and would be below the income bondholders. The effect of this arrangement, where it exists would make additional credit a little more difficult to secure with income bonds outstanding than with preferred stock. If the income bonds were junior to the general business creditors, it would increase the risk of the income bondholders receiving nothing in the event of liquidation, but the investors would still be in a better position than the preferred stockholders.

Income bonds must have a maturity date and in this respect differ from perpetual preferred stock. A maturity date is considered by the tax courts to be a necessary condition for there to be debt (although there is no essential reason for this requirement). A maturity date imposes more risk on the borrower. If the firm does not have the funds for repayment at the maturity date, it may be forced into receivership. Preferred stock has no such risk because there is no way the preferred shareholder can force the issuing firm into bankruptcy. There have been issues of preferred stock with provision for repurchase each year or with provision for mandatory redemption, but these issues are relatively rare.

In summary, income bondholders generally have substantially greater rights against the corporation than holders of preferred stock and fewer rights than bondholders. Income bondholders have the right to demand their money at maturity, and the right to interest if earned. Compared to regular bonds, income bonds are less risky to the corporation because the holders do not have the right to demand interest as it falls due. The risks associated with income bonds are between the risk normally associated with preferred stock and that associated with bonds.

If income bonds can provide a large degree of risk avoidance for issuers compared to bonds, why are they not used more? One reason is that income bonds have been used extensively in connection with reorganizations, and thus they tend to be associated with weak corporations. The historical association of income bonds with weakness seems to be fading slowly.

A second reason offered for not using income bonds is that strong companies do not need to issue income bonds because they can bear the burden of fixed charges on bonds. Although this argument is superficially attractive, it should be noted that even a strong corporation can issue only a limited amount of low-cost debt with low risk. At a given point in time it may be logical for such a corporation to pay the interest premium that income bonds would cost compared to the cost of other debt.

One fear of financial officers that is preventing the widespread use of income bonds may be that, if many corporations used this type of security to raise capital, the government would react and change the internal revenue code and disallow the deduction. This is a somewhat confused and incomplete analysis. The present code has a bias in favor of fixed-payment type of securities (interest payments being deductible and dividends not). This is undesirable from the point of view of the economy because it leads to corporations being more unstable. Corporations are more susceptible to ruin if business activity slackens. Income bonds used instead of regular debt adds to the survival power of a corporation rather than reducing it, and as such should be welcomed by government decision makers. The market may have to be educated as to the nature and advantages of income bonds. Perhaps a new title is needed. In any event, given the present tax code, it is apparent that there is a place in the capital structure of a corporation for income bonds. The corporate financial officer who does not investigate the possibility of their use is giving up the opportunity for tax savings (where the income bonds are used instead of equity-type securities) or reducing risk (where the income bonds are used instead of pure debt).

Other Types of Bonds

Characteristics of bonds are continuously changing to accommodate the needs of investors and borrowers. With high rates of inflation, lenders like bonds whose interest rates reflect the changes in the price level. A few bonds have been indexed to the price of commodities such as oil, silver, or gold.

Bonds can also be made convertible into stock in order to make them more attractive to investors. Although bells and whistles can be added to a bond, it must be remembered that a bond is no better than the company that issued the security, and the contractual provisions of the bond.

MEASURING DEBT

Accountants implicitly or explicitly make use of the present value principles in the measurement of long-term debt. For example, when the bond is issued, the liability is recorded at the amount received from the creditors; for a bond with a maturity value of $1,000, the liability is measured by the amount of cash received. This eliminates the need for the firm to compute explicitly the present value of the future payments. When the effective interest rate is equal to the contractual rate of the debt, the amount received at time of issue is equal to the amount to be paid at maturity, assuming the interest is paid periodically. That is, the cash received is equal to both the maturity amount and the present value of the debt using the current effective interest rate.

An important operational weakness of this practice is that it complicates interfirm comparisons because the debt-type cash flows are implicitly discounted using different discount rates. Consider the following example:

Company A issues $10 million of 20-year 0.05 bonds at 0.05, its effective rate of interest, and the debt is recorded at $10 million.

Exhibit 1: Present Value Computations Using the 0.04 Default-Free Rate

Dollar Amounts	Present Value Factors (.04)	Company A	Company X
$10,000,000	0.4564	$4,564,000	$4,564,000
500,000 per year	13.5903	6,795,000	
1,000,000 per year	13.5903		13,590,000
Present value of the liabilities		$11,359,000	$18,154,000

Company X issues $10 million of 20-year 0.10 bonds at 0.10, its effective rate of interest, and its debt is recorded at $10 million.

In an important sense, the two companies have different amounts of debt outstanding, and that conventional accounting fails to note this. Company A has promised to pay only $500,000 of interest per year for 20 years; Company X has promised to pay $1 million a year interest for the same period. Both companies have promised to pay $10 million at maturity.

In the example, we assume that both sets of bonds were issued at par and at the same time. Therefore, the difference in the quoted yields (which are equal to the contractual rates in this case) must be due to differences in risk in the two firms and not to differences in general economic conditions. Since we conclude that the yield differences result mainly from investors' evaluation of and reaction to the risk of default (assuming the bonds have similar call protection and other such contract provisions), we examine how this reaction may lead to the observed differences. Potential investors may not analyze default risk in the exact manner adopted here but the computations are illustrative.

If there were no risk of default, it would be possible to obtain a reliable predictor of the value of the bonds of Company A and of Company X (and therefore a predictor of how much the companies would obtain by selling them) using the yield on U.S. government bonds of similar maturity. Suppose that when the bonds were issued U.S. government bonds of the same maturity have a 0.04 yield. The present values of the liabilities of Companies A and X using a 0.04 interest are computed in Exhibit 1. These present values are predictions of the value of the bonds if they were default free. We cannot assume there is no risk of default for the securities of A and X. Investors do not expect to receive the amounts listed above, because they do not consider the bonds to be default free. There is no objective means of determining exactly the probabilities of default that investors actually assign.

USING DEBT TO REDUCE RISK

There are two ways of using debt to reduce risk to the stockholders. One is to use a large amount of debt, thus reducing the total amount of capital committed by the equity investors to be close to zero.

A second type of risk reduction takes place when the investment being undertaken with debt capital has very little risk. Thus the addition of the investment, even where there is a large amount of debt added, still reduces the risk to the firm. Imagine a situation where an investment earns $1,000 per month and the associated debt payments are $800 per month. If the $1,000 is certain, the overall risk of the firm is reduced by the $200 per month net increment, which can be used to pay other bills. The same conclusion follows if there is just a little risk, but does not hold as the amount of risk becomes large.

DEBT CHARACTERISTICS

Each characteristic of the debt contract affects the cost of the debt. For example, each of the following characteristics has a direct bearing on the interest rate the firm will have to pay if the debt is going to be issued at par:

1. Length of time until maturity (or the duration of the debt).
2. Degree of protection (e.g., a mortgage) or subordination to other debt.
3. Length of time till it can be called and the call price.
4. Financial protections (minimum current ratios, working capital, etc.).
5. Protection against event risk (event risk is the risk that a corporate restructuring will lead to an increase in credit risk).

The way that the debt contract is written will depend on the strategy considerations of the firm. For example, if it is important that the firm not be locked into a high-cost debt contract, the firm will want to make the debt callable as rapidly as is feasible.

Also, if the funds are going to be used to finance long-lived assets, the firm will prefer the use of debt with long maturities. It is important that long-lived assets be financed with long-term debt in order to keep the level of risk at a manageable level, and to increase the likelihood that the cash is available to pay the debt. It is a risky financial strategy to use short-term debt to finance long-lived assets. If the debt comes due before the assets have generated the cash flows necessary to repay the debt, the firm is then at the mercy of the lenders and the level of interest rates. While theoretically other lenders should be willing to step forward and supply the financing, one might not want to risk the situation where management knows the prospects are good, but the lenders do not have the same view of the world.

The Investor and Debt

The issuer of debt should have an appreciation of the risks that an investor faces. The investor has many risks. The primary risk is the risk of default. Not being paid back the funds which have been lent is the worst fate in the minds of most lenders, but there are several close contenders.

With long-term debt an increase in the market rate of interest will result in a decrease in the market value of the security. While the loss might not be recorded, it still exists. Each period the investor has a loss of interest revenue arising from being locked into a low-paying security. A comparable loss arises from having invested in a fixed-income security when a period of surprise inflation occurs. The loss in purchasing power might not be avoidable, but it is still a loss.

If the investor has a security paying a high interest rate, the risk of having the security called by the issuing firm is real. A bond that is noncallable has protection for the investor against a situation where interest rates go down. Without that protection an investor is apt to find a high-yielding bond replaced by a new low-yielding bond.

Why Use Debt?

Why should a corporation use debt? The most obvious reason is that it needs an infusion of capital. But why debt rather than common stock?

An important reason for using debt is that it is a fixed claim; thus its use offers the possibility of large gains to the stockholders if the expectations of profits are realized. This "trading on the equity" is a powerful reason for using debt. Debt amplifies the returns to stock equity capital.

It is conventional wisdom that debt costs less than common stock because of the tax laws. There is no question that the tax shield of debt interest is very attractive. Aside from the tax shield, debt will appear to cost less than common stock because the conventional calculation omits the effect of debt issuance on the cost of the common stock. One must also consider the cost of financial distress.

In a situation where the present stockholders do not want their ownership control to be diluted, debt is a useful form of capital. Also, the existence of the capital need may be viewed as relatively short term, and debt gives flexibility, since its retirement on maturity automatically shrinks the size of the firm.

A common reason for using debt is that it is a bad time to issue common stock. The common stock price is temporarily depressed, or the price-earnings ratio is too low. The lack of faith in an efficient capital market is widespread. It is not unusual for management to think the market to be efficient (the stocks are reasonably priced) for other common stocks but not properly priced for its own stock. A much more acceptable strategy, in the absence of significant insider information, would be to conclude that the market has considered the same factors as management and, given all factors (including current interest rates and business condition expectations), has set the market price. Thus "timing" would be downgraded in importance in determining whether debt or common stock should be issued.

If management wants to bet that the market for its common stock is temporarily depressed, then a strategy of issuing short-term debt as a temporary source of capital is reasonable. When the market price of the common stock approaches its intrinsic value, the debt is replaced by the common stock. The objection to this strategy is that one does not know when this increase in stock price is going to occur. In fact, it is not clear the common stock is actually depressed. It might just be that management's expectations are excessively optimistic. Thus an alternative strategy is to issue common stock directly rather than first issue debt.

The advantages of debt as a method of raising capital are many. The following items are by no means independent of each other, and some of the items listed may be questioned, since they may be accompanied by disadvantages that outweighs the advantages.

1. Trading on the equity (this implies that debt has a lower cost than stock equity).
2. Tax savings arising because of the deductibility of interest expense in computing taxable income.
3. Retention of ownership control by stockholders (no dilution of the stockholders' voting position).
4. Flexibility (after the need for the cash is over, the size of the firm is easily shrunk if debt is used to meet the temporary cash need).
5. Ease and quickness of obtaining the capital (especially valid if the firm has a line of credit or credit agreement with a bank).
6. Hedge interest rate changes (if the debt payment coincides with certain investment cash flows from assets such as marketable securities, a perfect hedge against interest rate changes may be arranged).
7. Timing; if it is not a good time to issue stock because the market value of the stock is currently less than the value estimated by management, and if management expects the stock's market value to increase in the near future, then debt may be a desirable short-run substitute for stock equity.
8. Lower risk (the total exposure of stockholders to the loss of capital because the total amount of the stockholders' investment is less than it would have been if no debt had been issued. This is related to the retention of control (item 3), trading on the equity (item 1), and the limited liability characteristics of a corporation.)

Arguments Against Debt

The primary argument against the use of debt is that debt may cause the stockholders to lose their ticket to future profits if an unforeseen bad event occurs. The variance of the outcomes to stockholders (both ROE and earnings per share) is increased, with the result that a bump can throw off the stockholders. This prospect is not pleasant, and unfortunately its occurrence is inevitable (not for any one specific firm in a given year, but over a long enough period for many firms, the probability of financial difficulty becomes larger with an increase in the amount of debt used).

In addition to the increase in the amount of risk, there is the loss of managerial freedom. It is a rare debt covenant that does not restrict the actions of management in a manner that management would prefer did not exist.

A primary reason for not issuing debt is that there is a loss of financing flexibility as debt is issued and the firm approaches debt capacity. Management frequently will prefer a margin of safety (flexibility) that means the firm can issue more debt if it needs more capital.

The amount of debt a firm can issue is limited. The limit may exist in the minds of management (a formulation of corporate financial strategy), or they may actually be specified by the outstanding debt contracts. The preference of the bond rating agencies may also be highly significant. There are many types of barriers. For example, a firm might not want more than a 0.35 debt/equity ratio (debt divided by common stock) or less than a three times interest coverage ratio ($75 million of income before taxes and interest divided by $25 million of interest, or some variation of this). Once these barriers have been set, they preclude the issuance of debt that will violate them. The amount of debt is also limited by the earnings prospects of the assets being financed. Perhaps the exact limits cannot be determined, but estimates can be made.

DURATION OF DEBT

Consider two companies with identical expected cash flows for the next year and both having debt/equity ratios of 0.40. This information may lead us to believe that there is equal interest rate risk in granting a dollar of credit to either but suppose that we now inform you that the former company has all its debt due in 1 year while the latter has no debt due for 10 years. Now, all other things being equal, the former is more risky, since its cash needs are greater in the first year. One measure of the immediacy of debt repayment is the average duration of the debt. The duration of a series of debt payments is the weighted average life of the cash flows, where the weights are the present values of the cash flows. The duration of a single-payment debt coming due in 20 years is 20 years. The duration of a 2-year $1,000 bond paying $100 a year interest for 2 years, issued at par (the current market interest rate is 10%), is 1.91.

$$d = \frac{1 \times \$100(1.10)^{-1} + 2 \times \$1,100(1.10)^{-2}}{\$1,000}$$

$$= \frac{\$90.91 + \$1,818.12}{\$1,000} = 1.91$$

The duration (or average life) of a conventional interest-paying bond is always less than its maturity. If the bond only makes a payment at maturity (a zero-coupon bond), the duration is equal to its maturity. A zero-coupon bond is a discount bond that only promises a single payment at maturity. Zero-coupon bonds have no explicit interest payment. The difference between their purchase price and maturity (face) value is the interest earned.

In addition to measuring the average life of the debt, duration measures are useful for judging the sensitivity of the market value of a debt (or investment) to changes in prevailing interest rates. It can be shown, for example, that if two equal debts have the same duration, then a small change in the entire structure of interest rates will result in the same change in market values of the two debts.

It is frequently said that the longer a bond's maturity, the more risk there is due to interest rate fluctuations. The value of a 20-year bond will change more than a 2-year bond for a given interest rate change. It is more accurate to say that the larger the duration, the more the value will change. The value change for small discrete changes in the interest rate is approximately equal to the product of the duration, the negative of the change in the interest rate, and the present value of the debt.

THE BOND REFUNDING DECISION

The question is whether or not to refund an outstanding long-term debt (that is callable) now, assuming that refunding in the future will be less desirable than refunding now (implicitly, the possibility of future refunding is not considered). The primary objective is to reconcile different approaches to making this type of decision and to illustrate a procedure that resolves the question of which rate of discount to use in making the refunding decision. It will also be shown that alternative investment opportunities available to the firm are not relevant to its bond refunding decision.

Two alternative approaches to the bond refunding decision to be compared are

1. Assume that the liabilities before and after refunding are to be kept at the same present value.
2. Assume that the maturity amounts of the debt before and after refunding are the same (if the same par value bond is used, the same number of bonds will be issued as are currently outstanding).

Finally, it will be shown that the decision whether or not to call the present debt is independent of the amount of debt issued in the refunding process.

In the 1980s, corporations issued debt with higher than normal historical interest rates. As long-term interest rates have decreased to levels close to historical averages, many firms are faced with decisions of whether or not to refund outstanding callable long-term debt.

The bond refunding decision is one of the few business decisions for which the cash flows are known with reasonable certainty: nevertheless, it is a decision about which there has been a great deal of confusion, and there have been misleading recommendations.

Bond refunding is actually a combination of two decisions that can be separated in some circumstances. The first is the decision to retire the outstanding bonds before their normal maturity by exercising the call option. The second is the decision to issue new bonds. To justify a bond refunding, two separate determinations should be made: first, that it is desirable to call the existing debt; second, that it is desirable to issue new debt. If both decisions are made, there still remain the questions of how much new debt to issue, for what maturity, and with what other characteristics (callable, convertible, etc.). Sometimes one or the other of the two decisions may be desirable, but not both. It is possible for a firm to call bonds without issuing new bonds if sufficient cash is on hand or can be raised in some other manner, for example, by selling some assets.

We first consider the decision to retire the outstanding bonds by calling them. The first step is to compute the present value of the cash flows associated with calling the existing bond. Callable bonds usually provide that the issuer may call the bonds by paying the book value and a call premium. The call premium is usually large when the bonds can first be called and gradually approaches zero. The cash outlay associated with calling the existing bonds is the sum of the debt's face value and the call premium (including any call expenses). The present value of the benefits from calling the bonds will be equal to the present value of the future interest and principal payments that will not be paid if the bonds are retired now. These should be discounted at the current cost of debt. There are other alternatives, e.g., calling the bonds later, that should be considered. But we consider only two alternatives: call the bonds now or wait until they mature. Under these assumptions the bonds should be called if the present value of their future payments is greater than the immediate cash outlay and the other costs associated with retiring them now.

Suppose the calculations indicate that retiring the existing bond issue is desirable, but no excess cash is available. It is then necessary to consider the second decision, to issue new bonds.

Example

There is presently outstanding $100 million of bonds coming due in 20 years paying 0.10 interest per year. The current interest rate is 0.07. The call premium and transactions costs associated with refunding would be $5 million. Management wants to keep the present value of the debt constant. Assume a zero tax rate.

Should the debt be replaced with 0.07 debt? Using 0.07 discount factors, we obtain

Present value of $100,000,000 = 0.2584 × $100,000,000   = $25,840,000
Present value of $10,000,000 per year = 10.594 × $10,000,000 = $105,940,000
Present value of currently outstanding debt $131,780,000

    $131,780,000 (present value of outstanding debt)
    105,000,000 (cash outlays at retirement)
    $26,780,000 (net present value of refunding)

The net benefit from refunding is $26,780,000.

If $100 million of new 0.07 debt is issued, the firm saves $3 million per year. The net present value of the savings minus the refunding costs is again $26,780,000

$$NPV = \$3,000,000(10.594) - \$5,000,000 = \$26,780,000$$

The net present value of the savings from refunding is independent of the amount of debt issued in the refunding process. Since the present value of the new debt is assumed to be equal to the cash proceeds arising from its issuance, this conclusion is reasonable. The amount of the debt to be issued depends on the needs of the firm. The decision to call the present debt depends on the present value of the outstanding debt and the cash outlays of calling that debt. The value of refunding does not depend on the amount of new debt issued.

If the transaction costs are a function of the new debt issued, then the answer would be more complex, since the problem then becomes one of determining the optimum size of debt issued with a given rate of utilization of cash.

The Maturity Date

We made the maturity date of the new debt equal to the maturity date of the old. This was convenient, since it enabled us to compute the interest savings without explaining what happens if the lives of two debts differ. However, just as the amount of debt issued does not affect the desirability of refunding, neither does the maturity date of the new issue. The refunding depends only on the present value of the old debt and the dollar outlays of retiring that debt. A lengthening of the maturity can be considered to be a plus factor in favor of refunding.

Computation of the Relevant Cash Flows

Sunk costs should not be included in the analysis. For example, consider the bond issue expenses discount associated with the currently outstanding bonds. Except as they might affect the income tax computation, these costs and discounts are not relevant to the decision. The call premiums and call expenses, the issue costs of the new bonds, duplicate interest payments during the period of issue (taking into account the return earned by investing the excess funds in short-term securities), and the savings in interest resulting from the new issue are relevant factors. The cash flows should be on an after-tax basis.

The Choice of the Rate of Interest

The choice of the rate of interest to be used in discounting the future cash flows is important. There are essentially three choices:

1. The weighted average cost of the capital.
2. The rate of interest on the new securities.
3. The rate of interest on default-free securities.

Consider a situation in which the possible interest saving associated with refunding is $100,000 a year and the life of the current bonds is 10 years. If we use a 0.20 weighted average cost of capital as the rate of discount, the present value of this saving is $419,247. If we use a 0.10 discount rate (the interest rate of the new issue), the present value of the saving is $614,457. If the cost of the refunding is $500,000, should the refunding be made? Using the interest rate on default-free securities would make the present value of the saving even larger than $614,457.

Should a firm reject the refunding if the funds can earn more elsewhere in the firm? The risks associated with the refunding are much less than with the normal investment (the cash outlays for incremental interest on the present debt are certain from the viewpoint of the corporation's treasurer). Also, after refunding if the firm issues the same present value of debt as the outstanding debt, it will have more cash. The firm is better off accepting the refunding and then the desirable investments.

Most important, we have shown that if the debt is refunded with the same present value of debt being issued, the amount of cash on hand will actually increase if the refunding is economically desirable. The use of the cost of debt to discount the cash flows is consistent with this economic analysis.

Timing

The timing problem of bond refunding has not been solved in this chapter. Assume that the ABC Company has issued a 0.10 bond. After issue, the treasurer may compute the interest rate that is required to make refunding desirable (a break-even interest rate). Each moment of time requires a different break-even rate, since the bond is continuously approaching maturity. Fortunately, the changes in the break-even rate will be slight, and for practical purposes the same rate may be used for several time periods. The treasurer of the firm will watch the bond market, and when the market rate of interest for bonds of comparable firms (or for its own bonds) reaches the break-even rate of interest, the firm has its first decision. Let us assume the current interest rate is a shade below the break-even rate. Should the refunding take place? If we ignore possible future decreases in interest rates, the analysis would indicate that it should. However, a more complete analysis suggests that we should be interested in the question as to whether the interest rate will soon be going lower than the current rate. If the rate is expected to decrease, then maybe the firm should wait for the reduction. The firm has an option to call the bond, and it might be desirable to delay exercising the option.

Obviously, the refunding problem has become complex. We must know not only what the future interest rates will be, but also when the changes in rates will occur. The present value of the saving that will occur if we refund at a given interest rate will be a function of when the refunding takes place, which, in turn, will be a function of when the interest rate that triggers the refunding is encountered.

The Call Provision

A call provision enables the corporation to refund a bond at a contractual amount and make a gain. Most corporate bonds have provisions that allow the corporation to "call" or retire the bond before maturity. The call price is generally above the face or maturity value at the time that the bonds may be first called. (The time of first call tends to be some reasonably long period, such as five years, after issue.) Corporations attach call provisions to bonds so that if interest rates fall, the bonds can be replaced with cheaper debt. It is because of the presence of call provisions that bond refunding can lead to an economic gain for the issuer. However, the presence of a call provision on new debt increases the interest rate that must be promised in order to sell the debt.

CONCLUSIONS

In evaluating the cost of borrowing, one must consider both the priority status of a debt issue compared with other existing issues, and the type of protection the debt carries against the possibility of subsequent issues of debt with equal or higher priority. We doubt that a firm can lower its real cost of borrowing by issuing at the same moment in time debts in many priority categories. Such attempted discrimination can be expected to be effective only if potential lenders are restricted to a narrow range of securities and if a limited group of corporations is able to issue their securities. These limitations are not characteristic of modern capital markets.

The types of subordination and the extent of protection against subsequent issues are only two of the many ways in which a debt issue can be characterized. However, an understanding of how these characteristics affect the cost of debt is necessary to an understanding of the overall cost of raising capital.

We find the tax status of a firm affects the cost of debt for a corporation.

In the U.S. Navy there was a saying that one never wanted a brilliant navigator, who always knew the location of the ship. A less brilliant person was apt to be unsure and to check position constantly. In like manner a treasurer who is a bit uncertain about the use of debt is apt to better serve the financial objectives of the stockholders. Once this uncertainty of understanding is recognized, a corporate treasurer can move to the formulation of a financial strategy using debt in a manner that will tend to maximize the well-being of the stockholders.

Chapter 5

The Analysis of
Buy versus Lease

P ick up an annual report of a major corporation and inspect the footnotes.
There is likely to be a footnote describing operating leases that the company
has contracted. It would be a rare corporation that had zero operating leases
(not shown on the balance sheet) and capital leases (shown on the balance sheet).

Leasing is jointly a method of financing and a method of acquiring an
asset. Almost any item that can be leased can also be bought; thus there is a decision to be made as to whether to buy or lease. The objective of this chapter is to
suggest an approach to evaluating the economic costs of buying as compared with
leasing. Unfortunately it is easier to describe errors that are likely to be made than
to recommend a simple universally accepted method of analysis. Two workable
solutions will be recommended.

THREE BASIC PROBLEMS

There are three basic problems in analyzing buy versus lease decisions. One is the
definition of the cash flows to be used. The second is the choice of the rate of discount. The third problem is to match the appropriate rate of discount with the
choice of cash flow.

We shall recommend the use of after-tax cash flows. For purposes of sim-
plification, a zero tax rate will initially be used so that the before-tax and after-tax
cash flows are identical for the first example.

A major problem with the cash flow calculation is the inclusion or exclusion of the debt component of the lease flows. The objective is to make the lease
analysis comparable in terms of debt characteristics with the buy analysis. Generally
this means extracting debt equivalent tax deduction elements of the lease cash flows.

There are three basic choices for the rate of discount to be used:

1. the after-tax borrowing rate
2. the before-tax borrowing rate
3. some type of risk-adjusted rate such as the weighted average cost of capital

If we assume that there are four possible sets of cash flows (there are
more) and three possible discount rates (again, there are more), there are then
twelve different ways of combining the two elements. If we then recognize the
possibility of using different rates of discount to discount different types of cash

flows for either the buy or the lease component, we can readily see why there has not been agreement on the method of analyzing buy versus lease decisions.

It is necessary to compare the cash flows and the present value of one alternative (buy) with the other alternative (lease). Rather than reviewing the basic theory and practice of capital budgeting, we shall jump into the middle of that discussion and conclude that one should use the net present value method since it is at least as good as any other method and, for many purposes, better.[1]

THE NET PRESENT VALUE METHOD

The alternatives will be evaluated using the net present value method. Future cash flows will be transferred back to the present moment in time using present value factors. Each present value factor is equal to $(1 + r)^{-n}$, where r is the discount rate being used and n is the number of time periods in the future when the cash is to be received. Multiplying the future cash flow by $(1 + r)^{-n}$, gives a present value equivalent. The sum of these present value equivalents for all cash flows gives the net present value of the alternative.

For example, if $100 is to be paid at time 2 and if the interest rate is 0.10, we have for the present value factor:

$$(1 + r)^{-2} = (1.10)^{-2} = 0.826446$$

The present value factor is 0.826446 and the present value equivalent of the $100 to be paid at time 2 is $82.64.

An investment is acceptable if its net present value is equal to or larger than zero. For example, assume a firm has a 0.10 time value factor and the cash flows of an investment are as follows:

Time	Cash Flows
0	−18,000
1	11,000
2	12,100

We want to compute the net present value of the investment by multiplying each cash flow by $(1.10)^{-n}$, where n represents the time the cash flow takes place. We now have

Time: n	Cash Flows	Present Value Factors	Present Values
0	−18,000	$(1.10)^{-0}$	−18,000
1	11,000	$(1.10)^{-1}$	10,000
2	12,100	$(1.10)^{-2}$	10,000

[1] The reader not accepting this statement might read H. Bierman Jr., and S. Smidt, *The Capital Budgeting Decision*, 8th ed. (New York: Macmillan, 1993).

The net present value of the investment ($2,000) is positive; thus the investment is acceptable.

The explanations just presented omit many complexities. But these complexities would not alter the basic calculations or the two basic decision rules. Accept an investment if its net present value is positive.

We will now consider one incorrect method of choosing between leasing and buying.

One Incorrect Method

In this section we assume the firm is paying zero taxes so that we can concentrate on the basic elements of the buy versus lease decision. We also assume that there is no uncertainty. In the example following we know that the equipment is to be acquired, that the life is three years, and that there is no residual value. The cost of the equipment if purchased is $90,000, and it can be leased for $36,829 with the lease payments being made at the end of each of the next three years. Capital can be borrowed at the bank at an interest cost of 0.10. The repayment schedule is flexible. The lease is not cancelable by the lessee. The lease is a method of financing.

Should the equipment be bought or leased? Since it has already been decided that the equipment should be acquired, the only question is as to the method of financing. While the problem has been described as a buy versus lease decision, actually it is more accurately described as a financing decision.

The firm has the following capital structure with a weighted average cost of capital of 0.14.

Method of Financing	Cost	Capital Structure Weights	Weighted Cost
Debt	0.10	0.5	0.05
Equity	0.18	0.5	0.09
Weighted average cost of capital			0.14

The present value of the lease payments using 0.14 as the discount rate is $85,504.

Time	Lease Payment	Present Value Factors	Present Values
1	36,829	1.14^{-1}	32,306
2	36,829	1.14^{-2}	28,339
3	36,829	1.14^{-3}	24,859
Present value of leasing			85,504

The cost of buying is $90,000 and the present value of leasing cost is only $85,504; thus leasing would seem to be more desirable than buying.

We have just illustrated a major error in buy versus lease analysis. One has to be very careful about the cash flows that are being used and the rates of discount. The above calculations are not correct.

Let us assume that the analyst is a naive but intelligent person who fortunately does not understand present value analysis. Instead of doing the calculations, the analyst phones the bank lending officer and asks one question: "How much will the corporation have to pay at the end of each time period to repay a loan of $90,000?" The 0.10 interest rate and the three-year time period have already been defined. The bank lending officer makes a relatively simple calculation and responds that the required annual payments are $36,190 at the end of each of three years. With that payment schedule the bank will earn a 0.10 return each year and the company will pay interest at the rate of 0.10 per year.

Now the analyst has the choice of recommending the buying of the equipment and paying the bank $36,190 or leasing and paying the lessor $36,829 each year. With the choice described in this manner, the preference for buying in this situation becomes obvious. The firm would rather write three checks to the bank for $36,190 than write three checks of $36,829 to the lessor.

The present value calculation led to an incorrect decision since the choice of the rate of discount was wrong. If 0.10 (the borrowing rate) had been used, we would have obtained $91,588 for the present value of leasing.

Time	Lease Payment	Present Value Factors	Present Values
1	36,829	1.10^{-1}	33,481
2	36,829	1.10^{-2}	30,437
3	36,829	1.10^{-3}	27,670
Present value of leasing			91,588

Now leasing has a larger present value of costs ($91,588) than does buying ($90,000). Again, buying is more desirable than leasing. The use of the borrowing rate will give sensible answers.

The Two Correct Methods

Two correct methods of analysis have been presented. One is to determine the cash outlay per period for buying using debt ($36,190) as compared with leasing ($36,829). Note that the buy analysis assumed the use of debt to finance the asset so that buying could be compared with leasing, which is an alternative type of debt. In a real sense we are comparing two different types of financing.

The second method of analysis computed the present value of the lease payments and compared the debt equivalent or the present value of leasing ($91,588) with the $90,000 cost of the asset. The cost of debt was used to compute the present value. The use of the weighted average cost of capital led to an incorrect decision. It caused leasing to appear to be less costly than buying when in fact it was more costly. The inclusion of a risk adjustment in the discount rate led to an incorrect observation.

Residual Value

In the example presented, buying was more desirable than leasing despite the fact that the residual value of the equipment was equal to zero. Now we will change the assumptions. The lease payments are now reduced to $36,000 per year. With zero residual value, leasing is now more desirable than buying. But now assume that the asset's residual value at time 3 is $1,500. How should this information be incorporated into the analysis? There are several possible approaches, but only one will be suggested here. First, compute the present value of the lease payments using the 0.10 borrowing rate. This is $89,527. Then, subtract the present value of the residual value from the cost of the equipment. Using 0.14 as the discount rate, we would have

$$\text{Net cost of buying} = \$90,000 - \$1,500(1.14)^{-3} = \$90,000 - \$1,500(0.6750)$$
$$= \$88,987$$

and buying is less costly thus more desirable than leasing. But someone could object to the use of the 0.14 rate of discount for the residual value, so we must relax that assumption. The cost of buying (net of residual value) is equal to the cost of leasing if the residual value is equal to $1,500 and if the residual value is discounted at a discount rate of 0.47.

The calculation of 0.47 is as follows:

$$\$90,000 - \$1,500(1 + r)^{-3} = \$89,527$$
$$(1 + r)^{-3} = 0.3153$$
$$r = 0.47$$

The cost of leasing is not affected by the use of different rates of discount being used for the cost of buying. The cost of leasing has been computed using the borrowing rate defined to be 0.10. The borrowing rate is held constant. The rate at which the residual value is discounted may be varied. We find that buying is preferred to leasing over a wide range of discount rates (as long as the discount rate is less than 0.47).

The Investment Decision

Let us return to the situation in which there is zero residual value and the lease payment is $36,829 per period. The weighted average cost of capital is again 0.14.

If the benefits each year are forecasted to be $38,000, what should the firm do? We assume that the decision to acquire the asset has not yet been made.

A straightforward capital budgeting analysis using the 0.14 weighted average cost of capital indicates that the investment has a negative net present value of $1,778 and should be rejected.

Time	Cash Flow	Present Value Factors	Present Values
0	-90,000	1.14^{-0}	-90,000
1	38,000	1.14^{-1}	33,333
2	38,000	1.14^{-2}	29,240
3	38,000	1.14^{-3}	25,649
Net present value			-1,778

Shifting to the consideration of leasing where the lease payment is $36,829 per year, we see that each year has a positive cash flow of $1,171: $38,000 − $36,829 = $1,171. The present value of leasing is positive using any interest rate.

It would seem that the firm should lease, but this conclusion is in error. It has already been shown in the previous section that with these facts buying is more desirable than leasing.

In the calculations using 0.14 as the discount rate we obtain a present value of benefits of $88,222. The present value (using 0.10) of leasing outlays has already been computed to be $91,588. Thus if 0.14 were to be accepted as the appropriate rate for discounting benefits and 0.10 as the rate of discounting the lease flows, leasing, as well as buying, would have to be rejected.

If the leasing alternative were to be accepted, then we should reconsider (and restructure) the buy decision analysis. Using $90,000 of debt and a 0.10 debt cost we know that the debt payments each year will be $36,190. The net benefits of buying each year are $38,000 − $36,190 = $1,810, a figure that exceeds the yearly $1,171 net benefits of leasing.

Using 0.10 as a discount rate leasing has a present value of costs of $91,588, which is larger than the $90,000 cost of buying. A method of analysis that indicates that leasing is acceptable but buying is not, given the facts of this example, must be deficient.

Comparing the annual $38,000 benefit with the $36,829 lease payment is analogous to subtracting the debt payment of $36,190 from the $38,000 benefit if the asset is purchased. One cannot include the debt payments of leasing in the cash flows, without including the debt payments in the buy analysis. A second alternative is to exclude the debt payments from both alternatives. The buy and lease alternatives must be made comparable relative to the inclusion or exclusion of the debt flows.

Should the equipment be acquired? The lease analysis clearly shows that, if $38,000 of benefits is certain with lease payments of $36,829, this is a good alternative. The buy analysis makes the point more forcefully since the debt payments are less with buying than with leasing.

However, if the benefit stream is not certain, it is no longer obvious that buying (or leasing) is acceptable. Should the equipment be acquired? It depends on the risk analysis for the investment. Thus we must stop short of declaring that the acquisition is desirable. What we can say is that, if the equipment is acquired, with the facts as given, the equipment should be bought not leased. We need a method of analysis that will lead to sensible decisions.

We are assuming that the necessary funds can be borrowed at a cost of 0.10. We are also assuming, for simplicity, that the debt will be repaid in equal installments. This latter assumption is not necessary for the basic analysis but is used to illustrate the fact that buying is clearly superior in the present situation.

We have been comparing leasing with a buy alternative in which the financing is being accomplished using borrowed funds. Having decided that borrowing to buy is better than leasing, the firm might then decide that the use of common stock is even better than borrowing the funds. We have definitely not proven that debt is more desirable than common stock. It has only been shown that straight borrowing is more desirable than leasing with the given facts.

If with the given facts a firm concluded that the common stock were more desirable than straight debt, but that leasing were more desirable than common stock, this would be upsetting. Transitivity of choice must apply here. If debt is less costly than leasing and if common stock is less costly than debt, then it is not possible to conclude that leasing is less costly than common stock.

This section has introduced two of the primary complexities of buy versus lease analysis: the computation of the cash flows and the choice of the rate of discount. With cash flows, the lesson to be learned is that buying and leasing must be placed on a comparable basis. With the rate of discount, one has to be careful using a risk-adjusted rate of discount for some of the cash flows but not for others. The choice of the rate of discount is not separable from the calculation of cash flows problem. It is interesting that a high level of complexity can be introduced even when the tax rate is assumed to be zero. Taxes add their own complexity.

We have presented a relatively simple method of choosing between buying and leasing. However, we have assumed an artificial situation of zero taxes. The next step is to review the buy versus lease decision assuming the existence of corporate income taxes.

THE LEASE DECISION WITH TAXES

We shall now assume that there is a 0.35 corporate income tax. All business decisions must be made on an after-tax basis and the buy versus lease decision is no exception. Several analytical problems arise from the fact that a lease is a combination of an investment and a financing. For example, when an asset is purchased, the firm will deduct depreciation expense in computing taxable income. With a lease there is no depreciation expense, but the entire lease payment is a tax deduction. We want to separate the lease payment into two components, one an equivalent to interest on debt and the second an equivalent to depreciation expense.

If we start with the before-tax lease payment (say, $36,190 per year) equal in each year of the asset's life to the debt payment accompanying the purchase of the asset, we have indifference on a before-tax basis if there is zero residual value. With indifference with zero taxes the preference between buying and leasing rests with the value of the tax deductions associated with interest and depreciation if the asset is purchased and the total lease payment if the asset is leased. Later we will make the choice using the depreciation deduction of buying and the depreciation equivalent of lease payments.

Assume that the lessor offers to lease an asset at a cost of $36,190 per year, first payment one year from now. This is exactly the same cash outlay (amount and timing) as with the buy-borrow alternative. The life is three years and there is zero residual value. With a zero tax rate, there would be indifference.

With a 0.35 tax rate, which alternative is to be preferred? Conventional wisdom says that leasing offers tax advantages. Rather than accepting this generalization, we will compare the tax deductions of buying with leasing. The cost of the asset purchased outright is $90,000 and the leasing alternative has a before-tax present value of $90,000, using a 0.10 discount rate. If $90,000 were to be borrowed at a cost of 10 percent, the debt amortization schedule with equal repayments would be as follows:

Time	Amount Owed Beginning of Period	Interest at 10 Percent	Principal Payment	Total Payment
1	90,000	9,000	27,190	36,190
2	62,810	6,280	29,910	36,190
3	32,900	3,290	32,900	36,190

If the asset is purchased using borrowed funds, the total tax deductions resulting from borrowing at 10% and the use of straight-line depreciation are shown alongside the tax deductions from leasing.

Time	Interest	Straight-Line Depreciation	Buy-Borrow Tax Deductions	Lease Tax Deductions
1	9,000	30,000	39,000	36,190
2	6,280	30,000	36,280	36,190
3	3,290	30,000	33,290	36,190
Total tax deductions			108,570	108,570

The total tax deductions from buying and leasing are equal in this example. The timing pattern of the deductions with buying is to be preferred since the deductions are accelerated as compared with leasing. The use of any of the accelerated depreciation methods would further enhance the tax advantages of buying.

We started with zero taxes and indifference between buying and leasing. The addition of taxes moved the choice to the buy alternative. The present value of the tax deductions with buy and borrow is larger than with leasing with any positive discount rate.

If the borrowing rate (after taxes) is used to discount the cash flows, we can compute the after-tax costs of the two alternatives.

We define the net cost of buying to be equal to the cost minus the present value of any tax savings associated with the asset. For the example, the net cost of buying is equal to $90,000 minus the present value of the tax savings from depreciating the asset. Since the depreciation deductions of each year are equal, we will use the present value of an annuity with an interest rate of 0.065 (that is, 0.10 times one minus the tax rate) to compute the present value of the tax savings. The present value of an annuity of $1 for three years using 0.065 as the discount rate is 2.6485.

Net cost of buying = $90,000 − 0.35($30,000)(2.6485)
= $90,000 − $27,809 = $62,191

The after-tax present value of leasing is

$36,190(1 − 0.35)2.6485 = $62,302

Leasing costs more than buying.

The interest tax shield is omitted from the buy analysis since the inclusion of the debt flows would result in their washing out completely (the net present value of the debt flows is equal to zero) when the after-tax borrowing rate is being used as the discount rate. Their inclusion if a different rate were used would result in distortion of the investment analysis.

If an interest rate other than the after-tax borrowing rate of 0.065 were to be used, and if debt flows were excluded from the buy analysis, the computation of the present value of the leasing costs would be more complex than that illustrated. One can only compute the after-tax cost of leasing by computing a present value of after-tax lease payments using an annuity if the after-tax borrowing rate is used.

Risk-Adjusted Discount Rates

If the after-tax borrowing rate is used in computing present values, the calculations of the net costs of buying and leasing are straightforward (they were illustrated earlier). If discount rates are used that attempt to reflect the existence of risk, the calculations are much more difficult. The objective is to treat leasing (which includes debt flows) and buying the asset using debt financing on a comparable basis. This issue is bypassed if the after-tax borrowing rate is used, but it becomes alive with any other discount rate.

Thus if some rate of interest other than the after-tax borrowing rate is used to accomplish the time discounting, complexities are introduced. We cannot then take the after-tax cash outlays of the lease and compute a present value that is comparable to other investment cash flow present values (the lease includes debt flows). With more than one time period, the error introduced by discounting the after-tax lease payments by the firm's risk-adjusted required return and comparing the present value obtained with the present value of buying is well hidden.

With a lease that can be cancelled it is not necessary to compute a debt equivalent of a lease if the firm can cancel the lease with the equivalent of a phone call. Thus the calculations are much simpler than with a financial type of lease since the present value may be computed with no special adjustments. With a financial lease we have a problem if we compute the after-tax present value of the lease using something other than the after-tax borrowing rate. The present value of leasing obtained using the unadjusted lease cash flows and a risk-adjusted discount rate is not comparable to the present value of the buy alternative's cash flows.

If the lease payments differed from $36,190, the before-tax present value of the lease payments would differ from $90,000 and the nondebt-related tax deductions would also differ from the numbers that have been used. It is necessary to split the lease payments into "interest" and "principal" to compute the annual tax savings if a discount rate other than the after-tax borrowing rate is used. If the after-tax borrowing rate is used, it is not necessary to make the split.

The Calculation That Is Not Made

One calculation is not made. We do not take the lease payment, multiply by one minus the tax rate to convert it to an after-tax cash flow measure, and then compute its present value using a risk adjusted discount rate. This type of calculation is correct if the after-tax borrowing rate is used, but it is not acceptable if any other discount rate is used unless the buy analysis is also adjusted to include debt flows. Including debt flows in the buy analysis is not a recommended procedure.

If the analyst were to insist on this calculation for the lease alternative, it would be necessary to include all the debt flows in the buy analysis to place it on a comparable basis.

Cash Flows and the Rate of Discount

Analysis of buy versus lease alternatives requires that we decide on the definition of the cash flows and the rate of discount to be used. Both the cash flows and the discount rate should be on an after-tax basis. Unfortunately, this statement does not remove all ambiguity. We will first consider the definition of cash flows with a debt and then with an investment and finally with a lease.

Cash Flows and Discount Rate: Debt

Assume that $1,000 is borrowed for one year at a cost of 0.10. The tax rate is 0.35. The after-tax borrowing rate is $0.10(1 - 0.35) = 0.065$. If the before-tax cash flows and the before-tax interest rate are used, the net present value of the cash flows is equal to zero.

$$\$1,000 - \frac{\$1,100}{1.10} = 0$$

If the after-tax cash flows and the after-tax borrowing rate of 0.065 is used, we again have a net present value of zero.

$$\$1,000 - \frac{\$1,100 - \$35}{1.065} = 0$$

The $35 is the tax savings resulting from the $100 of interest deductions at time 1.

If the $1,065 of net cash outlays of period 1 had been discounted at the before-tax rate of 0.10, the net present value would have been positive and this would have been in error. Funds can be borrowed at an after-tax cost of 0.065, and this should be used as the discount rate for the after-tax cash flows.

If the tax deduction cannot be used, the cash outlay at time 1 becomes $1,100 and 0.10 becomes the appropriate rate of discount since it represents the effective cost of debt.

The presence of taxes combined with the desire to use risk-adjusted discount rates introduces complexities into the present value calculations. It is very easy to introduce biases into the analysis without knowing that biases have been introduced.

A simple solution is to use the after-tax borrowing rate as the discount rate in buy-versus-lease analysis. Using this rate one can compute the present value of leasing by merely reducing the lease payment to an after-tax measure and applying the annuity present value factor. This simplicity disappears when a rate of discount different from the after-tax borrowing rate is used.

The acceleration of lease payments was shown to enhance the leasing alternative. However, we still conclude that if buy-borrow is being compared with leasing it is necessary actually to make the present value calculations to determine which alternative is the more desirable. Safe generalizations are very rare in the area of buy-lease analysis.

PROS AND CONS OF LEASING

So far we have considered the economic analysis of the buy-lease decision. Now we review the qualitative pros and cons of leasing. We shall see that there are valid reasons for leasing assets, just as there are valid reasons for buying.

Financing

Leasing is a method of 100% debt financing. A lease is frequently easy to obtain and the asset is quickly available. Since leasing is debt financing, it should be recognized that some of a firm's debt capacity has been utilized when a lease is signed. The signing of a lease reduces somewhat the lessee's ability to issue more debt in the future.

While some lease contracts are standard and merely require two sets of signatures, other lease contracts are specific to a given situation and are thicker than *Webster's* unabridged dictionary.

Flexibility

A short-term lease or a cancelable lease offers flexibility. If technology changes, only a phone call is needed to change to the more advanced equipment. There may be no loss to the lessee on the switch.

The disadvantage of the short-term lease is that the lease terms might be adjusted upward by the lessor at the end of the lease term. The lessee has no protection against an upward price spiral. While there is less risk of being stuck with a bad asset, the lessee has given up the chance of having a large residual value at the end of the lease contract. The lessor gains that value.

Flexibility is probably one of the two primary reasons why firms lease. A lease reduces one type of risk exposure.

Bankruptcy

With non-lease debt it is clear that failure to pay opens up the possibility of bankruptcy. While a lease can be written so that a lessee can walk away from the lease, it is more likely that failure to pay a lease payment will also lead to the same magnitude of bankruptcy risk as straight debt. One should not think that substituting a lease for conventional debt eliminates financial risk.

Maintenance is Cheap and Certain

With leasing the maintenance may be contracted. The certainty of maintenance and the fact that its cost is certain is said to make leasing attractive.

More exactly, these characteristics make maintenance contracts attractive. These contracts can generally be obtained with purchase as well as with leasing. They do not affect the merits of leasing compared with buying but, rather, are a separate decision.

Off-Balance-Sheet Financing

Before FAS 13, leases were largely off-balance-sheet debt and this was thought to be an advantage of leasing. Now capital leases are recorded as liabilities, and in the distant future we can expect to see the Financial Accounting Standards Board recommend that more leases be classified as capital leases.

Sophisticated analysts are likely to capitalize all leases, independent of the recommendations of the accounting profession. Most experts reconstruct financial statements so that all liabilities are taken into consideration. The artificial distinctions recommended by FAS 13 are not likely to be followed rigorously by a person attempting to use the information to make a decision.

When limits are set by top management on total capital expenditures, there is apt to be an expansion in leasing. The use of leases for this reason is likely to be an expensive manner of conforming to an artificial restraint.

Higher Return on Investment

With an operating lease there is no asset recorded; thus it is easier for management to justify an investment. A higher return on investment is likely to occur because the asset is not recorded. It is somewhat easier to earn a high return on investment if there is little or no investment. All that is required is a positive income.

Just as the off-balance lease does not fool the expert computing the total debt, the use of leasing does not fool the expert computing a return on investment. The asset base should be recorded consistent with the present value of the lease obligation.

A well-managed corporation will control the signing of leases so that leasing is not used as a device to inflate an operating division's return on investment.

Higher Incomes

An operating lease will tend to inflate the incomes of early years of life compared with the expenses resulting from buying the asset. Of course, there might be lower incomes in later years, but management taking a short-run point of view might lease in the hopes of inflating the incomes of the next few years.

Lower Property Taxes

Leasing leads to lower property taxes. This is true, but the lessor pays the taxes and the lessee pays the lessor. There is no reason to see an advantage relative to property taxes unless the lessor is tax exempt.

Income Tax Savings

We have shown that the income tax effects must be computed; they cannot be assumed. All things equal, it is difficult for the normal leasing contract to overcome the tax advantage associated with buying, namely, the use of accelerated depreciation in the calculation of taxable income. Tax rate differentials and interest rate differences can require a modification in the above conclusion.

A Well-Defined Cost

For certain purposes (for example, in the case of a government contract), it is useful to have the well-defined costs offered by a lease contract. Buying an asset requires estimating the asset's life, its salvage value, and its depreciation per year. With leasing, one only has to produce the canceled check showing the amount paid the lessor.

With buying, there are differences of opinion. With leasing, there are hard facts.

ARGUING IN FAVOR OF LEASES

This section reviews some of the arguments that have been used in advocating leases. You should evaluate the arguments and the comments.

"Defers the expenditure of capital."

A lease contract does not defer the expenditure of capital. It does defer the expenditure of cash and is itself a source of capital. It is debt capital but of a different nature than straight debt. The primary differences are the tax effects.

"The rentals are a fully tax deductible expense."

The depreciation expense and interest expense of buying are also tax deductible. If the tax deductions of leasing are better than for buying, it must be because their present value is larger. This is not likely to occur given the possibility of using accelerated depreciation if the asset is purchased.

"With a tax rate of 50%, the actual net cost of each rental dollar will be $0.50 compared with a cost of $1.00 with buying."

The first part of this statement is true, but the second part is not. Do not compare the after-tax cash outlays of leasing with the before-tax cost of buying. The cost of buying must be reduced by the depreciation deductions. In addition, the implicit debt cost of leasing must be considered in a manner consistent with the way that the buy alternative is analyzed.

"A lease is 100% financing."

Yes, and so is debt.

"A tax timing advantage will result from leasing."

This is very unlikely, given the possibility of accelerated depreciation with buying the asset. The timing advantage is likely to go to the buy alternative.

"The term of payment is frequently longer with leasing than with alternative financing."

All things equal, this would result in reduced payments per year with leasing, but more payments. Whether or not it is true is an empirical question. Whether or not it is an advantage depends on the size and timing of the payments, that is, on the present value of leasing compared with the present value of buying.

"Flexibility."

A lease does offer considerable flexibility. For example, one can lease a car for a day. This is a real advantage of leasing. However, the costs may increase through time as successive leases are signed.

"Inflation heightens the value of leasing."

The impact of inflation on a fixed (in dollar amount) stream of obligations is well known. The real value of a future payment is decreased by inflation. However, the same conclusion is true with straight debt. In addition, buying has the added advantage of the residual value's increasing in value.

While inflation will increase the value of leasing, it is apt to increase the value of buying even more. There is no obvious reason why inflation should tip the scale in favor of leasing.

"Profits are earned on saved capital."

If lease payments are $20,000 before taxes and $10,000 after taxes and if an asset costs $110,000, there is $100,000 of cash saved. If cash earns 0.15, the extra earnings for year 1 are $15,000.

This calculation compares apples and oranges. It depends heavily on the comparison of leasing with the use of equity capital. If an asset is financed with $110,000 of debt-paying interest of 0.10 (before taxes), we know that the cash flows of year 1 will be in favor of buying (the after-tax interest outlay is only $5,500 versus $10,000 with the lease and there are the tax savings of depreciation deductions).

"Leasing offers larger cash flows."

This is not likely to be true in the early years if leasing is compared with buying and using debt. Again we need the present values.

"Borrowing capacity is not reduced by leasing."

This implies a myopic vision on the part of analysts. A lease is a legal promise to pay and this is debt, no matter what FAS 13 requires.

"Leasing offers obsolescence protection."

A short-term lease does offer obsolescence protection, but at a cost of losing the inflation protection mentioned earlier. A short-term lease opens the possibility of increased lease payments. A long-term lease does not offer obsolescence protection.

"Leasing bypasses budget ceilings."

Spending ceilings should be defined so as to include lease contracts. If they do not limit lease arrangements, they are not effective and will encourage managers to lease rather than to buy for short-term cash spending strategy reasons rather than for economic (present value) reasons.

"Leasing from a tax-exempt entity offers advantages."

A tax-exempt entity that can issue tax-exempt debt and does not pay property taxes is an ideal owner of an asset. Whether the entity should be a lessor or lessee will depend on the tax laws in effect. The loss of the depreciation tax deductions is a disadvantage.

"Leasing places the tax deductions where they can be used."

If the depreciation deductions cannot be used by the lessee, leasing enables them to be shifted to a lessor who can use them. This is a substantive advantage of leasing. But one has to be careful about generalizations relative to the advantages of shifting tax depreciation shields. Different tax rates lead both to different values of tax deductions and different time value factors, and generalizations must be made carefully.

THREE DECISIONS

Firms have three decisions if an asset can be leased. First, the firm has to decide whether or not the project is worthwhile. Second, a decision has to be made whether the financing should be done with straight debt or with leasing. Third, the firm must consider using equity rather than leasing or debt. We are not concerned with the sequence in which the decisions are made as long as it is recognized that there are three decisions. For example, it might it decided that, if the project were accepted, buying is more desirable than leasing, but that it is not desirable to acquire the project.

The financing can influence whether or not the project is desirable. For example, a buy analysis might lead to a reject analysis, but since the lease terms are so favorable, leasing might cause the project to be acceptable. Acceptability implies that the asset passes some type of risk and present value analysis.

If it is decided that straight debt rather than leasing is desirable, it is still possible that the firm will decide to use common stock or some other type of financing. The buy versus lease decision should be made comparing the lease contract with straight debt financing so that the two alternatives are as comparable as we can make them. But after that decision is made it may still be correct for the firm to reject debt in favor of some other type of financing.

CONCLUSIONS

Many reasons are offered as to why a firm should lease. This chapter suggests that not all the reasons offered are valid. Several, however, are very important for leasing to be mutually beneficial for the lessor and the lessee. Most importantly, leasing is a method of financing.

1. The lessor may have made incorrect calculations.
2. The lessor may have economies of scale in purchasing (price discrimination in favor of large buyers).
3. The lessor may have lower borrowing costs than the lessee.
4. The lessor may have different estimates of life, cost of capital, or salvage than the lessee.
5. Different tax and borrowing rate situations may exist.
6. A difference of opinion of the lessor and the lessee may exist as to the appropriate method of evaluating the lease alternative (or computing a fair and profitable price).

Until the calculations are made, one cannot guess as to whether or not buy-borrow or leasing is to be preferred. Make the present value calculations.

Leasing has its advantages. Leasing also has its disadvantages. A hospital leased computers at a terrifically favorable price. Right after the hospital's check was cashed by the lessor, the lessor went bankrupt. The hospital lost its computers and the cash (actually it only lost the cash, it never had the computers).

Does leasing cost less than buying? Do the suggested calculations.

Chapter 6

Convertible Bonds

Finance officers are constantly seeking cheaper sources of capital. Convertible debt and convertible preferred stock are types of securities that receive attention because they offer the issuing firm a considerable amount of flexibility. Because of the difficulty of valuing these securities, they are extremely useful in situations where there is not agreement as to the appropriate cost of debt for a firm given a large amount of risk or where the cost of straight debt would be very large.

We will refer to convertible debt in this chapter, but an analogous analysis could be prepared for convertible preferred stock, or debt with detachable warrants.

MOTIVATION FOR ISSUING

There are several valid reasons for issuing convertible bonds. The primary reason is that it is an indirect means of issuing equity at a premium, though it might take some time for the debt to be converted into common stock. It is useful where the firm wants an expectation of permanent rather than finite-lived capital.

In a situation where it is perceived that the common stock price is depressed, a firm might prefer to issue the convertible bond rather than issue common stock at a low price. However, it can properly be argued that there is more risk to the firm with the issuance of the convertible bond than with the direct issue of common stock. If the firm's fortunes were to tumble, there would be debt outstanding with resulting bankruptcy implications if payments were not made on time. This threat is not present if common stock is issued.

A primary attraction of convertible bonds is that a relatively low interest rate can be set compared with a straight debt. This is a saving of cash paid out as interest as well as a reduction in the recorded (accounting) interest expense of the period. The accountant records the explicit cost of the capital (interest) but not the implicit cost of the dilution associated with the stock equity portion of the capital raised. Thus if straight debt costs 0.10 and convertible debt costs 0.04, $1,000,000 of straight debt would have a recorded interest cost of $100,000 and the convertible debt would have an interest cost of $40,000. Remember these are accounting measures of cost and not the economic cost that should be the basis of the decision when one is choosing between convertible and straight debt. The number of shares committed to the convertible bonds is ignored in computing the explicit cost.

In some situations a firm cannot issue straight debt. Because of the high risk, a straight debt bearing the necessary high interest rate would likely force bankruptcy. The addition of a conversion feature allows a lower interest rate while at the same time giving the investor an equity kicker which will have value if the firm is successful.

In a situation where there is considerable risk, an investor might be able to evaluate exactly the acceptability of the rewards offered by straight debt. The payments are explicit and contractual. The rewards have an upper limit. With convertible debt, confusion as to the exact value of the debt is introduced. The immediate value of the conversion feature is difficult to determine. Setting the conversion price (the conversion premium) and the period of no-call (as well as the call price) will greatly affect the value of the conversion feature. Bringing these factors together to determine value is difficult. There is apt to be disagreement as to value among investors. A security does not have to appear to be attractive to all investors to be successful. The fact that a conversion feature disperses the judgments of the investing community is likely to make the inclusion of a conversion feature a good strategy when there is considerable risk in a firm's operations.

Why Not Issue?

The primary valid argument against the issuance of convertible debt is that it does result in a dilution in the stockholder's equity position. The holder of a convertible security can share in the winnings if the events turn out to be desirable. This is real dilution. If events do not go well, with the result that the stock price does not increase, then an overhang of potential dilution is created, and there is still debt outstanding.

An important consideration is that financial analysts tend to consider convertible bonds as common stock equivalents in evaluating the common stock, and bond rating agencies tend to consider convertibles as debt in arriving at bond ratings. This is looked at by financial officers as a double penalty, and is considered as a negative factor arguing against the issuance of convertible debt.

Tax considerations work both for and against convertible bonds. The tax deduction of convertible bond interest gives the bonds an advantage compared to common stock. But the lower explicit interest costs than non-convertible debt result in lower tax shields thus there is less value added per $1,000 bond as a result of using the convertible bond (which is part equity capital).

WHAT IS CONVERTIBLE DEBT?

Assume a situation where a one-period $1,000 convertible bond paying 0.066 is convertible into four shares of common stock. Straight debt would have to yield 0.10. The common stock of the company can either be $259.44 (with 0.9 probability) or $90 (with 0.1 probability). The possibility of only two events is chosen for simplicity. Assume the interest is received and then the bond is redeemed or converted.

Event	Probability	Conditional Value	Time 1 Expected Value of Bond
Stock Price = $259.44	0.9	4(259.44) = $1,038	0.9(1,038) = $934
Stock Price = 90	0.1	1,000	0.1(1,000) = 100
			Total 1,034

At time 1 the investor will either convert into four shares if the stock price is $259.44 or take the $1,000 bond maturity value if the stock price is $90. The value including the present value of the $66 of interest is:

$$\text{Value of bond} = [934 + 100](1.10)^{-1} + 66(1.10)^{-1}$$
$$= (1{,}034)(1.10)^{-1} + 60 = 940 + 60 = \$1{,}000$$

Thus in this example the value of the bond is equal to the present value of the interest plus the sum of the expected value of the converted bonds and the bond redemption price times the probability of no conversion. A second interpretation is to define the bond as the sum of its value as debt plus an option to buy four shares of stock.

Assume the bond can only be converted at maturity. The value of the bond as debt is equal to its contractual flows as debt discounted at the cost of straight debt:

$$\frac{\$1{,}066}{1.10} = \$969$$

The option has value if the conversion takes place and the investor receives the value of the common stock, or $259.44 \times 4 = \$1,038$. The $1,038 outcome has an expected value of $1,038 \times 0.9 = \$934$. But the investor gives up the $1,000 redemption value with 0.9 probability. The net value of the option at time 1 is:

$$\$934 - \$900 = \$34$$

The present value of the option is:

$$\frac{\$34}{1.1} = \$31$$

The value of the convertible debt is equal to the sum of its value as debt plus the present value of the call option to convert. This is:

$$\text{Value of bond} = \text{Value of debt} + \text{Value of call option}$$
$$= \$969 + \$31 = \$1{,}000$$

The third and final interpretation of a convertible bond is to define the bond as common stock with downside protection or insurance (the investor has a put to sell the bond to the corporation for $1,000).

The common stock has an expected value at time one of $242.50.

$$\begin{aligned}
\$259.44 \times 0.9 &= \$233.50 \\
90.00 \times 0.1 &= 9.00 \\
\hline
&\$242.50
\end{aligned}$$

The expected value for four shares is $970.

But if the stock price is low, conversion will not take place and the investor will receive $1,000 (with 0.1 probability). This is an expected value of $100. However, the $90 per share, or $360 for four shares, is then forsaken. This has a 0.1 probability, so the expected value is $36. The value of the insurance is $100 less $36, or $64. We now have:

$$\text{Value of bond} = \text{Value of common stock} + \text{Value of insurance} + \text{Interest}$$
$$= (\$970 + \$64 + \$66)(1.10)^{-1}$$
$$= (\$1,100)(1.10)^{-1} = \$1,000$$

Three ways of interpreting a convertible bond have been described. All three ways stress the hybrid nature of convertible debt.

Conversion Premiums

There are many ways of computing conversion premiums. Basically all of the calculations try to measure the gap between where the stock price is now and where it has to go for the investor to start making something from the existence of the conversion feature.

Assume the bond is going to be issued for $1,000 and is to be convertible into 40 shares of common stock. The conversion price is then $1,000/40 = $25. If the current market price of the common stock at the time of issue is $20, the conversion premium at the time of issue is:

$$\frac{\$25 - \$20}{\$20} = \frac{\$5}{\$20} = 0.25, \text{ or equivalently } \frac{\$1,000 - \$800}{\$800} = 0.25$$

The market will compare this 0.25 conversion premium with premiums of other convertible bonds. The smaller the conversion premium, all things equal, the more desirable the convertible security.

The conversion value of the convertible debt is equal to 40 times the market price of $20, or $800, at the time of issue. We can expect the conversion value of the debt to change through time. For example, if the stock price were to increase to $38, the conversion value would be $38 × 40 = $1,520. The conversion value represents the value of the bond if it were immediately converted into common stock.

One of the more important decisions involving convertible securities is the setting of the initial conversion premium. To attract investors, a large conversion premium would necessitate a higher interest rate than with a smaller premium. Also, a smaller premium would increase the probability of conversion. Most corporations issuing convertible debt hope that the debt will be converted so that the debt overhang is eliminated.

Through time we would expect the price of the bond and the price of the common stock to change, and these changes will change the conversion premium being paid by the investor. Assume the bond price goes to $800 and the stock price to $17. The conversion value of the bond is now $17 × 40 = $680, and the conversion premium associated with the current bond price is now:

$$\frac{\$800 - \$680}{\$680} = 0.176$$

but compared to the face value the conversion premium is

$$\frac{\$1,000 - \$680}{\$680} = 0.47$$

What Decisions Associated with Issue Are There?

The firm must first decide on the interest rate that it wants to pay on the debt and then put together a conversion feature that will lead to the bond being accepted by the market with that interest rate. Other factors greatly impinging on value are the period of no-call, the call premium, and the maturity of the debt. The difference between the time of maturity and when the bond can first be called is of particular significance to the investor.

Why Should an Investor Convert Voluntarily?

There is a basic incentive for an investor not to convert. Holding the bond supplies protection, while at the same time the investor has upside potential because of the ability to convert into common shares if such a conversion is desirable.

If the common stock's cash dividends become larger than the payments on the debt, the investor has a decision. The choice is between more cash flow with the larger risk associated with common stock dividends and a safer but smaller amount of cash. If the investor converts, the investor is making an assumption that the expected present value of cash dividends is larger than the present value of the interest payments. In addition, it is expected that the price of the common stock will remain sufficiently high so that one does not lose in the future by giving up the maturity payment of the debt. If all these conditions are satisfied, the investor has a conversion decision, but because of the risk it is not obvious that the investor should convert voluntarily. Except in rare situations where there are high relatively safe cash dividends, the investor is better off holding the convertible bonds than converting. The put option has value.

If the bond's market price is larger than the conversion value it is better to hold or sell than it is to convert voluntarily. The investor does not want to give up the call option (the right to convert to common stock) or the put option (the right to the face value of the convertible debt at maturity).

Why Should a Firm Force Conversion?

The opportunity for a firm to force conversion arises when the conversion value of the bond is larger than the call price. Normally a price cushion is required to reduce the likelihood of the firm paying out cash. There are several reasons why a firm might want to force its investors to convert into common stock by calling the bond. It might be a way to strengthen the capital structure so that new debt can be issued. Another reason for the firm to force conversion is that the cash outlays of outstanding common stock are less than with debt. For example, a growth stock may be paying zero dividends; thus the after-tax interest payments are saved if conversion is forced. Also, calling the bonds results in the elimination of the implicit put option held by the investors.

Assume a $1,000 bond paying 0.10 interest is convertible into 40 shares of common stock. The common stock pays $1 per year dividend and is selling at a price of $50. The call price of the bond is $1,080. Should the company call? The corporate tax rate is 0.35.

The company can call, since the conversion value, $50 \times 40 = \$2,000$, is larger than the call price. If the bonds are called, the rational investors must convert rather than accept the call price ($2,000 is larger than $1,080). The bonds converted into common stock will require $40 per bond of cash outlays for dividends. The bonds now require $100 of interest outlays, which are $65 after tax. The $40 is less than $65. The bonds should be called so that they will be converted into common stock. The investors will receive $40 of dividends instead of $100 of interest; thus they do not have their position improved by the call. The position of the present stockholders is improved by the call, since the firm's cash outflow is reduced. In addition, the downside protection offered by the bond (the put option held by investors) is eliminated.

Earnings per share will also be affected by the conversion. Interest costs will be reduced, and the number of shares outstanding will be affected (the exact effect will depend on whether we are computing earnings per share with and without dilution and the nature of the conversion feature).

In some situations the amount of debt not yet converted has become very small and calling the debt is a reasonable way of eliminating an unnecessary financial complexity.

There is a sound financial theory that convertible bonds should be called as soon as the market price of the bond is high enough above the call price to insure conversion. If called at lower prices there would be cash outlays associated with the retirement of the debt. Just as an investor prefers to hold the convertible bond rather than convert because of the downside protection offered by the bond, the corporation wants to force conversion so that the legal obligation to pay interest and principal are replaced by the more flexible commitments to common stock.

Maximum Bond Price and Call

With straight debt that is callable, the maximum price of the debt is set by the call price of the bond. The market is not likely to pay more than the call price plus accrued interest if the bond is callable, since the corporation has the right to call and retire the debt. With a convertible debt the price of the bond can go above the call price to the conversion value, since the holder of the bond can convert the bond when it is called rather than submit it for cash redemption.

Despite the fact that a convertible bond can rise above the call price, before the event occurs we have to assume that as soon as the bond rises somewhat ("the cushion") above the call price, after the no-call period has ended, the bond will be called. Thus if the conversion value is above the call price and if the bond can be called immediately, the investor should not place a large value on the value of the bond's put option component based on the hope that management will allow the bond price to rise above the call price without calling the bond.

The Overhang

If the common stock price does not increase sufficiently so that the firm can force conversion, it is said that the bonds "overhang" the firm. Sometimes the threat of a bond overhang is offered as a reason for not issuing convertible debt. Let us consider the arguments. Assume a straight debt of 20 years maturity can be issued to yield 0.10 and a convertible debt of the same maturity is issued to yield 0.04. Unfortunately the common stock price does not go up, and after 20 years the debt is retired with a cash outlay. Should the company be happy or sad with its decision to use convertible debt?

For 20 years the company paid 0.04 interest rather than 0.10. At maturity the same amount was paid as would have been paid with straight debt. At the end of 20 years the company is better off because of the 20 years of lower interest rates associated with the convertible bonds.

It is true that the company is sad that the common stock did not go high enough to justify conversion. But that is a separate question and should not be confused with the basic strategy question as to whether to use straight debt or convertible debt. If the price of the common shares does not increase, the firm may be sad that the convertible debt was not converted, but should be happy that the convertible debt was issued compared with the issuance of straight debt (it might have been even better to have issued common stock).

The First Call Date

Setting the first call date for a convertible bond is extremely important. After the first call date, if the bond's conversion value goes above the call price it is likely that the bonds will be called. Since the bondholder has been receiving low interest payments from the date of issue until the call date, and since the call premium is likely to be a small percentage of the issue price, the actual yield to call may be less than could have been earned on straight debt (that is, the cost to the corporation may be less than the cost that would have been incurred on straight debt).

If the common stock price increases rapidly during the period before the company can call, then the investor can earn a relatively high return. The value of the bond can rise high above the purchase price, and the return can be much larger than could have been earned on straight debt. This is assuming that the increase takes place before many years of low interest payments have taken place.

Thus the cost of convertible bonds may be high or low to corporations (*ex post*), depending on how rapidly the common stock price increases as well as how long the no-call period is. The longer the no-call period, the more valuable is the bond to the investors. The initial conversion premium is important, since it sets how high the common stock must go before forced conversion is feasible, and also helps determine the profitability (cost to the firm) of any given stock price increase.

The Power of the Call Feature

The call features of a convertible bond are extremely important factors in determining a bond's value. Assume a situation where a $1,000 convertible bond is paying 0.06 interest and a straight bond would be paying 0.10. The call premium is $80 and the bond is callable anytime after time 2.

The investor's opportunity cost of buying the convertible bond is $40 per year. If the bond is called at time 2, the investor earns an extra $80. The cash flows arising because of the interest payments and the conversion feature are:

Time	Interest Opportunity Cost	Call Premium	Total
0			
1	−40		−40
2	−40	+80	+40

If the bond is called at time 2 and the investor receives the call price, the investor earns a zero return from investing in the convertible bond rather than investing in straight debt yielding 0.10.

If the bond is not called at time 2, but rather the corporation calls after time 2 as soon as the bond reaches a price slightly above $1,080, the return to the investor will be less than 0.10. The holder of the debt has to hope that the stock price increases rapidly enough to drive the price of the bond above $1,080 before time 2.

We can actually solve for the maximum number of periods that can pass without conversion for the investor to earn a 0.10 compound interest return (the same return that could be earned by investing in the straight debt). Remember, once the bond is callable, the holder cannot expect to receive significantly more than the call price. It is only during the no-call period that the investor has hopes of making a large return on investment. The longer the period of no-call, the better is the probability of a large gain by the investor, since the common stock has a long period of time to increase above the conversion price.

Each period without conversion the investor is losing $40 of interest that could be earned. If the stock price does not increase rapidly (before the bond can be called), then the best that the investor can expect is to receive the call premium or slightly more.

Now let us assume the same facts but now the call premium is $120 instead of $80. If the bond is again called at time 2, the investor earns 100% incrementally on the convertible debt compared with the interest of the straight debt:

Time		Cash Flow
1		−40
2	+ 120 − 40 =	+80

However, if the stock price does not go up rapidly and the debt is not called until time 3, the investor earns a zero return incrementally (compared to straight debt) on the convertible debt:

Time		Cash Flow
1		−40
2		−40
3	+ 120 − 40 =	+80

If the bond is not called until after time 3, even a lower return will be earned. These conclusions are all based on an assumption that the corporation calls the debt as soon as the conversion value equals the call price.

Solving for the maximum delay time in calling, we find that with the given facts (including the two-year no-call period and the $120 call premium) the debt must be called on or before time 2.75 years or the investor will not earn the 0.10 return available on other comparable investments. If the period of no-call was five years, then the investor would have five years in which to have the opportunity of large gains without the threat of call. With call being possible at time 2, the investor only has 2.75 years. The number of years would change with a change in the call premium or a change in the difference between the interest rate on convertible debt and straight debt.

If bonds with short periods of no-call and low call premiums result in low returns for investors, they will also result in a low cost for corporations. We can expect the market to insist on reasonable periods of no-call, high call premiums, and appropriate interest rate differentials.

Other Conversions

We have been discussing the conversion of long-term debt into common stock. There is no reason why other possible types of conversions could not exist. For example, short-term debt could be convertible into long-term debt or long-term debt into short-term debt (this latter conversion would be dangerous to the firm, but in a sense it exists when a creditor can call a loan if a covenant is not fulfilled). Bonds may also be convertible (or exchangeable) into the stock of a second firm.

Warrants

Instead of issuing convertible debt, some firms choose to issue bonds with detachable warrants. The advantages of this security are that the debt remains outstanding (this may also be a disadvantage depending on the capital structure objective) and that new capital is brought into the firm on exercise of the warrants. There are also differences in the accounting for convertible debt and debt with warrants, and these differences may affect the choice. A synthetic convertible is a bond issued with warrants where the bond may be used to satisfy the warrant's exercise price.

Dilution

Anytime a convertible security or a security with warrants is issued, the present common stock ownership is being diluted. The amount of effective dilution will depend on the numbers of shares being introduced by the securities, the number of shares outstanding, and the terms of the conversion feature or the warrant. A warrant that offers the right to exercise at a price of $50 anytime in the next year when the stock price is currently $20 dilutes the present stockholders' position very little. On the other hand, the issuance of 1,000,000 warrants with an exercise price of $0 dilutes the ownership represented by 1,800,000 outstanding shares a large amount.

Double Jeopardy

There are many business corporations which would not issue convertible bonds. One reason for this strategy is that bond rating agencies consider convertible bonds as debt and the bonds enter all calculations as debt. The accountant records the convertible bonds as debt. Thus convertible debt, dollar for dollar, has approximately the same negative effect on bond ratings as straight debt. While bond rating agencies consider a convertible to be debt, it is perceived by many financial managers that common stock financial analysts consider convertibles to be effectively common stock.

Even if the securities are not always considered debt and common stock simultaneously, certainly the potential for the position does exist. It exists because convertible debt is part debt and part an option to acquire common stock. Thus the security is part debt and part common stock.

The calculation of an equivalent number of implicitly outstanding shares of common stock that is represented by the conversion feature of the convertible is not easy. There is apt to be considerable difference of opinion. In a situation where a $1,000 bond is convertible into 40 shares of common stock, there is not likely to be an argument against the position that the number of shares implicitly outstanding ranges from zero to 40 depending on the price of the common stock. If the conversion price is $25 and the common stock price is currently $89, there are effectively 40 more shares of common stock outstanding. If the common stock price is $1, the number of shares resulting from the conversion feature (a conversion price of $25) is closer to being zero than 40.

Other Equity Kickers

The president of the R Company said that it could profitably increase sales if only it had working capital. The loan officer of the bank said it would like to make a loan but the R Company had a large amount of risk and a conventional interest-bearing loan was not adequate compensation. How can we bring these two parties together? If the profit prospects are dim, there might not be any way of achieving a loan. But let us assume the president's optimism is justified and the banker believes it to be justified.

The first step is to make the debt convertible into common stock or to add warrants to the debt instrument. This gives the bank an opportunity to share in the good events if they occur. Unlike the fixed claim of interest, the bank now has an equity kicker that has no limit on the upside.

But both the conversion feature and the warrants depend on the market value of the common stock for their value. The bank may be optimistic about the firm's future, but is not willing to bet on the whims of the stock market. A way around this bind is to add a provision that ties the bank's receipts to the after-tax income measures of the firm. The banker has to be satisfied that the bank can live with the income measures resulting from generally accepted accounting principles. If it cannot, the exceptions must be carefully defined. Again the objective is for the bank to share in the profitable years by a larger amount than the fixed interest payments allow.

This is not meant to imply that banks should always lend funds to risky firms. It does mean that if truly profitable opportunities exist, it should be possible for the firm needing the capital to obtain it from a lending institution.

It is true that a lending institution can structure the loan so that it only receives interest and the equity kicker is omitted. But this type of debt instrument can jeopardize the existence of the firm, and management might not be willing to accept the magnitude of the probability of bankruptcy that very high interest rates impose on the firm. The equity kicker arrangement with the bank is a way of spreading somewhat more risk to the bank but at the same time allowing the bank to have the protection of the basic loan agreement. In many senses the bank is still first in line, at least for part of its investment.

CONCLUSIONS

There will always be situations where a firm cannot raise capital using straight debt because the interest rate would be excessively high ("excessive" refers here to a comparison of what the borrower would be willing to make a commitment to pay and the rate needed to attract debt capital). An equity kicker can be used to reduce the contractual interest rate. One type of equity kicker is to make the debt convertible into common stock.

There is an implication in the above that only high-risk firms should follow a strategy of issuing convertible debt. A conclusion of this sort would be too strong; on the other hand, there is no question that the addition of a conversion possibility adds to the likelihood of a risky firm being able to issue debt. It is a way of reducing the contractual interest payments and at the same time offering the investor more protection than would be given by an investment in newly issued common stock of a risky business entity. A convertible debt reduces the ability of the borrowing firm to use a strategy that exploits the vulnerable position of a debt-holder, since the debtholder would own a call option on the stock. The convertible debt tends to reduce agency costs for the investors who buy convertible bonds.

Chapter 7

Financial and Operating Leverage

W hat do a fully automatic lathe and a debenture bond have in common? The answer to the question is that they add to the leverage of the firm. The lathe affects operating leverage. The debenture affects financial leverage. It is argued in this chapter that it does not make a basic difference to investors buying the stock whether the leverage is caused by a real asset or the type of financing used.

The more operating leverage there is, the more a slight swing in sales will cause a wide swing in earnings before interest and taxes. In like manner, the more financial leverage there is, the more a slight swing in earnings before interest will cause a wide swing in income after interest. But there is an important difference between financial and operating leverage. Operating leverage affects the risk of all of the firm's investors. Financial leverage risk can be eliminated by investors using a suitable strategy.

OPERATING LEVERAGE

Firm F has 100% fixed costs of $1 million. If sales were to double, the total expenses would remain at $1 million. Within the feasible range of sales, the total expenses are constant.

Firm V has 100% variable costs of $5 per unit. If 200,000 units are produced and sold the total expenses are $1 million (same as Firm F). But if sales increase to 400,000 units the total expenses will increase to $2 million.

We define Firm F to have a large amount of operating leverage and Firm V to have zero operating leverage.

FINANCIAL LEVERAGE

A firm may be said to be levered financially when there are securities representing ownership, which have different priorities of payment, and when some of the promised payments for the use of a form of capital are of limited amount (so that if more than the limited amount is earned, the holder of a different type of security benefits). Bonds and preferred stock are the securities commonly used to attain leverage for the common stockholders. In this chapter, we deal only with the use of bonds as a form of financial leverage.

The Measurement of Financial Leverage

We want to measure the amount of leverage, since we associate leverage both with the risk and the opportunities for profit. The measure of leverage is an important input into our evaluation of the value of common stock and also the value of debt.

We define financial leverage as the use of debt in the capital structure. The measurement of the amount of financial leverage is not exact. There are many ways of measuring the amount of leverage, and they may not give consistent measures when comparing different firms. However, with any reasonable measure, the addition of more debt in substitution for stock will lead to an increase in the measure of financial leverage from the viewpoint of the common stockholders. We briefly consider the following measures of financial leverage:

1. Static: book values
2. Static: market values
3. Flows: interest and income
4. Flows: cash flows

Static: Book Values

A conventional measure of financial leverage is the ratio of debt to total capital:

$$\frac{\text{Debt}}{\text{Total capital}} \quad \text{or} \quad \frac{\text{Debt}}{\text{Common stock plus debt}}$$

where all the inputs are book values (some analysts use a ratio of debt to common stock).

The advantage of this calculation is that the inputs are very easily obtained, and the computations are well understood by management. The disadvantage of the procedure is that it uses book values, and the book values may not be relevant measures of the values of the debt or common stock.

Static: Market Values

Although deficiencies in the book measure might lead one to adjust the book values based on available information, in practice, book values are sometimes discarded, and the market values of debt and common stock are substituted. This procedure has the advantage of leaving behind the accounting measures based on sunk costs and uses the market's collective judgments of value.

Flows: Interest and Income

An alternative to the use of the static measures (either book value or market value) is the use of the several flow measures.

Define EBIT to be the income before interest and taxes. One of the most important measures of financial leverage is the income interest coverage ratio:

$$\frac{\text{Income (before interest and taxes)}}{\text{Interest}} = \frac{\text{EBIT}}{\text{Interest}}$$

This is sometimes called the "times interest earned" measure. It relates the net inflow into the firm compared to the debt payment requirements identified as interest. Calculations of interest coverage are made including and excluding tax effects and interest deductions.

This measure has the advantage of being reasonably well defined and easily computed. It is widely used and is probably the best single measure of the impact of the debt on the riskiness of the firm. A low coverage ratio (say less than 2) indicates that a slight downward shift in income will cause the firm to approach the point at which it will not be able to pay the interest on the debt.

Cash Flows

The income interest coverage ratio described above has two difficulties. First, it requires a measure of income, and second, it omits other types of debt payments than interest. The cash flow coverage ratio corrects both of these deficiencies:

$$\frac{\text{Cash in}}{\text{Cash out in payment of debt}}$$

The numerator is a measure of the cash flows coming into the firm (essentially the income plus depreciation and other noncash utilizing expenses). The denominator measures the interest, debt retirement, and lease payments. Thus the cash flow coverage ratio is a broader measure of debt obligations than the income interest coverage ratio. Instead of "Cash in" the measure of earnings before interest, taxes, depreciation, and amortization (EBITDA) is used in the numerator.

One deficiency of this measure is that it is "near-sighted," and unless it is computed for a series of years extending into the future, significant debt retirement payments could be omitted from the computation (thus leading to an understatement of the amount of leverage).

In addition to computing static and flow measures, we can also combine the two types of measures. For example, the present value of the debt can be related to the net cash flows from operations:

$$\frac{\text{Present value of debt}}{\text{Cash flows from operations}}$$

to obtain the "number of years of debt," assuming the cash flows are on an annual basis. Variations of this computation deduct the current assets from the total debt of the firm to obtain a "debt net of current assets" measure (alternatively, the liquid disposable assets can be deducted). This measure has the advantage of combining what is happening to the firm (its flows) and the information about its current financial position.

Which Measure is Relevant?

To some extent, all the above measures are relevant. If the investing public uses a measure to evaluate the value of the firm's securities, that measure becomes relevant to the financial decision maker. If we start with a given financial structure, all the above measures will show an increase in leverage if debt is substituted for common stock. Although the measures may not be reliable in comparing different firms, still if the cash flow from operations divided into the present value of debt for one firm is 0.6 (say it has $6 million of debt and $10 million of cash flows) and is 4.5 for a second firm (say it has $45 million of debt and again $10 million of cash flows), then, unless some other facts are introduced, we can strongly suspect that the second firm has more leverage.

Leverage and Risk

The substitution of a dollar of debt for a dollar of equity adds risk to the common stockholders. As the number of dollars of debt increased, the amount of risk to the stockholders is increased. This increase in risk is inevitable, although it is possible to conclude mistakenly that the amount of risk is still so small that for "practical purposes" one can ignore the effect on the stockholders. However, in the same manner that one more straw may cause a camel difficulties, one more dollar of debt can cause a corporation's stockholders to have difficulties.

There should be a clear understanding of the risk consequences to the firm's stockholders of adding debt. While it is possible for the individual investor to adopt an investment strategy that will reduce risk, the fact remains that generally debt does add to the overall risk of the stockholders of the corporation. Planning requires that management consider the long-term consequences of decisions. The consequence of adding debt is to increase the variability of the return per dollar of common stock investment.

Financial Leverage and Earnings Per Share

Let us assume that a new firm wants to raise $35 million of initial capital. It can use either common stock and debt. Although it would be incorrect to suggest that one could only look at earnings per share (EPS) data to evaluate debt versus common stock alternatives, since the risks to the stockholders are not held constant, managers are greatly interested in how the EPS is affected. We need to determine the amount of earnings before interest necessary for the firm to be indifferent between debt and common stock. Second, for any given earnings before interest and taxes, do we prefer debt or common stock?

We consider different capital structures and the effect of different earnings before interest and taxes on the earnings per share of the firm. Suppose the stock could be issued at $25 per share, and the debt costs 0.08 for any amount of debt. The tax rate is 0.40.

To raise the $35 million of capital using only common stock issued at a price of $25 per share would require 1.4 million shares of common stock. However, if 50% of the capital is debt, only 0.7 million shares will be required. Should the firm issue debt or common stock? Assume that the board of directors wants to know the effect on earnings per share of different capital structures.

Let the total earnings (EBIT) be X, then with zero debt:

$$\text{EPS} = \frac{X(1-0.4)}{1.4}$$

With debt of B paying 0.08 interest and a 0.4 tax rate:

$$\text{EPS} = \frac{X - 0.048B}{1.4 - \dfrac{B}{25}} = \frac{(X - 0.08B)(1 - 0.4)}{1.4 - \dfrac{B}{25}}$$

The two EPS numbers are equal if $X = \$2,800,000$. With zero debt:

$$\text{EPS} = \frac{2,800,000(0.6)}{1,400,000} = \$1.20$$

With $10,000,000 of debt, 1,000,000 shares would be issued:

$$\text{EPS} = \frac{0.6(2,800,000 - 800,000)}{1,000,000} = \frac{1,200,000}{1,000,000} = \$1.20$$

If the EBIT were known to be $2,800,000, the firm would be indifferent to all possible capital structures, since the EPS will be $1.20 regardless of the structure. The interest rate times the amount of capital gives the indifference income before interest and taxes.

If the earnings before interest and taxes are expected (are known?) to be larger than $2,800,000, the more debt in the capital structure the better for the common stock investor. If the earnings are expected to be less than $2,800,000, an all-common-stock capital structure is to be preferred by common stockholders. If the earnings are unknown, the board should be aware that the choice of financing methods is contingent on the probabilities of different earnings taking place and the risk preferences of the decision makers. Financial managers will generally not know their firms' future earnings; thus the value of EBIT that will occur is uncertain. If uncertainty is acknowledged, the analysis being illustrated is a technique that is helpful in understanding the consequences of the decision alternatives, rather than a procedure for clearly defining the right decision.

Raising New Capital

The above example assumed that the capital was to be raised by a newly formed firm. We assume the same facts, except that an existing firm is now going to raise $10 million of new capital. In addition, assume that the initial capital structure consists of 1.4 million shares of common stock and no debt. Debt will again cost 0.08, and 400,000 shares of common stock could be issued at a price of $25 per share.

For any amount of debt paying 0.08, if the earnings before interest and taxes are $3,600,000, the EPS will be $1.20. If the earnings (EBIT) are expected (are known?) to be larger than $3,600,000, the more debt the better for a common stockholder. If the earnings are expected to be less than $3,600,000, an all-stock capital structure is to be preferred.

PLANNING CONSIDERATIONS

There are companies that will not use debt because it is too risky, and there are companies that will use a lot of debt but will not undertake a real investment with significant risk. This chapter points out that operating risk adds to the amount of risk faced by investors, and that one should consider the overall risk to the firm. Financial leverage increases the risk to stockholders. The planner should attempt to optimize jointly the amount of operating leverage (or product risk) and the amount of financial leverage.

The sensitivity of stockholder profitability to changes in sales depends both on the amount of operating leverage and the amount of financial leverage. Thus the planner must understand the inherent risk of the product (the fluctuation in sales), the economies of sales and production (the fixed costs and profit margin), as well as the amount of stock equity and debt under the several alternative financing plans.

In addition to the sensitivity of income and return on investment to the two types of leverage we should know the expected values that result from different decision combinations. Also, we should know how operating and financial leverage affects the way in which the firm's common stock is correlated with the overall market basket of securities. One should understand that increased operating leverage and increased financial leverage both have the effect of increasing the swings of a firm's common stock earnings relative to the swings in the market.

This chapter deals with the effect of substituting debt for equity on the risks to investors in common stock. The next chapter will consider the effect on an investor who follows an investment strategy that neutralizes the risk consequences of the firm's financial leverage decision.

Chapter 8

Capital Structure: The Weighted Average Cost of Capital

The financial officers who have conscientiously deciphered the academic literature to determine what decisions should be made relative to capital structure (the mixture of debt and common stock financing) have had an interesting time over the past 40 years. They would have begun by concluding that there was an optimum capital structure (the so-called classical position). In 1958 they read the classic Miller-Modigliani *The American Economics Review* article, which informed them that the value of a firm was invariant to capital structure decisions.[1] There were later modifications of the Miller-Modigliani position that indicated that in the presence of corporate income taxes a firm should have as close to 100% debt as it can achieve. Finally, just as the assumptions behind this latter recommendation were being understood, theoretical finance literature suggested that perhaps the optimum capital structure is somewhere between no debt and 100% debt given the costs of financial distress and investor taxes.

The chief financial officers of corporations are likely to ask three questions involving capital structure:

1. How is the overall weighted average cost of capital of the firm changed by decisions affecting the capital structure?
2. How will the firm's value be affected?
3. What is the firm's cost of capital and what is its relevance to investment decisions?

Answers to the first two questions influence the types of securities that are issued to investors. The answer to the third question conventionally becomes the cut-off rate (or the rate of discount) for investments. The answers to these three questions are not obvious.

---

[1] See Franco Modigliani and Merton H. Miller, "The Cost of Capital, Corporation Finance, and the Theory of Investment," *The American Economic Review* (June 1958), pp. 261-297; "The Cost of Capital, Corporation Finance, and the Theory of Investment: Reply," *The American Economic Review* (September 1959), pp. 655-669; and "Taxes and the Cost of Capital: A Correction," *The American Economic Review* (June 1963), pp. 433-443. Also David Durand, "The Cost of Capital, Corporation Finance, and the Theory of Investment: Comment," *The American Economic Review* (September 1959), pp. 640-654.

DEFINITION OF COST OF CAPITAL

We define the cost of capital as the cost to the corporation of obtaining funds. To simplify the discussion, assume that the rates at which the corporation can borrow and lend funds are equal. The definition is appealingly simple and leads to simple decision rules. If the average cost of obtaining funds is 0.10 and if the corporation has an investment with comparable risk that yields more than 0.10, it should accept the investment. Unfortunately, this decision rule glosses over considerations of uncertainty and risk preferences that we cannot ignore if we expect the investment decision rule to be operational in the real world.

The weighted average cost of capital (WACC) is equal to sum of the costs of several different types of capital each weighted by its proportion in the capital structure. Thus if the following capital structure and costs apply (there are zero taxes), we obtain a cost of capital of 0.10:

	Amount of Capital	Proportion	Cost	Weighted Cost
Debt	$20 million	0.4	0.08	0.032
Common stock	30 million	0.6	0.113	0.068
			WACC	0.100

Define the value of a firm as equal to the present value of all the cash distributed to all capital contributors. Initially we assume that there is no taxes, no costs of financial distress, and the firm is not growing. If the rate of discount used in computing the present value can be decreased without decreasing the cash flows, by manipulating the capital structure, the total value of the firm will be increased.

Since the 1958 Miller and Modigliani article on capital structure and the cost of capital, a continuing controversy has raged about the sensitivity of the cost of capital of a firm to changes in its capital structure. The controversy is of importance to financial officers, since the effect of capital structure on the cost of capital affects the debt versus common stock decision and the determination of the cost of capital affects the cut-off rate that is frequently used to determine which independent investments are acceptable.

The broad assumptions made by the several parties to the discussions are worthy of review. The capital structure debate implicitly assumes that

1. There is a definable cost that we can label "cost of capital."
2. It is possible to compute the cost of capital with reasonable exactness and meaningfulness.
3. The cost of equity capital is the factor used (either explicitly or implicitly) by investors in common stock in making their investment decisions.
4. Different risk classes of firms have different costs of capital.
5. We can use the firm's or the division's cost of capital in making investment decisions. Using the net present value method of making investment

decisions, it is the rate of discount to be used in choosing the best of a set of mutually exclusive investments, and it is the cut-off rate for accepting or rejecting independent investments.

Assumption 5 is convenient because it enables a firm to implement the very logical net present value procedure, which works in excellent fashion as long as we do not ration capital or allow uncertainty.

Although assumption 1 may be satisfied, there is no reason for assuming that the other four assumptions hold under conditions of uncertainty. No one has shown in a logical manner that the firm's cost of capital can be generally and effectively used in evaluating a wide variety of investments, if uncertainty is taken into consideration. In this chapter we attempt to determine the effect of leverage on the cost of capital and on the value of the firm, but do not attempt to determine the exact rate of discount to be used in investment evaluation. It can be shown that it is not always correct to use the firm's cost of capital to evaluate investments since each cash flow has its own appropriate discount rate.

THE OPTIMAL CAPITAL STRUCTURE

How much debt should a company have? It would be useful if we could answer that question in a simple definitive manner, but unfortunately the answer is complex and inexact. In this chapter we shall suggest some approaches to the basic type of capital mixture question, aiming to eliminate some misconceptions and suggesting some useful methods of analysis.

First, we will assume there are zero taxes. While this is an unrealistic assumption, it is useful in highlighting the necessary conditions for one or another forms of capital structure. It has been shown that in the absence of taxes and costs of financial distress that the value of a firm is not affected by its capital structure.

CAPITAL STRUCTURE AND FINANCIAL ARBITRAGE

Modigliani and Miller, in their 1958 article, stated (pp. 268-269) that "the average cost of capital to any firm is completely independent of its capital structure." If this were not true, "an investor could buy and sell stocks and bonds in such a way as to exchange one income stream for another stream, identical in all relevant respects but selling at a lower price."

Modigliani and Miller illustrated the "arbitrage" process by borrowing on personal account to obtain an equivalent amount of leverage as that obtained by owning a highly levered firm. They also discussed the possibility of "undoing" leverage of a firm by the investor buying stock and bonds. The objective of this section is to explore in some detail a method of attaining equivalency and to define the necessary conditions for being able to do so. We see that it is not always easy (and sometimes not possible) to obtain equivalency in the presence of financial distress. We define equivalency as being a situation in which the two investment alternatives available to an investor lead to the same earnings. For example, an investor buys both the bonds and stock of one levered firm to obtain the same characteristics as buying the stock of a zero levered firm. If the two firms have identical operating characteristics, these two investment alternatives may be equivalent.

Several assumptions are made that run throughout this section:

1. There are no transaction and information costs (it costs the same to supervise two investments as one).
2. There are no taxes.
3. Limited liability does not exist.
4. Financial distress and resulting transaction costs are assumed to be zero.

Delevering a Firm: Buying Stock and Bonds of a Firm

An investor can delever a firm by splitting the investment between the common stock and debt of the firm. If the investor buys 0.01 of an unlevered firm, the investor buys 0.01 of the common stock and 0.01 of the debt of a levered firm with identical operating characteristics (the investment in the levered firm is equivalent to an equal percentage of ownership in an unlevered firm).

Example

Let the size of the unlevered firm be $10 million. The levered firm has $6 million of common stock and $4 million of debt. The investor has $100,000; thus 0.01 of the unlevered firm can be purchased. The debt pays 0.08. The two firms have identical operating results.

To delever the levered firm the investor should buy $60,000 of common stock and $40,000 of debt, where these amounts are 0.01 of the outstanding securities:

Common Stock: $0.01(\$6,000,000) = \$60,000$
Debt: $0.01(\$4,000,000) = \$40,000$

The investor delevering the levered firm will earn the same return as if the company were financed entirely with common stock. Exhibit 1 illustrates four different possible earnings (EBIT) and two different capital structures. Note that the earnings with all common stock are identically equal to the total earnings with 40% debt for each of the four possible earning levels if 0.01 of both securities are purchased.

The total interest on the $4 million debt is $320,000. The investor has claim to 0.01 of this amount or $3,200 interest. We are assuming that interest cost is incurred even if it is not earned (more complex assumptions can be incorporated).

Exhibit 1: Earnings to Delevered Investor
(Owning 0.01 of Both Securities)

Earnings (EBIT)	Common Stock Earnings after $320,000 Interest	Earnings if Capital Structure All Common Stock (0.01 of Stock)	Capital Structure: With 40% Debt Buying 0.01 of Securities		
			Common Stock Earnings	Debt Interest (0.08)	Total Earnings
0	−320,000	0	−3,200	+3,200	0
100,000	−220,000	1,000	−2,200	+3,200	1,000
500,000	+180,000	5,000	1,800	+3,200	5,000
1,000,000	+680,000	10,000	6,800	+3,200	10,000

The investor buys the vertical slice of the securities (0.01 of each security type) has the same earnings as would be earned if the firm were fully financed by stock and the investor owned 0.01 fraction of the stock. The conclusion is that a levered firm cannot sell at a discount compared to a less levered firm. If a levered firm is selling at a discount, an investor can sell the stock of an unlevered firm, buy the stock and bonds of the levered firm selling at a discount, and be better off than holding the unlevered firm. Too much debt should not scare investors, since they can delever the firm.

Can a levered firm sell at a premium compared to an unlevered firm? Not if personal borrowing is available at the same cost as the corporation can borrow. It can be shown that an investor can use personal borrowing combined with investment in a lightly levered firm to be equivalent to an investment in a highly levered firm (remember there are zero taxes). Consistent with this logic, the weighted average cost of capital curve is unaffected by capital structure decisions, unlike the classical view that there is an optimum capital structure. A third point of view discussed in the next section is that the use of debt decreases the cost of capital if we consider corporate taxes.

Until we bring in taxes, there is no reason why the possibility of changing the capital structure should lead to the possibility of increasing the value of a firm. The strategies of buying the firm's debt and common stock or buying a mixture of low levered and high levered firms can delever firms using a large amount of debt. Also firms using too little debt can be levered by the use of personal debt to achieve leverage. Only when taxes or financial distress costs are introduced is there a logical justification for expecting there to be a value change from classification of ownership claims as debt rather than common stock.

There are complexities. The limited liability characteristic of a corporation enhances having the corporation do the borrowing rather than the individual. Also, there may be different transaction costs associated with the different strategies.

Since the publication of the 1958 Modigliani and Miller article, the terms "arbitrage" and "homemade leverage" have been widely used in the context of corporation finance. This section attempted to describe one way in which arbitrage can be accomplished.

Substituting Debt for Equity

At zero leverage the cost of stock is equal to the weighted average cost of capital, and at 100% leverage the cost of debt is equal to the weighted average cost of capital. There are logical reasons for assuming that the cost of debt and the cost of common stock capital both increase as the amount of leverage increases.

We cannot be sure of the shape of the weighted average cost of capital curve when debt is substituted for stock. With zero taxes and no costs of financial distress there are good reasons for assuming that the weighted average cost of capital (WACC) is constant for all amounts of leverage. Given taxes and costs of financial distress, conventional wisdom among financial executives is that the WACC curve goes down (because of taxes) and then goes up (because of financial distress). That is, there is an optimum capital structure and management should find the mixture of debt and common stock that leads to a minimum WACC.

The location of the minimum point of the WACC, in fact the existence of a minimum point, is heavily dependent on the corporate taxes and taxes on investors, the mix of investors, and the institutions connected with bankruptcy situations, and the economics of financial distress. Under certain conditions (e.g., zero taxes and zero financial distress costs) the WACC curve is flat and the value of the firm is indifferent to all capital structures. With corporate taxes but no taxes on investors and no costs of financial distress, there are logical reasons for assuming that 100% debt is the most desirable capital structure. With more realistic assumptions, it is less clear that either one of the two extreme positions is correct. Certainly the evidence represented by the financial statements of corporations indicates a general belief that the use of some debt is desirable, but practice does not approach 100% debt (though banks use a large percentage of debt).

Consider an operating financial executive attempting to decide whether it is desirable to move from a leverage of 0.35 to 0.40. An analyst can indicate the effects on earnings per share and the increase in risk, and can offer an evaluation of the effect on the firm's bond rating, but cannot give definite answers as to whether or not 0.35 or 0.40 debt is desirable from the viewpoint of shareholder value. In some situations it is useful to know where exact conclusions cannot be reached, instead of pretending that exact answers are possible when they are not.

OPTIMAL CAPITAL STRUCTURE: CORPORATE INCOME TAXES

We have argued that without income taxes and costs of financial distress the value of a firm is independent of its capital structure. With corporate income taxes the value of a firm is greatly affected by the fact that interest is deductible for tax purposes and dividends are not. In this section we assume the investors have zero personal tax rates.

Example

A firm is considering a $2,000 investment earning $100. Debt is available at a cost of 0.05 per year. There is a 0.35 corporate marginal tax rate. There are zero investor taxes. With three different financing arrangements, the results would be as follows:

	100% Stock	50% Stock 50% Debt	100% Debt
Earnings before tax less: interest	100	100.00	100
Interest	___	50.00	100
Taxable income of issuer	100	50.00	0
Income tax (0.35)	35	17.50	0
Income after tax	65	32.50	0
Interest	0	50.00	100
Total contributions to investors	65	82.50	100

There is a larger after-tax distribution with 100% debt than with the two other financial arrangement. If the stockholders buy the debt, there is no additional risk to the stockholders compared with raising the required capital using common stock. Since the total payoff to the capital contributors can be increased by using more debt, the value of the firm can also be increased, if we assume zero costs of financial distress.

The question about whether the overall cost of capital of a firm is changed by decisions affecting its capital structure is answered with a yes. If it were not for the income tax laws the answer would be different. The present tax laws, allowing interest on debt but not dividends on stock to be deducted in computing taxable income, results in a bias in favor of issuing debt. The reason for this bias is most easily seen where the debt is issued to the common stockholders. In this situation there is no increased risk to the stockholders, since they own the debt, but the amount of the distribution of earnings is changed.

With all the capital in the form of stock, the cash distributions to the owners would not result in a tax deduction. With all the capital in the form of debt, an amount equal to the tax rate times the cash distribution in the form of interest would be a tax saving. To avoid being identified as a "thin corporation" the firm would want less than 100% debt, and to avoid arousing the Internal Revenue Services it would not want to issue all its debt to the stockholders. But assuming the firm did not go too far, it is clear that in the presence of current corporate income tax laws one can change the value of a corporation's earning stream by changing its capital structure. The clearest illustration of benefit arises when we merely change the form of the distribution (a dividend changed to interest) but where the payments are made to the same capital contributors. Where all the debt payments are made to a third party who is not presently a stockholder, the analysis becomes more complex because the risk changes for the common stockholders.

A corporation that has debt outstanding, or is issuing debt, is better off with interest being deductible than with a cash distribution not deductible, for tax purposes. For example, assume that interest is deductible and that debt is outstanding with an interest rate of 0.05 and the marginal corporate tax rate is 0.35 (the after-tax interest rate is 0.0325). We further assume that the time value of money of both stockholders and bondholders is 0.05. In this situation, the deductibility of interest for tax purposes enables the firm to consider investments for the benefit of the stockholders with yields of less than 0.05 (but with after-tax yields of at least 0.0325). Without the deductibility of interest, investments yielding less than 0.05 would be rejected. Insurance (risk-reducing) type investments are not considered here. The investments are desirable with yields larger than 0.0325 because of a combination of tax deductibility of interest and trading on the equity.

With investments yielding over 0.05, financed by the 0.05 debt, we have a situation of pure trading on the equity, and the acceptability of the investment is not the result of the tax deductibility of interest (although the fact that interest is deductible may make the investment more desirable).

Substituting Debt for Equity — No Investor Taxes

It can be shown that:

$$V_L = V_u + t_c B \tag{1}$$

if investors are not taxed, where

V_L = the value of the levered firm
V_u = the value of the unlevered firm
t_c = the corporate tax rate
B = the debt to be substituted for common stock
X = the earnings before interest and taxes (EBIT)
I = the interest paid on B of debt

The stockholders of the unlevered firm with a value of V_u earns $(1-t_c)X$. If B of debt is substituted for stock and if the investor buys (owns) all the stock and $(1-t_c)$ of the debt, the investor will also earn $(1-t_c)X$.

Equation (1) for V_L shows that $t_c B$ of value is added by substituting debt for equity. The investor determines the risk of the investment. For more risk than investing in the stock of the unlevered firm buy the common stock of the levered firm. For less risk buy the debt of the levered firm. For the same risk buy all the stock and $(1-t_c)$ of the debt.

It is interesting that with zero debt the amount available for capital contributors is $X(1-t_c)$ each year, and with debt paying kB interest the cash flow is increased to $X(1-t_c) + kBt_c$. This amount is independent of risk attitudes and discount rates. This is partial analysis, since to be complete we should also consider investor income taxes.

Exhibit 2: Earnings Needed to Pay Investors

	Before Interest, Before-tax Earnings	(1-Tax Rate)	Necessary Earnings (Cash Distributions)
Bonds	100		100
Preferred stock	154	0.65	100
Common stock	154	0.65	100
	408		300

Exhibit 3: Corporation's After-Tax Cost

	Necessary Earnings	Tax Saving	Net Cost to Corporation
Bonds	100	35	65 or 0.065
Preferred stock	100	0	100 or 0.10
Common stock	100	0	100 or 0.10

For example, if $X = \$100$ and $t_c = 0.35$ with zero debt the stockholders net \$65. With $B = \$1,000$ and $k = 0.10$, $kB = \$100$ the cash flows for investors is:

$$X(1-t_c) + kBt_c = \$65 + \$100(0.35) = \$100$$

The value added each year by the use of debt instead of common stock is \$35. The present value is $t_c B = 0.35(1,000) = \$350$ or

$$\frac{\$35}{0.10} = \$350$$

The investor who can earn \$65 per year by buying the stock in the unlevered firm can buy 0.65 of the debt and all the stock and again earn \$65: $0.65(\$100) = \$65$ from the debt. The stock earns zero if $X = \$100$ and the interest equals \$100.

Tax Considerations and Costs of Different Capital Sources

Assume for illustrative purposes that holders of bonds, preferred stock, and common stock of the ABC Company all required a return of 0.10, and there is a 0.35 tax rate. There are \$1,000 of each security outstanding (the return to each type of security is \$100).

In order to have \$100 to distribute to each type of security, the company will have to earn \$408 before tax. Since the bond interest is deductible for tax purposes, we need only \$100 of before-tax earnings to satisfy the interest payment to the bondholders.

But let us consider more exactly the after-tax cost of debt. The \$100 of interest results in a tax saving of \$35, thus the net cost of the debt is \$65 or $0.065(\$65/\$1,000 = 0.065)$. We extend Exhibit 2 to show the after-tax cost of each security (Exhibit 3).

We have three sets of costs. These are set forth in Exhibit 4.

Instead of assuming that the returns of each type of security are equal, we now assume that the required returns are 0.10 for debt, 0.12 for preferred stock, and 0.20 for common stock. Exhibit 5 shows the costs of the alternative sources.

Exhibit 4: Costs of Each Type of Capital

	Necessary Earnings Before Tax	After-Tax Distribution As a Fraction of Capital	After-Tax Cost
Bonds	0.100	0.10	0.065
Preferred stock	0.154	0.10	0.10
Common stock	0.154	0.10	0.10

Exhibit 5: Costs of Each Type of Capital
(Changed Assumptions)

	Before Tax Necessary Earnings	After-Tax Distribution	After-Tax Cost
Bonds	0.100	0.10	0.065
Preferred stock	0.185	0.12	0.120
Common stock	0.308	0.20	0.200

In the current example, the common stockholders require twice as large a return as the bondholders, but the before-tax cost of common is more than three times as large as the debt cost. The difference in cost between preferred stock and bonds is also interesting. The preferred stock is almost twice as expensive (before tax) as the bonds, despite the fact that the return to the preferred stockholders is only 0.12 compared to 0.10 for bondholders.

The differences in the costs would be less dramatic if a tax rate less than 0.35 were used. A higher tax rate would make the cost differences more dramatic.

PERSONAL TAXES AND THE
OPTIMAL CAPITAL STRUCTURE

The study of the optimal capital structure question has proceeded in three stages. First there was the no-tax situation offered by Miller and Modigliani in their 1958 article in which a firm's cost of capital is not affected by the amount of debt. Second, the corporate income tax was introduced with the conclusion that a firm should issue as much debt as the Internal Revenue Service will allow. The third stage was the introduction of personal income tax considerations. If we agree that business decisions cannot be made on a before-tax basis, the logical conclusion is that the investors' tax position as well as that of the corporation must be taken into consideration.

It is well known that the fact that a corporation can deduct interest in computing its taxable income acts as a significant incentive for corporations to issue debt. In fact it can be shown (without personal taxes and costs of financial distress) that firms should be financed by as much debt as the Internal Revenue Service will allow. This position has been stated frequently in the finance literature. It is argued here that the optimal capital structure of a corporation cannot be determined without consideration of the personal income taxes of the investors in the corporation.

There are three tax factors at work that must be considered in making capital structure decisions. First, there is the different tax treatment awarded at the corporate level for interest and earnings of stockholders. Second, there is the possibility of a firm acting to defer the personal taxation of its stockholders by retaining rather than paying dividends and issuing new stock. Third, there is the differential tax rate applied to capital gains compared to that applied to ordinary income for investors. The deductibility of interest moves a firm toward the use of debt, but the other two factors are strong incentives for issuing stock. The advantages of retention of earnings compared to cash dividends and issuing new stock to the present stockholders are well known. If interest payments are recognized to be the economic equivalent of dividends (although taxed differently), it can be seen that the twin advantages of tax deferral and capital gains with common stock may balance the disadvantage of losing the deductibility of interest.

The implication here is that the personal tax structure and tax situation of a corporation's investors should affect the capital structure of a corporation as well as the type of securities different investors buy. The tax deferral and capital gains associated with common stock may outweigh the tax shield of debt interest.

Assume the value of an unlevered firm is V_u and the common stock investor, taxed at t_s, earns

$$X(1-t_c)(1-t_s)$$

If B of debt is substituted for common stock and if ordinary debt income is taxed to the investor at a rate of t_p, the investor buying all the stock and

$$\frac{(1-t_c)(1-t_s)}{1-t_p}$$

of the debt will earn the same as $X(1-t_c)(1-t_s)$ which is the return earned by the investor buying the stock of the unlevered firm.

With this one type of investor it can be shown that:

$$V_L = V_u + B + \left[1 - \frac{(1-t_c)(1-t_s)}{1-t_p}\right] \tag{2}$$

Whether or not the substitution of debt for stock adds value depends on the values of t_c, t_s, and t_p. There are some investors for which $t_s = t_p$, and for those investors, we again have $V_L = V_u + t_c B$, if these investors are buying the firm's securities.

THE CLIENTELE EFFECT

The relationship for V_L given by equation (2) is somewhat complex, but unfortunately additional complexity is required. The investors will buy the type of security that is best for them. Thus investors who do not pay taxes will buy bonds and high tax investors will buy stocks. In fact, the high tax investors will tend to buy stocks that do not pay dividends (thus affecting the value of t_s). Thus the value of the levered firm is more complex than the formulas offered if we consider the clientele effect. The clientele effect occurs anytime that different groups of investors are taxed differently, and thus have different financial strategy preferences both because of tax differences and wealth differences.

An example of a clientele effect is the preference of high tax investors for low cash dividend stocks. The first assumption we must make is that in a dynamic world, cash will be flowing to investors who are not taxed or to taxed investors who have special accounts that are not taxed or are taxed at low effective tax rates. Now assume that there are zero taxed investors who buy the new corporate debt. The unlevered firm leads to annual benefits for its stockholders taxed at a rate of t_s of:

$$X(1-t_c)(1-t_s) \tag{3}$$

where X is the firm's earnings before interest and taxes.

After substitution of B debt (paying I interest to investors who are not taxed) for equity the benefits for all its investors are:

$$(X-I)(1-t_c)(1-t_s) + I = X(1-t_c)(1-t_s) + I[1-(1-t_c)(1-t_s)] \tag{4}$$

The benefits added by the debt substitution are $I[1-(1-t_c)(1-t_s)]$ with a present value, using the interest rate cost of the debt as a discount rate, of $B[1-(1-t_c)(1-t_s)]$.

Assuming $t_c = 0.35$ and $t_s = 0.071$ we have:

Value added = $B[1-0.65(0.929)] = 0.396B$

Without considering the investor taxes (or with zero investor tax rates) the value added would be $0.35B$. The value added is increased to $0.396B$ by considering investor taxes, if we allow a clientele effect. Zero taxed investors are assumed to be buying the firm's debt.

Now assume a larger value for t_s. With $t_s = 0.20$ the value added is now:

Value added = $B[1-0.65(0.80)] = 0.48B$

The value from substituting debt is increased since the after-tax desirability of the stock is decreased. A dividend-paying stock with investors who churn their portfolio could have a tax rate of 0.20. Each firm will have a dividend and retention policy that leads to different implied values for t_s. The range would be from 0.396 (assuming all the gains are dividends taxed at 0.396) to zero (assuming all the gains are capital gains that are deferred forever).

The ability of a firm to find zero taxed investors will depend on many factors including the amount of funds flowing to these investors and the amount of debt being issued by the corporate sector.

OBSERVED CAPITAL STRUCTURES

Most corporations use some debt, but not a dramatically large amount. There are many factors which effectively limit the proportion of a firm's capital structure that is debt. Among these factors are:

1. the firm's top managers do not want to jeopardize their positions (and financial rewards) because of financial difficulties caused by a large amount of debt. The financial decisions are made from the viewpoint of managers, not the stockholders.
2. an assumption of a larger value of t_p for the purchasers of the debt than is realistic.
3. a pessimistic estimate of the probability of financial distress and the size of the financial distress cost.
4. a pessimistic estimate of the likelihood of being able to use all the firm's tax deductions.
5. a fear of the restrictions imposed by the covenants of the debt.
6. the ability of the firm to use its debt capacity and the tax deductions in ways other than issuing debt.
7. the retention of financing flexibility to take advantage of opportunities.
8. the debt capacity based on book values is small compared to the effect on the firm's market value capitalization.
9. the perceived operational risk precludes the use of a large amount of debt.
10. the debt will be "unfriendly" debt not bought by stockholders.

It is reasonable that given the existence of the above factors that we find the average corporation has less debt than the tax saving model with clienteles would lead us to conclude should exist. It is only when we shift to the leverage buyout model, where the stockholders are making the financial decisions, that we find the amount of debt that the above values for V_L suggest.

We could assume one specific set of tax rate relationships where the corporation is then indifferent to different capital structures. For given values of the tax rate on common stock returns (t_s) and the corporate tax rate (t_c) there is a value of the tax rate on ordinary income (t_p) for which all capital structures are equally desirable (assuming no costs of financial distress and no differential transaction costs).

When there are investors with very low tax rates who have investible funds, they will find the purchase of debt to be attractive. The presence of these investors makes it possible for the value added by the substitution of debt for equity by a corporation to be larger if investor taxes are considered than if there were no investor taxes. The tax rates consistent with an assumed equilibrium situation are not the only tax rates that should be considered.

WACC AND INVESTMENTS AND TAXES

We want to show that if the return required by debt and stock can be defined for a given investment and a given capital structure, that the use of WACC as the required return will lead to the investors receiving their required returns. The analysis will include taxes.

Assume a corporation uses $\frac{1}{3}$ debt and $\frac{2}{3}$ stock to finance an investment. The stock has a cost of 0.15 and the debt costs 0.10 before tax. The tax rate is 0.4. The WACC is

$$\text{WACC} = (1 - 0.4)(0.10)\tfrac{1}{3} + (0.15)\tfrac{2}{3} = 0.02 + 0.10 = 0.12$$

Since the WACC is 0.12, an investment with equivalent risk earning exactly 0.12 should just satisfy the investors. Assume an investment costing $300 is financed with $100 debt costing 0.10 and $200 stock equity costing 0.15 (this is consistent with the WACC of 0.12). The investment has a life of one year. To earn 0.12, an investment of $300 should earn $336 of cash flow or $36 of income. The projected income statement for the project, exclusive of financing considerations is

Sales		$800
Cost of goods	$440	
Depreciation	300	
Tax	24	764
Income (before interest)		$36

The after-tax cost of debt is 0.06, or for $100 of debt it is $6, and the after-tax return to stock equity on their $200 investment is 0.15 or $30. The $36 of project income satisfies these earning requirements.

The funds flow at time one is $36 + $300 = $336. This allows the payment of $6 after tax interest and $100 of principal to debt, $230 to stock, in the form of a $30 dividend and $200 return of capital.

The income statement, including the $10 interest expense, is

Sales		$800
Cost of goods	$440	
Depreciation	300	
Interest	10	
Tax	20	770
Income to stockholders		$30

The funds flow to stock equity and debt principal payment (interest effects have already been considered) is $30 + $300 = $330, which is enough to return the $230 to stock equity investors and to pay the $100 principal of the debt.

CONCLUSIONS

This chapter has argued that the capital structure decision of a corporation depends on the personal tax rates of the investors in the corporation. Whether debt is more desirable than stock depends on the corporate tax rate, the investors' ordinary income tax rate, and personal capital gains tax rate as well as the length of time that personal taxes will be deferred.

Business decision making is constantly searching for rules that will lead to clearly defined accept-or-reject decisions. It is reassuring when we can direct our attention to one number and justify the decision using this number. One could recommend using the weighted average cost of capital and accepting only those independent investments that have positive net present values. Unfortunately, this is an incorrect decision rule. We do not know that one should automatically reject investments that yield less than the firm's estimated cost of capital; in fact stockholders may want firms to accept many such investments where the investments are relatively safe or where they have risk characteristics that reduce the overall risk of the firm. In like manner many investments yielding more than the cost of capital should be rejected because of their unacceptable risk characteristics.

The use of debt in the capital structure of a corporation may enable the firm to reduce its cost of raising capital, since the interest payments are deductible for tax purposes. The desirability of debt compared to common stock is dramatized when the debt is purchased by the common stockholders, since in this situation there is no increase in the risk to the investors. One could be led to the conclusion that a firm should issue as much debt as possible, with the stockholders purchasing the debt if they fear an excessive increase in risk arising from the highly levered capital structure. The addition of debt, even where the debt is a relatively cheap source of capital because of the tax structure, does add risk. If there is no taxable income, the full cost of the interest falls on the corporation and ultimately on the stockholders. Thus the present corporate tax structure offers strong incentives to issue debt but that there are forces (the risk of bankruptcy, the costs of financial distress, and the conventions of the investment banking community) that restrain the corporation considering the issuance of unusually large amounts of debt compared with common stock. In addition, there is the complexity of investor taxes.

We conclude that with the institutional facts of taxes and financial distress costs, the cost to a firm of obtaining capital is a function of its capital structure. Thus, with real-world institutions the cost of capital is a variable dependent on decisions of corporate managers.

It is possible to eliminate the risk considerations of capital structure by having the stockholders buy a mixture of stock and debt. If investors want to buy either debt or stock, the capital structure decision becomes interwoven with the entire question of capital asset evaluation, since the expected return and the risk of the investor's returns will vary with the proportion of debt.

With the investors in a low tax bracket for all returns, there is a tendency for debt to be more desirable than stock, and this preference switches if all the investors are from a high tax bracket for debt and a low tax rate for stock returns. These conclusions assume that all the investment funds are to come from the present investors so that risk considerations arising from the nature of the capital do not enter the analysis.

Corporations generally have stockholders and debtholders with tax rates ranging from zero (foundations, universities, and retirees) to stockholders paying the maximum of the federal plus state and city taxes. In such a situation, the analysis of the chapter cannot be applied directly. It provides a reminder that different parties may desire the corporation to take different actions. The more information an investor has relative to corporate plans, the more likely the investor will be able to make decisions that are consistent with maximizing their own well-being (a clientele effect).

We conclude that the cost to a firm of obtaining capital is a function of its capital structure if there are taxes structured like the U.S. tax system. Thus with real-world institutions, the "cost of capital" is a variable dependent on the decisions of corporate managers. The next step would be to estimate and include the costs of financial distress for each specific corporation and determine the tax characteristics of the available investors.

Chapter 9

Dividend Policy

W hen the Motor Car Corporation designs an automobile, it designs a car for a specific segment of the market. When the Motor Car Corporation arrives at a dividend policy, it implicitly attempts to please all those who invest in common stock. Walk into a financial vice-president's office of a major firm and announce that you have just advised a potential buyer not to buy the company's common stock. After the announcement, duck. Rather than the vice-president asking about the economic characteristics of the investor and why the purchase would not be reasonable, the reaction will be one of indignation. However, it is entirely appropriate that not all corporations appeal to all investors and that corporations design their common stock (and other securities) in the same way they design their consumer products. A corporation should have a financial personality resulting from its various financial policies (especially capital structure and dividend policies) that is attractive to a given group of investors, and is inappropriate for other groups. Corporate securities should have clienteles.

Define the price (and value) of a share of common stock as being equal to the present value of the next dividend (assumed to be declared and paid one period from now) and the price of the share at the time the dividend is paid. If we keep repeating the substitution process, we find that the value of the firm is equal to the present value of all future dividends, where the word "dividend" is used to include all cash distributions made from the firm to its investors. We replace the price at each future moment in time by the dividends that causes the stock to have value.

The fact that the value of a firm depends on future dividends does not mean the firm has to pay dividends now to have value. The cash dividend may be a liquidation payment on termination of activities. It is only necessary that there be an expectation that someday there be a dividend (or some cash flow from firm to investors).

In the absence of investor taxes and transaction costs, the funds necessary to achieve growth targets may either be obtained from retained earnings or as a result of new investment from the stockholders after a dividend (the funds are flowing in a circle from the firm to investors and back to the firm). Thus with a given investment policy, in the absence of taxes and transaction costs, logically dividend policy should not affect the value of a firm. Since investor taxes are necessary for dividend policy to matter, we shall focus on the interrelationship of dividend policy and tax regulations.

There have been two "dividend policy golden rules" followed by publicly held corporations. First, it is necessary to pay cash dividends to common stockholders, and second, the dividends through time must increase. It is far from obvi-

111

ous that these policies are optimum from the point of view of maximizing the well-being of all stockholders. In this chapter and the next, we consider the effect of different dividend policies on the well-being of the common stockholders.

Before launching into examples that imply "exact" answers to the dividend versus no dividend decision, we describe several valid reasons for dividends. Some of these reasons cannot be quantified; thus they must be kept in mind in evaluating the decisions that result from the mathematical models.

REASONS FOR DIVIDENDS

One of the more popular reasons for a corporation to pay a dividend is that the corporation does not have good enough earning opportunities internal to the firm. But there are better ways for the corporation to distribute cash to its investors.

There is a provision in the Internal Revenue Code that penalizes the retention of earnings just to avoid income taxes. Although it is infrequently applied, this provision does exist as a threat to a corporation that retains and invests in passive investments. No corporation would want to pay the tax penalties associated with an excessive retention of earnings. The rule has not been applied (historically) to large publicly owned corporations.

The attitude of investors is an important factor to be considered. Consistently increasing dividends are generally welcomed by investors as indicators of profitability and safety. Uncertainty is increased by lack of dividends or dividends that fluctuate widely. Also, dividends are thought to have an information content; that is, an increase in dividends means that the board of directors expects the firm to do well in the future. This "signaling effect" might favorably affect the firm's common stock price.

Since trust officers can only invest in securities with a consistent dividend history, firms like to establish a history of dividends so that they can make the "trust legal list." This consideration sometimes leads to the payment of cash dividends before the firm would otherwise start paying a dividend.

Another important reason for the payment of dividends is that a wide range of investors need the dividends for consumption purposes. Although such investors could sell a portion of their holdings, this latter transaction has relatively high transaction costs compared to cashing a dividend check. The presence of investors desiring cash for consumption makes it difficult to change the current dividend policy. One group of investors may benefit from a change in dividend policy, but another group may be harmed. Although we see that income taxes paid by investors tend to make a retention policy more desirable than cash dividends, the presence in the real world of zero tax and low tax investors needing cash dictates that we consider each situation individually and be flexible in arriving at a dividend policy.

DIVIDENDS AND RISK

In many discussions of dividend policy it is argued that under conditions of uncertainty an increase in a firm's dividend payout can be expected to increase the share price. This conclusion is reached by assuming (1) that stockholders have risk aversion, and (2) that the uncertainty of a firm's dividends increases as the time of payment is far into the future. It is assumed that investors discount expected future dividends using higher interest rates than dividends received in earlier time periods. It is then concluded that if shareholders are faced with the choice of a certain increase in current dividends or the possibility of a larger future dividend they will tend to choose the former, though the difference in amount will affect the choice.

The dividend policy affects the magnitude and timing of investors' tax payments. Decreases in present dividends tend to reduce the size of immediate tax payments. This permits one to make a strong case in favor of reducing a firm's payout ratio where funds are needed for investment. If not retained, these funds would be obtained from the stockholders after they have paid taxes on the distribution.

There is little reason to believe that all shareholders will lose as a consequence of a decision to reduce dividend payments. To the contrary, many investors probably stand to gain. For the firm's shareholders (those paying taxes at a high rate) who desire to have their earnings reinvested, as well as other investors not yet holding stock in the firm, there are good reasons to value shares more highly after dividends have been cut back if earnings expectations are positive. The dividend-preferring shareholders could quite likely sell their holdings at attractive prices, reinvesting the proceeds in firms that have a high payout ratio, or all investors could be given a choice of dividend paying or non-dividend paying shares.

We are not arguing that all firms should discontinue dividend payments. There is a place for a variety of payout policies. We are suggesting, however, that there may be a high cost to investors if all firms cater to the dividend and reinvestment preferences of an average stockholder. The firm that combines dividend payments with a dividend reinvestment plan, for example, is causing some of its stockholders to pay unnecessary taxes. The firm can argue that it gives its investors a choice about whether or not they want to reinvest their earnings, but it does so at a high cost in terms of the additional taxes paid by a large number of its investors as well as the increased fees incurred by the firm.

There are stockholders who desire cash. A dividend supplies cash without the investor incurring brokerage expense. If cash is retained by the corporation, the stockholders wanting liquidity will have to sell a fraction of their holdings to obtain cash, and this process will result in brokerage fees. Retired individuals living off their dividends and tax-free universities are apt to prefer dividend-paying corporations to corporations retaining income. While a 100% earnings payout cash dividend has the advantage of giving cash to those investors who desire cash, the policy also results in cash being given to those investors who do not desire cash, and who must incur brokerage fees to reinvest the dividends.

The arguments in favor of retention of earnings by some firms do not require that all investors prefer retention of earnings, but that some fraction of the market has this preference. There is a need for well-defined securities that fit the investment preferences for a variety of investors.

RETENTION VERSUS DIVIDEND: TAX DEFERRAL

It has been "proven" that dividend policy is not relevant to the valuation of the common stock equity of a firm. However, the proof assumes zero investor taxes; thus it does not apply to a real-world situation in which such taxes exist. In the real world, an investor benefits from being able to defer the payment of taxes as well as the fact that some types of income (capital gains) for individuals are taxed at lower rates than other types of income (dividends).

If a company retains $100, earns 0.10 per one period, and then pays a dividend of $110, the investor taxed at a rate of 0.40 will net: $110(1 − 0.4) = $66.

If the same company had paid a dividend of $100 and if the investor also could earn 0.10 before tax and 0.06 after tax on the $60 reinvested funds, the investor receiving the $100 dividend ($60 after tax) would have after one period: 60(1.06) = $63.60.

The investor is better off by $2.40 with the one-period delay in cash distribution. The investor "defers" $40 of taxes that earns 0.06 or $2.40; thus the investor is better off by $2.40.

If desired, one could compute the return necessary for the firm to earn to justify retention. It would be equal to the after-tax return (0.06) available to the investor. Thus if the corporation could earn 0.06 and then pay a dividend, the investor would net: $100(1.06)(1 − 0.4) = $63.60. This is the same as the investor would net with an immediate cash dividend.

If the planning horizon is n periods instead of one period, then 0.06 still measures the return that the firm must earn to justify retention. If the earning opportunities available to the corporation are greater than 0.06, retention is more desirable than an immediate dividend.

If the planning horizon is n periods, the dollar advantage of tax deferral increases. For example, if the firm can earn 0.10 and the time horizon is 20 years with retention the investor has:

$$\$100(1.10)^{20} (1 − 0.4) = \$100(6.73)(0.6) = \$404$$

With an immediate $100 cash dividend and the investment of $60 by the stockholder to earn 0.06 after tax for 20 years, the investor would have:

$$\$60(1.06)^{20} = \$60(3.207) = \$192$$

With a planning horizon of 20 years, the advantage of tax deferral is $212 for the retention in the one year generating the $100 earnings. There will be

19 other years between now and the end of the 20 years that will generate comparable tax deferral savings (although of decreasing amounts).

Capital Gains

To this point we have assumed that all income is taxed at one rate. Now we assume that a capital gains tax rate of 0.20 applies to income that is deferred. This assumes that retention of earnings leads to stock price increases and that these increases can be realized by investors if they desire.

Returning to the 20-year horizon, with retention and then capital gains taxation of 0.20, the investor would have:

$$\$100(1.10)^{20} (1 - 0.20) = \$100(6.73)(0.80) = \$538$$

The cash dividend and an after-tax earning rate of 0.06 again leads to a value of $192 after 20 years.

The net advantage of retention is $538 − $192 = $346.

Capital gains taxation increases the value of retention from the $212 obtained above to $346.

Again, if we considered the tax consequences of the dividend decision for all subsequent years, the value of the difference would be even larger. Tax deferral and capital gains are two powerful factors.

A Constant Investment Policy

The previous examples implicitly assume that the amount of investment undertaken by the firm is affected by the dividend-retention decision. We now assume that the investment policy of the firm has been established, and the investments that will take place in the next n years will not be affected by the dividend policy. Further, we assume that if a dividend is paid, the funds required to implement the investment policy will come from the present stockholders.

This type of policy, although it seems strange (to give money to investors and then request the funds back), is frequently found in the real world. The situation exists when a dividend-paying company concurrently raises funds either in the form of common stock, preferred stock, or debt from its present stockholders. Also, dividend reinvestment plans are of this type.

The advantage of zero dividends compared to a series of cash dividends is equal to the sum of the present values of the taxes saved on *not* having the cash dividends *less* the present value of capital gains tax paid at the end of the time horizon, because the retained earnings (equal to the cash dividends) did not increase the investors' tax basis. A numerical example follows.

Example

Let the tax rate on ordinary income be 0.4 and on capital gains be 0.20. The investor can earn 0.03 after tax. The initial dividend is $1, and dividends will grow at 0.10 per year. We assume a 5-year planning horizon.

We would have the following dividends and present values:

Year n	Dividend	$(1.03)^{-n}$	Present Value of Dividend
1	1.00	0.9709	0.9709
2	1.10	0.9426	1.0369
3	1.21	0.9151	1.1073
4	1.332	0.8885	1.1826
5	1.4641	0.8626	1.2629
Total dividends	6.1051		5.5606 Present value of dividends

The advantage of zero dividends compared to current dividends increasing through time is the present value of taxes saved: $0.4(\$5.5606) = \$2.24$ less the present value of the tax basis lost since zero investment was made, times the tax rate:

$$0.20(\$6.1051)(1.03)^{-5} = \$1.05$$

The net saving of zero dividends is $\$2.24 - \$1.05 = \$1.19$.

The advantage of zero dividends for five years compared to the dividend policy of paying \$1 and increasing the dividend by 0.10 per year is \$1.19 per dollar of present dividends. The dividends have an after-tax present value of $0.6(\$5.5606) = \$3.34$ and this value can be increased by \$1.19 with retention rather than a cash dividend.

Because the investment policy is assumed to be independent of the dividend-retention decision, the value of the firm after n periods is common to both decisions (dividends or retention). This value drops out when we compute the net advantage of the zero dividend policy. Thus the advantage of retention is not dependent on a forecast of future value (remember the investment policy of the firm is assumed to be fixed).

Although the example seems far fetched (why would a company pay a dividend of $\$D$ dollars and have the investor invest the same amount back in the firm), most large firms have so-called "dividend reinvestment" plans whereby dividends are directly reinvested in the common stock of the same firm. The net results of plans such as this are very similar to the example of this section. Dividend reinvestment plans are inferior to the firm retaining earnings. They may be superior to the firm paying dividends without a plan (the plan results in the firm having more cash if newly issued shares are used). Dividend reinvestment plans are implemented by the corporation either issuing new shares (raising capital) or by buying shares in the market.

STOCK DIVIDENDS

With a stock dividend the holders of common stock receive additional shares equal to a given percentage of the shares currently held (the percentage must be small or the process is described as a stock split). One purpose of a stock dividend or a stock split is to reduce the market price per share to a level that is more attractive to the market.

Stock dividends are redescriptions of the holdings of the stockholders, but are not distributions of the firm's assets; thus they should not be considered to be the equivalent of a cash dividend. With a cash dividend the firm's cash and stockholders' equity are reduced by the amount of the dividend. With a stock dividend the stockholders' equity is not changed in total (individual components may be changed). If a stockholder will hold 10% of the company before the stock dividend, the stockholder will hold 10% after the stock dividend. The number of shares involved would change, but not the basic proportion of ownership.

It is sometimes thought that a firm could issue a stock dividend without affecting the stock price. This is naive and incorrect. Whatever the total value of the firm before the stock dividend, it is going to be approximately the same after the dividend. Since the number of shares is increased, we can expect all per share calculations to be proportionally reduced.

The IRS recognizes the nothingness of a stock dividend and the dividend is not taxed as income. Even the tax collector recognizes that a stock dividend is not income.

Stock Dividends and Capital Gains

A stock dividend can be combined with a process whereby the corporation sells the additional shares for the investors desiring this, thus converting ordinary income into capital gains. These investors not wanting cash do not sell, thus increasing their percentage of ownership.

Aside from the administrative complexities for the investors, this is a reasonable process given the differential between ordinary income tax rates and capital gain rates.

DIVIDEND POLICY AND CAPITAL STRUCTURE

Because of the tax shield associated with interest, debt has a tax advantage at the corporate level. But bond interest is taxed as ordinary income at the personal tax level, and this is a disadvantage. Common stock has an advantage for the high-tax individual both because of tax deferral and because of the distinction between ordinary income and capital gains.

Consider a firm which earns $100,000 before interest and taxes. The corporate tax rate is 0.35, the ordinary income investor tax rate is 0.4, and the investor capital gains tax rate is 0.20.

If debt is issued and $100,000 is paid as interest, the *investors* will have after tax: $100,000(1 − 0.4) = $60,000. If common is issued, the issuing *corporation* will have earned after tax: $100,000(1 − 0.35) = $65,000.

The investor will net $52,000, assuming the capital gains is equal to $65,000 and that it is taxed at 0.20 ($65,000(1 − 0.20) = $52,000). With zero capital gains realized, the tax would be zero and the capital gain $65,000 (competitive with the debt).

Assuming the corporate income of $65,000 is taxed to the investor at the personal tax rate of 0.4, the investor nets: (1 − 0.4)$65,000 = $39,000. With this assumption, stock is inferior to the use of debt.

Multiperiod Retaining

Now assume the retention for the above example is for 20 years rather than one year. The investor can earn 0.06 after tax and the corporation can earn 0.10 (before investor tax).

With debt and $100,000 interest taxed and then reinvested, the investor will have:

$$(1 − 0.4)\$100,000(1.06)^{20} = \$192,428$$

With common stock and retention of $65,000 and then a 0.20 capital gain tax rate the investor will have:

$$\$65,000(1.10)^{20}(1 − 0.2) = \$349,830$$

The example illustrates the fact that common stock may be better than debt from the point of view of a high-tax investor (paying 0.4 on interest income) if the gain is taxed at a 0.20 capital gains rate, and if the investment horizon is long enough. In this example we are only considering the question of how the capital should be classified, as debt or common stock. Risk considerations are omitted from the example. With a multiperiod case, the common stock alternative is helped by tax deferral.

This example brings together capital structure (debt versus common stock), dividend policy (the common stock alternative is enhanced by the retention of earnings), and investment policy (the retention implies a different investment strategy than if the cash were distributed to investors).

If we assume that different investors buy bonds than buy debt, then we can have the $100,000 of bond interest taxed at a zero rate and bonds again appear to be a sensible form of capital. Thus the investor tax consideration does not eliminate the tax shield advantages of interest, but rather gives common stock a possible advantage associated with tax deferral and capital gains treatment. This advantage depends on the assumption of the tax rates of the bond and the stock investors.

DIVIDEND REINVESTMENT PLANS: WITH A DISCOUNT

Most major U.S. corporations give their stockholders the opportunity to have their dividends invested in the common stock of the firm. The transaction costs and discount from market price vary from firm to firm. We will assume the firm pays the transaction costs and in addition gives the investor the opportunity to purchase the stock at a 5% discount from the market price. The advantage to the investor is a saving of transaction costs and a possible saving in purchase price (this latter saving will depend on whether or not all investors participate).

We will consider three alternatives for a firm which is considering raising common stock capital:

1. Implement a reinvestment plan with a 5% price discount.
2. Do nothing.
3. Issue securities to the market and incur a 5% cost (or issue at a 5% price reduction).

Assume there are 100,000 shares outstanding and an investor owns 1,000 shares. The market price is $50 per share.

The investors can subscribe at a cost of $47.50 for 0.1% of their holdings. For holdings of 1,000 shares this is one share. Assume 99 new shares are issued.

The total market value of the firm is initially $5 million. After issuance of 99 shares at a price of $47.50, new capital of $4,702.50 will be raised and the new stock equity will be $5,004,702.50 (assuming everyone does not invest).

If the holder of 1,000 shares does not reinvest, the value of the holdings of this investor decreases from $50,000 to:

$$\$5,004,702.50 \times \frac{1,000}{100,099} = \$49,997.53$$

To protect their holdings and maintain value the stockholders must reinvest.

Now assume that as a result of cash received the value of the firm increases to $5,004,950. The value for the investor who does not invest is:

$$\$5,004,950 \times \frac{1,000}{100,099} = \$50,000$$

the same as before the reinvestment. The investors who own 99,099 shares and have reinvested have their investment increase from $4,950,000 to:

$$\$5,004,950 \times \frac{99,099}{100,099} = \$4,954,950$$

Thus if the value of the cash obtained is higher than the amount of actual cash received, it is possible for all the stockholders to be benefited by the dividend reinvestment plan, but those who reinvest benefit more. The value of the stock is assumed to remain at $50 but the investors only paid $47.50 for the 99 new shares.

We do not know whether dividend reinvestment plans benefit all investors. In a situation where a dollar of cash received is only worth a dollar, except for taxes the investors who reinvest are not harmed. The investors who do not reinvest do have their holdings diluted. But these holdings would also be diluted if new capital were obtained by issuing new shares at a net price of $47.50. If the value of the cash received is larger than a dollar per dollar received, then it is possible for all holders of common stock to benefit. If all investors participate in the dividend reinvestment plan, the value of the discount is neutralized. It is as if all the stockholders were receiving a stock dividend. Since all the stockholders receive the same discount, they all (collectively) have received nothing. However, the company has avoided the dilution that would have taken place (or the cost) associated with a new issue of common stock to new shareholders at a net price of $47.50. If the amount of the discount is taxed as ordinary income, the participating stockholders are actually worse off than without the discount. If all investors reinvest, they all have the same proportion of ownership and have gained nothing, but they pay tax on the discount.

There are two different ways of evaluating dividend reinvestment plans with new shares issued. First, they can be compared to retained earnings. Retained earnings wins this comparison as long as there are investor taxes and transaction costs.

Secondly, if the corporation is going to pay a cash dividend when it needs capital, a dividend reinvestment plan may compare favorably on a cost basis with other ways of raising capital. Thus it may be that the corporation should not pay a cash dividend, but if it is paying a dividend, a dividend reinvestment plan might be better than no plan.

CONCLUSIONS

If investors in a high tax bracket expect the price of a stock to increase because of improved earnings (and a higher level of future dividends), they will be willing to pay more for a stock knowing that if their expectations are realized the stock can be sold and be taxed at the relatively lower capital gains tax rate. Whereas the lower capital gains tax rate tends to increase the value of a share of stock, we have shown that another powerful factor arises from the ability of the stockholder to defer paying taxes if the corporation retains income rather than paying dividends. Tax deferral is an extremely important advantage associated with the retention of earnings by a corporation.

The present tax law allows deferral of tax payment (or complete avoidance) on capital gains, and recognized gains are taxed at a lower (0.20) rate than ordinary income. Dividend policies of firms have relevance for public policy in the areas of taxation of both corporations and individuals. As corporate managers adjust their decision making to include the tax law considerations, the makers of public policy must decide whether the results are beneficial to society.

It is not being argued that all firms should discontinue dividend payments. There is a place for a variety of payout policies, but there is a high cost to investors for all firms attempting to cater to the dividend and reinvestment preferences of an average investor. The firm that combines dividend payments with the issuance of securities to current investors is causing some of its investors to pay unnecessary taxes, as well as incurring increased transaction costs itself in raising the funds.

A board of directors acting in the interests of the stockholders of a corporation sets the dividend policy of a firm. The ability of an investor to defer income taxes as a result of the company retaining earnings is an important consideration. In addition, the distinction between ordinary income and capital gains for purposes of income taxation by the federal government accentuates the importance of investors knowing the dividend policy of the firm whose stock they are considering purchasing or have already purchased. In turn, this means that the corporation (and its board) has a responsibility to announce its dividend policy, and attempt to be consistent in its policy, changing only when its economic situation changes significantly. In the particular situation in which a firm is expanding its investments rapidly and is financing this expansion by issuing securities to its stockholders, the payment of cash dividends is especially vulnerable to criticism.

Investment decisions, capital structure, and dividend policy must be coordinated so that the well-being of the firm's stockholders is considered in the planning process. The corporate planners should realize that the individual investors are also making plans, and the corporation can assist this planning process by making its own financial plans and strategies well-known.

Chapter 10

Repurchase of Common Stock by the Corporate Issuer

ajor U.S. corporations have repurchased significant amounts of their own common shares. The reasons for this development and its implications for the theory of share valuation and for public policy, however, have been subject to numerous, and often conflicting, interpretations. In this chapter we will reach some fairly definite conclusions concerning share repurchase. A number of explanations of the motivation behind this activity have been suggested. It has been argued, for example, that firms buy back their own shares to have them available to acquire other companies or to fulfill the obligations of stock option plans. Unquestionably, some repurchasing has been done for these reasons. Income tax considerations may make it possible for firms to acquire other companies more cheaply for stock than for cash, and the use of stock options as a form of executive compensation has been widespread. However, it seems quite unlikely that the growth of share repurchasing can be explained by merger and stock option plans. There is no essential reason why firms should use repurchased shares for these purposes, rather than newly issued shares.

Corporations also repurchase shares with the intention of retiring them, or at least holding them indefinitely in the treasury. Several motives for such repurchasing activities have been suggested, virtually all relating the repurchase of the shares to liquid assets which cannot be profitably invested internally by the firm in the foreseeable future. In particular, it has been suggested that firms with excessive liquid assets have one or more of the following motives to repurchase shares:

1. Repurchasing shares is the best investment that can be made with these assets.
2. Repurchasing shares has beneficial leverage effects.
3. Repurchasing shares, rather than paying dividends, has a significant tax advantage for stockholders.

Is a firm's purchase of its own common stock an investment? Does a firm repurchase stock to produce leverage effects not otherwise attainable? What are the tax advantages associated with buying back shares?

The next two sections are devoted to a discussion of the investment and leverage questions. In brief, we shall argue that repurchasing is not an investment and does not produce "special" leverage effects. We then shall consider the argument that repurchasing shares can have beneficial tax effects for stockholders.

SHARE REPURCHASING AS AN INVESTMENT

In this section we shall examine the logic underlying the argument that when a firm is generating more cash than it can profitably invest internally, share repurchasing is itself a good investment.

Share repurchasing does not possess the same general characteristics as other acts of investment by a firm, e.g., purchasing plant and equipment. Normal investments increase the size of the firm and do not decrease the stockholders' equity balance. A firm's repurchase of its own common stock, on the other hand, reduces the size of the enterprise. Specifically, the cash balance is decreased and the stockholders' equity balance is reduced. In short, repurchasing shares has few characteristics which identify it as a normal investment.

While share repurchasing is clearly not an investment by the firm, there is a change in the relative proportions of ownership if some stockholders sell their shares and some do not sell. The investors who do not sell are implicitly making an investment compared with the investors who do sell. Also, investors not selling make an investment in the firm compared with what would have happened if they had received a cash dividend.

Even though share repurchasing is not an investment, it may be the best use of corporate cash from the point of view of the present investors. This may occur if the present stock price is below the intrinsic value of the shares.

Market prices are set by investors based on available information. It is possible that decision makers of a firm may have more information than the market. In such a situation, ethical issues arise dictating against the firm acquiring its own shares, otherwise purchases might take place in order for one group of investors to take advantage of inside information. Lacking the resources to buy the stock themselves, they use the corporation as the vehicle for making their investment.

Another reason for purchase is that one group of stockholders currently controlling the corporation may seek to retain control. Again, lacking the financial resources as individuals, they use the corporation's resources to attain their own objective. We consider both of these reasons for purchase to result in improper activities by a corporation. The possibility of these situations developing is a cost of allowing corporations to repurchase their own shares.

However, let us assume that the market has all the available information, so that it is not a matter of ethics, but the stock price is lower than management thinks it should be based on the available published information. In such a situation, if the firm follows a policy of share repurchase, this may be the best use for the cash. Aside from market or contractual imperfections, advocating share repurchase rather than dividends requires the presence of either personal income taxes or transaction costs. Without taxes or transaction costs, there is no real advantage of stock repurchase compared to a conventional cash dividend.

REPURCHASING AND LEVERAGE

It has been argued that the repurchase of shares increases the percentage of debt in the capital structure (by reducing the amount of common stock equity). We are still faced with the question, why repurchase shares to change the debt/equity ratio, rather than pay dividends and accomplish the same objective? Buying back stock involves no changes in capital structure that could not also be obtained by a dividend payment. Both procedures have the effect of distributing cash to stockholders, reducing the firm's capitalization, and increasing the firm's leverage. Of course, leverage can also be increased by increasing the amount of debt without reducing the stock equity.

TAXES AND SHARE REPURCHASING

The current tax laws provide powerful incentives for firms with excess liquid assets to repurchase shares, rather than pay dividends. Under the present tax structure many individuals prefer capital gains to ordinary income. The reason for their preference is that the top marginal rate of taxation on ordinary income of 0.396 is higher than the 0.20 rate on capital gains.

Consider now a corporation with excess cash that it desires to pay out to stockholders in the form most attractive from its shareholders' point of view. If it distributes the assets as dividends, they will represent ordinary income to shareholders, and will be taxed accordingly. If, on the other hand, the corporation buys back shares, the tax basis of the stock will be regarded as a return to the shareholders' capital and will not be taxed at all, while that portion of the return which is taxed, i.e., the capital gain, will be subject to a lower rate than ordinary income. In addition, the investor who merely wants to reinvest and does not sell is not taxed at all.

Given these incentives for returning cash to stockholders by repurchasing shares, a relevant question would seem to be, why do firms ever pay dividends? One important answer is that many stockholders do not pay tax on the dividends they receive (e.g., Cornell University and low-income retirees). A second reason (related to the first) is that the receipt of cash dividends to low-tax investors reduces the transaction costs for those investors who need cash. But even if one were to accept the above explanations, the basic question still remains. Why do firms pay dividends to investors who are taxed at high ordinary income tax rates?

Example

A firm has 100,000 shares outstanding and $100,000 available for distribution. Should it pay a dividend or repurchase shares? Assume the personal tax rate is 0.396 and the capital gains tax rate is 0.20. The initial stock price is $20. Assume the tax basis is also $20. There is an investor who owns 1,000 shares. With a $1,000 cash dividend for this investor we have:

Dividend

Cash received	$1,000
Tax (0.396)	396
Net	$604

If the company acquires $100,000/20 = 5,000$ shares and the investor tenders 0.05 of the 1,000 shares held, we have:

Stock repurchase

Cash received (50 × $20)	$1,000
Tax	0
Net	$1,000

There is a $396 cash flow advantage for share repurchase compared to a cash dividend. With a zero tax basis and a 0.20 tax rate we have for the share repurchase:

Stock repurchase

Cash received	$1,000
Tax (0.20)	200
Net	$800

Not selling, the investor's percentage ownership goes up from 0.01 to 0.0105 (that is, 1,000/95,000). The investor has a choice of receiving cash (selling some stock) or increasing the relative investment in the firm.

When capital gains and ordinary income are accorded different tax treatment, the value of the firm's stock is influenced by the form of its cash distribution. In addition, with share repurchase and a positive-tax basis, part of the cash distribution is not taxed. There are three factors at work that cause buying back shares to be more profitable than dividend payments (from the stockholders' point of view) under any reasonable set of assumptions that includes taxation of income. For one thing, part of the distribution under the share-repurchasing arrangement is considered a return of capital and is not taxed. Secondly, that part of the distribution subject to tax (i.e., the capital gain) is generally taxed at a lower rate than ordinary income. Finally, the investor can avoid all taxes by not selling.

One must be careful about real and illusory changes that take place with stock repurchasing. Assume that investors own 0.01 of a firm (say 1,000 shares out of 100,000) and that the corporation has enough cash ($100,000) to buy back 5,000 shares or 0.05 of the outstanding shares at $20 per share. With a cash dividend, the investor will receive $1 per share, or $1,000 in total and will own 0.01 of the firm. With a stock repurchase program, the investors could decide to sell 0.05 or 50 shares. The investor would then receive $1,000 of cash and would retain 950 shares. The company would have 95,000 shares outstanding; thus the investors would again own 0.01 of the shares outstanding. In both cases (with a cash dividend and with stock repurchase), the investors have $1,000 cash and 0.01 ownership in the firm. The only true difference is the tax treatment the investors will face under the two different corporate policies.

SHARE REPURCHASE: STOCK OPTION PLANS

A sometimes neglected consequence of share repurchase programs is that such programs enhance the value of stock options compared to cash dividends by forcing the stock price up compared to a cash dividend of equal dollar amount (the number of shares outstanding is reduced). The stock price effect is not a real advantage to the investor, but it is an advantage to the holders of stock options.

For example, suppose a firm has 1 million shares outstanding selling at $40 per share. The value of the stock equity is $40 million. If it pays a $4 million cash dividend, the value of the stock equity will be $36 million. Then, as a result of the cash dividend:

Stock price per share	$36
Cash received	4
Total value to investor per share	$40

The investor is indifferent to the share repurchase and dividends (with zero taxes), but the holder of the stock options prefers the share repurchase.

Stock Price Effects of Share Repurchase

The firm could buy 100,000 shares with the $4 million. The value of the firm after purchase will be $36 million, and the stock price per share will be $40 (that is, $36,000,000/900,000 = $40). The investor is indifferent to share repurchase and cash dividend (with no taxes), but the holder of a stock option prefers the $40 market price to the $36 price with cash dividends.

The Long-Term Stock Price Effects of Share Repurchase

The stock price after one year is interesting. Assume the stock equity is again $40 million (the firm made earnings of $4 million during the year).

Having paid a $4 million dividend last year, the stock value per share would be $40. If the firm had repurchased 100,000 shares instead of a dividend, the stock value per share would be $40,000,000/900,000 = $44.44.

A share repurchase program, all things equal, will result in an increasing stock price through time compared to the price with dividends being paid. With a stock option contract (not adjusted for share repurchases) the increase in stock price resulting from a share repurchase strategy rather than a cash dividend is valuable for the call option holder.

STOCK REPURCHASE: A FLEXIBLE DIVIDEND

One real advantage of stock repurchase in lieu of cash dividends is that investors who do not want to convert their investments into cash do not sell their stock back to the corporation. By not selling, they avoid realization of the capital gain and do not have any taxation on the increment to the value of their wealth (they also avoid transaction costs).

The investors who want to receive cash sell a portion of their holdings, and even though they pay tax on the gain, it is apt to be less than if the cash distribution were taxed as ordinary income. By using stock repurchase as the means of the cash distribution, the company tends to direct the cash to those investors who want the cash and bypass the investors who do not need cash at the present time.

CONCLUSIONS

Three public policy questions concerning corporate share repurchasing become apparent. First, should firms be allowed to buy back their own shares, and secondly, if so, should they be required to give stockholders advance notice of their intentions for the future? Third, how should such distributions be taxed?

We have shown that repurchasing shares can have a significant impact on the after-tax returns of stockholders. Should the form of the firm's distribution, rather than its substance, influence the amount of taxes paid by stockholders? It seems clear that, as more and more firms become aware of the advantages of repurchasing shares compared with paying dividends, this issue will have to be faced.

Should corporations that decide to repurchase shares be required to notify stockholders of their intentions? The value of the firm's stock is a function of the form of its cash distributions. Thus it seems reasonable that shareholders be advised of a company's distribution policy, and of changes in that policy. The corporation that repurchases shares without giving its stockholders advance notice is implicitly, if not explicitly, penalizing those who sell their shares without this information.

Here is another situation (as with capital structure and dividend policy) in which corporate financial planning affects the plans of individual investors. It is reasonable for individual investors to be informed of the financial plans of the corporation, where disclosure of the plans will not significantly adversely affect the competitive position of the firm.

Chapter 11

Valuation of an Acquisition

In a narrow sense, the problem of valuation of a firm arises when the firm is being considered for acquisition. In a broader sense, the problem arises whenever the common stock of a corporation is being considered as an investment. We investigate only the former question in this chapter, although the procedures have broader application.

MEASURES OF VALUE

In periods of mergers and acquisitions the valuation of a firm is an important activity for both the corporations which are buying and selling. There are many ways of valuing a firm that is being considered for acquisition. Unfortunately, there are few, if any, exact answers and there is room for a wide range of differences of opinion. The objective should be to define a range of values. We will consider the following objective and subjective measures of value:

Relatively Objective Measures:

        a. market value of common stock
        b. current earnings times the price-earnings multiplier
        c. book value of stock equity
        d. cost basis of investors
        e. actual cash flows times cash flow multiplier
        f. asset valuation method
        g. replacement cost or price level adjusted value of assets
        h. $V_L = V_u + tB$ where V_u is the initial firm value equal to the number of outstanding shares times the observed stock price, t is the corporate tax rate, and B is the amount of new debt. V_L is the value of the levered firm.

Relatively Subjective Measures:

        a. present value of future dividends for perpetuity, that is, $P = D/(k - g)$
        b. present value of discretionary (free) cash flows
        c. present value of future earnings minus the present value of new investments
        d. present value of an earnings perpetuity plus the present value of growth opportunities (PVGO)
        e. present value of dividends for n years plus present value of the firm's value at time n (possibly determined using a multiplier). n-stage growth models

    f. multipliers times E, EBIT, NEBIT, EBITDA, NEBITDA where:

      E is earnings

      EBIT is earnings before interest and taxes

      NEBIT is the next period's expected earnings before interest and taxes

      EBITDA is the earnings before interest, taxes, depreciation, and amortizations (equivalent to cash flows)

      NEBITDA is the next period's EBITDA

    g. multiplier times free cash flow (dividends)

    h. $V_L = V_u + tB$ + operations improvements

    i. present value of economic incomes

In practice we would expect the valuation to be accomplished using a combination of the above measures, with the actual offer being as much a matter of game theory as basic valuation. That is, having determined the value of the firm to be acquired, it is then necessary to determine the minimum amount that can be offered and still have a reasonable probability of acquiring the firm and making an income.

Example

We will use the following notation:

X	=	EBIT
t	=	the corporate tax rate
b	=	the retention rate
Deps	=	the accounting depreciation
D	=	the dividend
$k = k_e(0)$	=	the cost of equity with zero debt
r	=	the return on new investments
g	=	the growth rate of dividends and earnings

Assume that

X	=	$100
t	=	0.35
b	=	0.4
Deps	=	$50
E	=	$65
D	=	$39
k	=	$k_e(0) = 0.12$
r	=	0.05
g	=	0.02

The following calculations apply to the above list of valuation measures.

$$\text{a,b. } P = \frac{D}{k-g} = \frac{\$39}{0.12-0.02} = \$390$$

Since $D = (1-b)E$ we can substitute for D.

c. $P = \dfrac{(1-b)E}{k-g} = \dfrac{E}{k-g} - \dfrac{bE}{k-g}$

where the second term is the present value of the additional investment outlays.

$$P = \frac{\$65}{0.12 - 0.02} - \frac{\$26}{0.12 - 0.02} = \$650 - \$260 = \$390$$

d. Using the present value of an earnings perpetuity plus the present value of the earnings growth:

$$\text{PVGO} = \frac{(1-b)E}{k-g} - \frac{E}{k} = \frac{k(1-b)E - Ek + gE}{k(k-g)} = \frac{E(g-bk)}{k(k-g)}$$

$$= \frac{\$65[0.02 - 0.4(12)]}{0.12(0.10)} = \frac{-\$1.82}{0.012} = -\$151.67$$

$$P = \frac{E}{k} + \text{PVGO} = \frac{\$65}{0.12} - \$151.67 = \$390$$

The growth of earnings is a negative value since the firm has a cost of equity of 0.12 and can only earn 0.05 on new investments. The investments are decreasing the firm's value.

Instead of assuming a constant growth rate of 0.02 for perpetuity, assume the growth continues for 11 years, and then there is zero growth and zero reinvestment. With 0.02 growth for perpetuity, the dividend and earnings at time 11 are:

Dividend at time $11 = \$39(1.02)^{11} = \$48.4916$
Earnings at time $11 = \$65(1.02)^{11} = \$80.81933$

The firm's value at time 10 with 0.02 growth after year 10 would be:

$$P_{10} = \frac{\$48.4916}{0.12 - 0.02} = \$484.92 \text{ with } 0.02 \text{ growth}$$

The present value is:

$$PV = (1.12)^{-10}\,\$484.92 = \$156.13$$

The present value of the first 10-years' dividends:

$$PV = \frac{D}{k-g} - \$156.13 = \$390 - \$156.13 = \$233.87$$

With zero growth after time 11, the value at time 10 is:

$$P_{10} = \frac{\$80.82}{0.12} = \$673.50$$

with a present value of:

$$PV = (1.12)^{-10}\,\$673.50 = \$216.85$$

The stock's value would be (with zero incremental investment at time 11 and thereafter):

$$P = \$233.87 + \$216.85 = \$450.72$$

The firm's value goes up since unacceptable investments earning 0.05 are not made after time 11.

With no growth (and no reinvestment at time 0) and with maximum debt of $833.33:

$$\text{Max Debt} = \frac{X}{k} = \frac{\$100}{0.12} = \$833.33$$

and if the value of the tax savings of substituting debt for equity is equal to tB, with a tax rate of 0.35:

$$tB = 0.35(\$833.33) = \$291.67$$

If $V_u = \dfrac{\$65}{0.12} = \$541.67$, then the maximum value of V_L is:

$$V_L = V_u + tB = \$541.67 + \$291.67 = \$833.33$$

where V_L is the value of the levered firm.

Relatively Objective Measures

Objective measures are attractive since their origin can be explained and there is a substance to the measures that is lacking as we move to the more subjective measures. The relevance of these objective measures varies considerably, but they are easy to compute.

The market value of the common stock is essential in establishing a buyer's offering price. It sets a floor for any offering price by a buyer. If the market price of the common stock is $20 per share rarely would a buyer consider submitting a bid less than $20. In fact, one would expect the acquirer to have to pay a premium over market. Thus the market price of the common stock is an important measure of value since it sets a minimum offering price if an offer is to be made.

If there is a market value for the firm's stock, an attempt might be made to compute the value of the stockholders' equity based on the market valuation. It can be argued that, with a closely held corporation, if the stockholders desire to unload their stock, they may not be able to, because the market is too thin. On the other hand, with a widely traded stock all investors holding or buying the stock are implicitly placing a higher than market value on the stock.

Can one obtain the value of the stockholders' equity by extending the market value for a few shares traded on the stock market? If more shares were offered for sale, it would not be surprising to see the price per share be somewhat lower than it is for normal daily trading. However, it should be remembered that the entire universe of investors is available as possible purchasers of the stock. It will not take a large price decline to attract the investors necessary to digest the additional shares of stock assuming the price before the shares were offered was set by the same market. An acquiring firm will generally expect to pay more than the market value for shares of stock. The market value sets a floor for the bid price rather than being a feasible method of valuation for purposes of acquisition.

The second objective measure is equivalent to the first. If one takes the current earnings and multiplies by the current price-earnings multiplier, one obtains the current market price. If a "normal" price-earnings multiplier is used, the amount obtained will be somewhat objective since the value is based on observed earnings, but it is also subjective since the P/E ratio used to obtain the value is different than the currently observed value. The expected earnings of the current year or an adjusted earnings can be used rather than the observed earnings. Another variation is to use the expected earnings of next year.

The use of the expected earnings times a price-earnings multiplier is a common technique for evaluating prospective acquisitions. If there is some type of synergy (2 + 2 = 5) associated with the acquisition, the acquiring firm's estimate of earnings will be higher than the market's estimate, and the firm can offer an attractive price to the present owners and still expect to profit.

At its best, the use of a price-earnings multiplier is a short-cut method of applying discounted cash flows. The following mathematical model illustrates this position.

Let

P = the market price per share
k = the discount rate
g = the growth rate in earnings and dividends
E = the earnings
b = the retention percentage

Since $P = \dfrac{(1-b)E}{k-g}$ we can divide both sides by E and obtain:

$$P/E = \frac{(1-b)}{k-g}$$

Thus the price earnings ratio (P/E) that can be expected is equal to the dividend payout rate ($1-b$) divided by $k-g$. The larger the value of the growth rate (g), the larger the value of the P/E ratio that will be justified, and if the market accepts the model, the higher the price-earnings multiplier that will be observed.

If one were to determine a price-earnings multiplier for a specific firm, in order to use the P/E ratio there remains the problem of determining the earnings to which this multiplier should be applied. Conceptually, it is easy to arrive at the fact that only future earnings are relevant. But the forecast of future earnings is apt to draw on the measurement of recent past earnings. The reported income of a firm cannot be accepted automatically as the number to be used for decision making or for analysis.

The third objective measure is book value per share. In theory the book value of the common stock is not a relevant consideration since the book value represents sunk costs and sunk costs are not relevant to decisions. However, if the investors who are selling consider book value to be relevant, then in a sense it becomes relevant. An offering firm should not set a price equal to book value just to satisfy the condition that the offering price should be equal to or greater than book value, but if the price that has been determined by economic analysis is less than book, the acquirers should recognize that some sellers will refuse to sell because the offering price is less than book value. Book value should not be a relevant consideration, but it may become one in the minds of some holders of the common stock.

Perhaps the most important consideration is that some of the present holders of the shares of the firm being acquired will consider the book value to be important, just as they might consider important the price that they paid, even though this too is a sunk cost, and thus it is not "relevant." Thus in some situations the book value may be thought to be floor for an offer, not for economic reasons, but because of the likely thinking of sellers.

With knowledgeable sellers and buyers, the book values of the assets become important only to the extent that they become the basis for recording the assets on the books of the acquiring firm (as they would with pooling of interests accounting). Aside from this, book value is not relevant to the economic analysis of the purchase (the book tax basis would be relevant). The accountant records sunk costs, and sunk costs are not relevant in evaluating an acquisition from an economic standpoint.

The liquidation value of the assets of a firm sets a floor for the value of the firm. If the owners of the firm can obtain x by liquidating, there is little economic reason for them to sell the firm for less than x. In like manner, the bidders may feel safe bidding the liquidation value because they believe that, if they cannot operate the enterprise successfully, they can liquidate.

The liquidation value may be defined as equal to the immediate sale value of the assets less the liabilities present (or that have to be assumed by the new owner). The liquidation value of assets, such as inventory and plants, may differ widely from the accounting measures, and there is no justification for assuming that the accounting measures of value have any use in this context. Hopefully, the accounting records will contain information relative to physical quantities and location that will be useful in searching out the value of the assets.

With the possible exception of patents, it is likely that the intangible assets will have little value on liquidation. Occasionally, the name of the firm or product may be sold, but where the firm is being liquidated, it would not be surprising to find that goodwill has reached a value close to zero. To compute the value of the stockholders' equity, the present value of the liabilities (which may be different than the book value) are subtracted from the liquidation value of the assets.

In some situations, the acquiring firm is only interested in the production capacity of the prospective acquisition. That is, it is not buying the goodwill, the managerial team, the customers, and so on, but only the production capacity. In this type of situation, the replacement cost of facilities is highly relevant information, since the facilities could be built rather than acquired. Timing is frequently offered as the reason for the acquisition of a firm rather than starting from scratch. An acquisition is a quick way of obtaining production capacity or position in an industry.

The fourth objective measure is also a non-relevant sunk cost. Above we discussed the relevance of the book value of the stock equity. There is another book value that is relevant and that is the book value or cost basis of the investor's investment. If an investor paid $30 per share and if $20 per share is being offered, there is apt to be a reluctance to accept the lower price. Admittedly this attitude is not rational, but it is human. If the stock price is currently at or close to being a historical high, the consideration is of less importance than if the stock is selling at a fraction of the price it has been selling at in recent years. The investors' tax basis may also be relevant.

The fifth objective measure is to multiply the cash flows (this period's cash flows or next period's) by a cash flow multiplier (the multiplier is subjective).

The sixth method is the "asset valuation method." One starts with the appraised values of the assets and multiplies each asset by the loan potential factor of the asset to obtain the amount that can be borrowed. To this amount is added the cash that can be realized by selling off other assets or by conserving cash. Any outstanding liabilities would reduce the bid.

The seventh objective measure is to start with the firm's market value and to that value add tB where t is the corporate tax rate and B is the debt to be added (investor taxes can also be considered). This calculation assumes $V_L = V_u + tB$.

Thus a very useful objective measure is the market value of the common stock, but this measure, from the point of view of the acquiring firm merely sets a minimum offering price. It is still necessary to determine a value for the firm from the point of view of the acquiring firm.

Relatively Subjective Measures

We move from measures having a relatively large element of objectivity to measures for establishing value that are relatively subjective. We can set a minimum value (offer price) using the market price, but we still need to estimate the value of the firm being acquired, and subjectivity cannot be avoided.

The risk-adjusted present value of future dividends is a theoretically correct method of computing the value of a firm's stock equity, if dividends are defined to include all cash flowing from the firm to the stockholders, whatever the form of the flow. Despite the correctness of using dividends, we will search for alternative methods for three reasons. First, the amount of dividends is a derived measure. It is derived from the projections of future cash flows or earnings of the firm. Second, in a situation where there are no cash dividends, it is difficult (but not impossible) to estimate the future dividends. Third, management tends to be more comfortable with the use of the target firm's cash flows or earnings. Where the target firm is paying a dividend the difficult estimation problem is to determine the dividend growth rate for perpetuity. An alternative calculation is to estimate the growth for n years and multiply the dividend at time n to represent the firm's value at that time.

One of the major problems is determining the appropriate rate of discount to be used. A useful solution is to determine the value of the firm for a wide range of different discount rates. For example, one might be interested in the present value using a default free government bond rate (assuming zero risk), the after-tax borrowing rate, the before-tax borrowing rate, and the weighted average cost of capital of the acquiring firm as well as the cost of capital of the firm being acquired. While the latter is a logical choice, it is not obvious that the decision should be made using this one measure, since the cost of capital is subjective. The evaluation of an uncertain stream is complex since both the cash flows and the discount rate are uncertain.

If the cash flows used above were defined after all future investments and financings we would find that the net cash flows (after additional investments) are exactly equal to the dividends to the stockholders. The two calculations turn out to be identical by definition if the cash flows include all investments (including investments in working capital).

We could stop with the above calculation since if we accept the cash flow estimates and the choice of the discount rate we have determined the value of the stock equity. However, there is a temptation for management to use earnings in the calculation of value, and therefore we will consider the use of earnings to determine the value of a firm.

Assume that the cost of the firm is $12,000, and the depreciation expense of each of the three years of life is $4,000 and that the cash flows of the above example apply. The present value of the below cash flows is $13,974. The projected earnings are:

Period	Cash Flows	Depreciation	Income
1	10,000	4,000	6,000
2	5,000	4,000	1,000
3	1,000	4,000	−3,000

The above measures of income have a present value of $4,027 using 10% as the rate of discount.

Income	Present Value Factors	Present Value
6,000	1.10^{-1}	5,455
1,000	1.10^{-2}	826
−3,000	1.10^{-3}	−2,254
	Present Value of Income	4,027

Using cash flows, the net present value is $1,974 and the present value is $13,974.

The present value of the unadjusted earnings cannot be used to establish the purchase price. It is necessary to make two adjustments to compute the present value of the stock equity. First, it is necessary to subtract from income the implicit interest on the book value of the depreciable assets being used ($12,000 in period 1, $8,000 in period 2, and $4,000 in period 3) to obtain the economic incomes.

	Net Assets Used	Implicit Interest	Income Before Interest	Economic Income Income less Interest	Present Value of Income less Interest
1	12,000	1,200	6,000	4,800	4,364
2	8,000	800	1,000	200	165
3	4,000	400	–3,000	–3,400	–2,555
				Net Present Value	1,974

Secondly, the depreciable cost must be added to the $1,974 net present value to obtain the firm's present value.

The present value of the above "economic incomes" plus the depreciable cost of $12,000 gives $13,974 which is the same present value as is obtained using cash flows.

Thus with the finite lived asset of this example, the value of the stockholder's equity is not simply the present value of the earnings but rather the present value has to be adjusted by two factors — the interest on the capital being used and the cost basis of the depreciable assets.

Now let us consider an asset that costs $100,000 and that has a cash flow in perpetuity of $10,000 per year. There are zero depreciable assets and zero depreciation. The discount rate is 0.10. The present value of the cash flows is $100,000. The implicit interest on the asset is $10,000, thus the economic earnings are zero. Adding the cost basis of $100,000 to the present value of the earnings, the value of the stock equity is again $100,000. In this case there are no "excess" earnings and no value is added to the cost basis. This is the same result as computed by discounting the cash flows. With a more complex example the present value of any residual value minus the book value would be added to the $100,000 computed in the above example.

It is possible to start with earnings and then make adjustments so that we end up with cash flows (dividends). If earnings are used then they have to be adjusted for the implicit interest and the cost basis of the assets.

If there is debt outstanding, an additional adjustment must be made. We obtained $13,974 for the present value of cash flows as well as for the present value of the economic incomes plus the depreciable cost. If there is $10,000 of debt (present value) then the $10,000 of debt should be subtracted from the $13,974. The stock equity would have a present value of $3,974.

Another type of subjective measure is the replacement cost of the assets. Assume a situation where replacement cost is reasonably well-defined and there are no intangibles. In this case the replacement cost tends to set a maximum value for the offering firm. Why offer more than replacement cost when the assets can be replaced at an amount equal to the replacement cost? An important reason for acquiring an operating firm is that an acquisition is instantaneous while construction of assets takes time.

Usually there are complexities that limit the use of replacement cost in setting a maximum value. There may be intangibles whose replacement cost cannot be computed. Even the replacement cost of tangible assets may be difficult to compute since assets generally would not be replaced in kind. Also, the time required to start from ground zero and grow to the same size as the firm being considered, might be an important element in the setting of the price. Finally, competitive considerations might dictate acquisition rather than duplicating the facilities currently in existence. The possibility of acquiring an ongoing facility is going to tend to be more attractive than starting up a new facility, even where it costs less to start fresh, if costs only include the explicit replacement cost, and leave out intangibles and time value.

Price level adjusted cost numbers are not very useful in establishing value since the price index used is a highly subjective input. By definition any price index is a result of an averaging process, and thus does not apply exactly to the assets being adjusted. Obtaining a value estimate by multiplying a recorded cost measure and a measure of the price level is not a reliable method of establishing the capability of that asset to earn cash flows in the future.

Multipliers

Wall Street uses many different multipliers. The multipliers are applied to either historical measures or forecasts for the next period. We will consider three different multipliers

M_0 applied to after-tax earnings: $M_0(E)$

M_1 applied to earnings before interest and taxes: $M_1(\text{EBIT})$

M_2 applied to earnings before interest, taxes, depreciation, and amortization: $M_2 (\text{EBITDA})$

Determination of M_0

Let P be the value now of a share of common stock. Then by definition of M_0:

$$P = M_0 E$$

or

$$M_0 = \frac{P}{E}$$

If $P = \dfrac{D}{k-g}$ then the theoretical value of earnings multiplier is:

$$M_0 = \frac{D}{E(k-g)} = \frac{(1-b)E}{E(k-g)} = \frac{1-b}{k-g}$$

Determination of M_1

Again, let P be the value now of a share of common stock. Then:

$$P = M_1(\text{EBIT}) = \frac{D}{k-g} = \frac{(1-b)E}{k-g} = \frac{(1-b)(1-t)X}{k-g}$$

Solving for M_1 we get:

$$M_1 = \frac{(1-b)(1-t)}{k-g}$$

since $X = \text{EBIT}$.

Determination of M_2

In this case, P is

$$P = M_2(\text{EBITDA}) = \frac{(1-b)(1-t)X}{k-g}$$

$$M_2 = \frac{(1-b)(1-t)X}{(k-g)(\text{EBITDA})}$$

Example

Assume that

$$X = \$100,\ t = 0.35,\ b = 0.4,\ \text{Deps} = \$50$$

$$E = \$65,\ D = \$39,\ k = 0.12,\ g = 0.02,\ \text{EBITDA} = \$150$$

Then,

$$P = \frac{D}{k-g} = \frac{\$39}{0.12 - 0.02} = \$390$$

Calculating the three multipliers

$$M_0 = \frac{1-b}{k-g} = \frac{0.6}{0.12 - 0.02} = 6$$

$$M_1 = \frac{(1-b)(1-t)}{k-g} = \frac{0.6(0.65)}{0.10} = 3.9$$

$$M_2 = \frac{(1-b)(1-t)X}{(k-g)(\text{EBITDA})} = \frac{0.6(0.65)\$100}{0.10(\$150)} = 2.6$$

We can use these multipliers to compute the value of a share (P). Using M_0 and E:

$$P = M_0 E = 6(\$65) = \$390$$

Using M_1 and EBIT, then:

$M_1 = 3.9$, EBIT $= \$100 = X$

$P = 3.9(\$100) = \$390$

Finally, using M_2 and EBITDA:

$$M_2 = \frac{(1-b)(1-t)X}{(k-g)(\text{EBITDA})} = \frac{0.6(0.65)\$100}{0.10(\$150)} = 2.6$$

$P = M_2(\text{EBITDA}) = 2.6(\$150) = \$390$

It is likely that these multipliers cannot be applied to a different firm with a different cost of equity and a different growth rate. Above, the multipliers were computed based on specific information. Other information will lead to different multipliers.

CONCLUSIONS

Many approaches to the problem of valuing a firm have been illustrated in this chapter. While the development of the certainty model has been in the context of an example, it is relatively simple to generalize the example into algebraic models. The important point is made that one cannot just compute the present value of the expected earnings to find the present value of the stock equity. The difficult part of valuing a firm is to obtain reasonable estimates of future cash flows or earnings, but it is important that once these measures are obtained, that they be summarized correctly.

We have attempted to show that there are a variety of measures, some objective and some highly subjective that can be used by the decision makers in attempting to determine the value of a firm. There are exact methods of calculation, but there are not exact reliable measures of value.

Accounting information must be adjusted for purposes of determining the value of a firm. The liquidation value of the assets sets a minimum price and value, but any value in excess of this minimum must find its justification in the present value of the projected cash flow expected to be generated in the future. The going concern value of the assets, with the assets gaining their value from the cash flow, is the relevant factor. The prime advantage to be gained by using cash flow versus conventional income is that it is theoretically correct and it does not tie us to the results of accounting procedures that are not designed for this specific type of decision. If the decision makers want to use the current income as the basis for making their investment decision, care should be taken since the computation may not be equivalent to the use of cash flows. However, even if they do not use the income measure directly, the decision makers will use it indirectly as the basis for their evaluation of future dividends.

Chapter 12

Mergers and Acquisitions

I n this chapter, we will consider several reasons offered for mergers and acquisitions and evaluate the validity of each. We also discuss other issues associated with mergers and divestitures.

REASONS FOR MERGERS AND ACQUISITIONS

There are many reasons for mergers and acquisitions to take place. Among them are:

1. Synergy (real and imaginary), the process whereby 2 plus 2 was supposed to equal 5, but sometimes equaled 3.
2. Financial considerations (including tax effects).
3. Bargain prices and availability of capital.
4. Psychological reasons (empire building by managers and raiders).
5. The P/E effect.
6. The reduction of risk (diversification).

Synergy

Two firms may be more valuable after a merger than as separate entities because:

1. One firm may be badly managed and the other firm may have managerial talent.
2. One firm may have assets (e.g. plant or liquid assets) that can be effectively used by the other firm, or intangible assets such as technological, marketing, or production know-how.
3. Horizontal integration — increase markets (and possibly reduce competition).
4. Vertical integration — increase operating efficiencies by integration of production.
5. Joint utilization of service facilities, or organization and elimination of duplication.

The likelihood of synergy cannot be assumed to exist in all merger situations. The expected increased efficiency of a merger may never be realized. Even though synergy cannot automatically be assumed, there are still situations in which the two component firms joined together are able to achieve efficiencies that increase the total of the earnings to a higher level than would exist if the firms were not merged.

Mergers and acquisitions sometimes supply the means of acquiring productive capacity that would otherwise take long periods of time to construct. The acquisition of an entire firm may be a cheaper and more rapid means of acquiring productive capacity than planning and building plants. Assume a firm has a mature product but has a new idea for a product that requires different production facilities and techniques and is to be sold in a different market. It can start from ground zero and build both new facilities and a new organization for the product, or it can seek out an established firm which it can acquire. Any firm interested in increasing its rate of growth must consider the strategy of mergers and acquisitions.

Financial Considerations (Tax Effects)

The financial reasons for mergers and acquisitions are both real and imaginary. Consider the position that new capital is easier to raise with a large corporation than with a small corporation. Although this position is generally accepted, it is not at all clear that a small, profitable, well-managed firm has more difficulty raising capital than a large poorly managed firm. The present tax laws do tend to encourage acquisitions, since a firm that has accumulated cash may find it more desirable to spend the cash acquiring another firm than paying a cash dividend or investing the funds internally. The tax laws as they affect investors are an incentive for acquisitions.

Another tax consideration is the estate tax. An impending estate tax bill may force an owner of a firm to go public so that the estate is liquid (and a public corporation is easier to value).

A third tax reason is that, if a firm has a tax loss that it cannot use, a second firm currently paying taxes will find the tax loss carryforward to be an asset. This same advantage occurs through time (one unit has a gain while another component has a loss).

Another tax consideration is the tax deduction of debt interest. The debt capacity of a potential acquisition has motivated many an acquisition. If a target firm currently has earnings of $12 million that are expected to continue forever, financed entirely by common stock, a potential acquirer can apply the following logic (assuming an after-tax time value factor of 0.10 and a corporate tax rate of 0.4). The before-tax earnings are $20 million, and the after-tax earnings are $12 million; thus the firm is worth $12 million/0.10 = $120 million to the present owners. However, if the $20 million were financed completely by debt costing 0.10, then theoretically the $20 million of earnings could support $200 million of debt. Thus, if the stock price were equal to $120 million, with debt financing the stock could be acquired at a cost of $120 million, and there would be $80 million of value left over for other uses. Although this analysis has some deficiencies (e.g., omitting investor taxes), the first-order explicit effects are as indicated. The tax shelter offered by debt is real if the analysis stops at the firm level. A firm without debt or with a small amount of debt becomes a potential acquisition candidate.

One must be careful in appraising the financial implications of a merger. A conglomerate acquired a steel company expecting a large cash flow throw off, but the actual cash flow was much less because of the necessity to replace and improve the steel-making facilities to maintain the cash flow from operations.

Bargain Prices and Availability of Capital

The most logical reason for acquiring a firm is that the present value of the cash flows from acquisition are greater than the cost. That is, if the firm can be acquired at a "bargain" price, acquisition is desirable.

Where the common stock price of the acquiring firm is too high (in the mind of the managers of the acquiring firm), it is easy to see why they would want to acquire other companies using the stock. That is, management might want to take advantage of the inflated stock prices to acquire real assets. The counterpart is also true — deflated stock prices tend to preclude the use of common stock. Until public accounting required the calculation of equivalent earnings per share, the use of convertible bonds, convertible preferred stock, and warrants were very popular because these securities had very low explicit costs. The real costs were the dilution of the current stockholders' position, and this dilution was effectively hidden from view.

Different expectations held by the buyer and the seller can lead to an acquisition because one of the parties sees a "bargain." If the seller thinks that earnings will be a constant $10 million, but the buyer thinks earnings will grow at 0.09 per year for perpetuity, the seller will capitalize the earnings at a $100 million value assuming a 0.10 time discount factor, and the buyer will see a value of $1 billion. The seller sees

$$\frac{\$10 \text{ million}}{0.10} = \$100 \text{ million}$$

and the buyer

$$\frac{\$10 \text{ million}}{0.10 - 0.09} = \$1 \text{ billion}.$$

Psychological Reasons

Growth for growth sake has undoubtedly been a factor in some mergers and acquisitions. Some managers measure their success by the size of the firm they manage, and to some extent their salaries are affected by size. One of the quicker ways of growing is via mergers and acquisitions; thus an impatient executive is apt to follow this path. The desire to build an empire, combined with the likely optimism associated with viewing new organizational structures arising from the merger of firms, leads naturally to mergers and acquisitions.

Fear has also stimulated mergers. Some firms have sought out mergers when it appeared that they would be gobbled up by a less desirable suitor (from the point of view of those controlling the firm).

The P/E Effect

Some mergers have taken place because of faulty arithmetic. It has been argued that a firm with a price-earnings multiplier of 20 should acquire a firm with a P/E of 10, since the earnings once acquired would be capitalized by the market using a P/E of 20. It is more likely that the P/E of the merged firm would be somewhere between 10 and 20 and that the acquired firm would be capitalized at about 10 times its earnings even thought it was part of a larger enterprise. For example, if the market used a P/E of 10 because it expected zero growth, the acquisition would slow the growth rate of the acquiring firm.

For example, suppose there are two firms, and A is thinking of acquiring B. The following facts apply:

Firm	Earnings	P/E Multiplier	Value of Firms
A	10,000,000	20	200,000,000
B	1,000,000	9	9,000,000
	11,000,000		209,000,000

If the P/E of 20 applies, the new firm will be worth

$11 million × 20 = $220 million

and A will gain $11 million by acquiring B. Now if the P/E of the firm after acquisition is 19, then:

$11 million × 19 = $209 million

and the sum of the two firms joined together is the sum of the two separate firms. We can compute the expected new P/E by weighting the P/E of each firm by the percentage of earnings it is contributing:

$$\text{Expected New P/E} = 20\left(\frac{10}{11}\right) + 9\left(\frac{1}{11}\right) = \left(\frac{209}{11}\right) = 19$$

If a stagnant firm has poor reinvestment opportunities, so that it faces a lower growth rate, or if the cost of stock equity is large because of a large amount of risk, the P/E will be relatively small. Merging this situation with a more promising situation may tend to hide the negative factors, but they will still exist.

Only using P/E factors bypasses all the assumptions that are implicit in a P/E measure (such as the level of risk, earnings opportunities, retention rate, etc.), thus is not a reliable form of analysis.

Managers tend to be concerned with the effect of the acquisition on earnings per share. The effect of a merger on the immediate earnings per share is one of the first numbers computed, and will heavily influence the willingness of an acquiring firm to proceed with the merger. The earnings per share will be increased by an acquisition if the price/earnings ratio of the acquirer is larger than the ratio of common stock price to be paid to the common stock earnings of the firm being acquired. This conclusion assumes common stock is being used to finance the acquisition.

We cannot use the relative size of the price/earnings ratios of the firms as the sole basis of making the acquisition. It may be that an acquisition that decreases the earnings per share now is a good acquisition (the earnings per share in the future will be increased sufficiently to compensate for the current decrease). How long will the earnings dilution persist? Can the dilution be avoided by using debt rather than common stock?

Diversification

In the 1970s an oil company (Mobil) acquired Marcor, which was a combined retail firm (Montgomery Ward) and packaging firm (Container Corporation). This was a dramatic example of diversification by acquisition. If previously Mobil was looked at as a rapidly growing energy company with a large number of profitable investments in the energy area, this evaluation had to be revised.

Is there any set of assumptions that would lead to great excitement about Mobil's eagerness to buy Marcor stock? If previously it was felt that energy was a bottomless pit for investment funds, with certain losses with "dry holes" and government regulation if oil was found, then the switch in investment direction might well be received with a sign of relief, and more enthusiasm for Mobil stock. There is little advantage investing in the common stock of a company engaged in a series of gambles when the firm cannot win whatever the outcomes (this does not have to be an accurate description of the world, but merely an accurate description of the analysts' perceptions).

The merger that is least likely to attract attention of the federal government regulators is the merger that crosses over industry lines, and where the operations of the entities are highly independent. The acquisition of Mobil Oil Corporation of Marcor was obviously an attempt by a company in a beleaguered industry (officials of the United States government including several presidents have indicated a distrust of "big oil") to move from an industry perceived to be rapidly heading for controls to industries not yet so fettered. If the federal government threatens to reduce the profitability of one industry, it can expect funds to flow from that industry to other more profitable activities. Mobil executives seemed to be betting that stockholders would welcome a shift from funds invested in a controlled industry. The talk of taxing excessive profits and breaking up vertically integrated companies is likely to have a multiplier effect in terms of discouraging investment in the industry being reviewed for such taxation and dismemberment. After many frustrating years the Mobil management finally realized that diversification has costs, and divested itself of Montgomery Ward.

With most acquisitions for diversification one would not expect there to be a drastic improvement in the common stock price of the acquiring firm. The selling firm has at least as much information as the buyer, and there is no reason to think that the buyer rather than the seller will reap the surplus. Also, the individual investors could have achieved the same diversification by directly buying the stock of the firm being acquired.

Reduction of Risk

Mergers and acquisitions are generally assumed to reduce risk, but this is not necessarily so. If the risk of the acquired firm is sufficiently large, it tends to contaminate the financial position of the firm acquiring it. Paying too much for an acquisition can also adversely affect the acquirer's risk.

Despite this disclaimer, certain types of mergers tend to reduce risk. Assume two firms have operations that are perfectly independent of each other, both in an economic and a statistical sense. In this situation, investors who keep their investment size the same in a merger will reduce their risk. We are assuming that a failure of one firm will not cause failure of the second firm and that operations are not affected by the merger. For example, say one group of investors owns a firm where there is 0.5 probability of success and 0.5 probability of failure; if that firm is merged with a second firm whose operations are independent, and if the original investors now own 50% of the merged firms, there will only be a 0.25 probability of both portions of the merged firm failing. Risk has been reduced (the expected return is unchanged).

For simplicity we generally assume the goal of a firm is profit maximization (in present value terms) in order to maximize the well-being of the common stockholders. Periodically we should question this assumption, since corporations are also in existence to serve other groups, for example, management.

When a firm diversifies by merging with or acquiring a firm in another industry, who benefits? Let us consider the position of the shareholder, and for purposes of focusing on diversification, let us assume zero investor tax rates. The objective of diversification is risk reduction. The advice is not to put all one's eggs in one basket is good advice if the objective is to avoid a feast-or-famine situation.

The individual shareholder can diversify easily by buying stocks in different firms in different industries or by investing in mutual funds. The stockholder of a company does not need that company to incur costs to achieve diversification.

If diversification can generally be achieved efficiently by investors, then why do firms diversify? In the first place there are many investors who are not well diversified and would like to have the corporation diversify on their behalf. But even more importantly, management has its major asset invested in the firm, and this asset is difficult to diversify. The major assets of managers are their careers. If a company goes bankrupt or enters a period of financial difficulty, the middle-aged manager pays a heavy economic price. It is reasonable for such a manager to seek a higher level of security by trying to stabilize the income of the corporation.

HOLDING COMPANIES

Holding companies had their day of glory in the 1920s in the United States, but the depression of the 1930s soured the investing community. However, one still sees several layers of companies that give the appearance of having many of the characteristics of a holding company.

The following example is meant to be illustrative of the species rather than any one company. It is artificially simplified, but it has the basic elements of a holding company. We assume there are five layers of firms, with A owning 50% of the stock of B, B owning 50% of the stock of C, and so on. In addition, we assume that each of the companies is financed with 80% debt and 20% common stock. The only real assets are owned by firm E, which owns $500 million of real assets. The example can easily be made more realistic by having each firm own some real assets.

	A	B	C	D	E
Assets	50,000	500,000	5,000,000	50,000,000	500,000,000
Liabilities	40,000	400,000	4,000,000	40,000,000	400,000,000
Common Stock	10,000	100,000	1,000,000	10,000,000	100,000,000

Investors who borrow $5,100 from the bank to buy the stock of A could control the $500 million of assets of firm E, if they were satisfied with owning just 51% of the stock of A (they would have to borrow $10,000 to have 100% of the ownership of A).

The consolidated balance sheet is informative:

Assets	500,000,000
Debt	444,440,000
Common Stock-Minority Interests	55,550,000
Common Stock	10,000

PURCHASE VERSUS POOLING

With any business combination accountants have a series of decisions. They must first decide whether the transaction should be treated as a purchase or a pooling of interests. If the pooling method is used, the accounting is well defined. However, if the purchase method is used, they must decide:

1. the valuation of any securities issued in the transaction to determine the total cost of the acquisition
2. the valuation of specific assets, such as marketable securities, accounts receivable, land, plant, and equipment
3. the amount to be assigned to goodwill and its disposition in the future.

We briefly describe the two methods, and then consider some pros and cons of the two methods and the criteria to be used in choosing between them.

If the pooling of interests method is used, cost based accounting is used to record the assets of the merged corporations. No goodwill is created, since the basis of the accounting is the asset values already on the books of the present firms.

Theoretically, pooling should be used when two firms merge and the surviving firm is merely an addition of the two old firms. An example of a transaction that would fit this description is a moderate-sized coal company merging with a moderate-sized steel company accomplished with an exchange of stock so that the surviving firm would be a vertically integrated firm with both sets of stockholders owning stock in the firm.

With pooling, the original costs, as recorded on the books of each company, are carried forward. This is consistent with the use of historical cost in normal going concern accounting. However, it is likely that the assets of the firm being acquired have changed drastically in value, and the acquiring firm (although the firms are being merged, it might well be that one set of management of stockholders will be in control because of size differences) although giving up stock with a value far in excess of cost, would still record the assets at cost.

The use of cost at the time of merger will affect future expenses and incomes. The fact that future incomes are not affected adversely by a high price paid now (in the form of common stock) for the acquired firm, means that a firm can inflate its total income by acquiring firms.

To illustrate the two methods, assume firm P acquired firm S by the issuance of 1 million shares of common stock currently selling for $20 per share and that immediately before and after the acquisition the balance sheets of the two companies were as follows:

| | Before | | After | |
	Firm P	Firm S	"Pooling"	"Purchase"
Assets	100,000,000	10,000,000	110,000,000	128,000,000
Liabilities	40,000,000	8,000,000	48,000,000	48,000,000
Stock Equity	60,000,000	2,000,000	62,000,000	80,000,000

Assume that firm *P* had 6 million shares of common stock outstanding before the merger and 7 million after the merger. The market value of the stock equity of *S* was $20 million, and that of firm *P* was $120 million. Assume that the value of *S*'s tangible assets is $10 million (there is $18 million of goodwill). *S*'s total assets are $28 million.

Shortly after the merger, firm *P* sells the assets of what was firm *S* (now a subsidiary) for $15 million. The income statement of *P* would be affected as follows:

1. With "pooling" there would be a $5 million gain, since the cost basis of the assets sold is $10 million.
2. With "purchase" there would be a $13 million loss, since the cost basis of the assets, including $18 million of goodwill, is $28 million (equal to the $20 million of common stock issued plus the $8 million of liabilities assumed).

The purchase procedure resulted in a loss of $13 million in this example, which is consistent with the sales of an asset that cost $28 million for revenue of $15 million. However, if the $18 million of goodwill had been charged to a capital account at the time of acquisition, the sale of the assets would have resulted in a gain of $5 million. Thus the immediate write-off of goodwill gives rise to a potential distortion when combined with the disposition of assets (an immediate write-off is not currently allowed unless the assets are sold).

One of the prime difficulties with purchase accounting arises because the cost basis of the assets of the acquired company are adjusted based on the market transaction, but the assets of the acquiring company are not adjusted. The market value of the stock equity of P is $120 million, but the book basis is only $60 million. The records of P were not adjusted to take note of this difference, since there was not a direct transaction involving the assets of P.

Thus the purchase method moves partially away from cost-based accounting by adjusting the assets of the acquired company to take note of the new values, but the accounts of the acquiring company are left unadjusted.

It is tempting to use the market transaction as the basis of adjusting P's books as well as S's assets. One difficulty would be to determine the size of the transaction necessary to trigger this adjustment. At the extreme, one could argue that any arms' length market transaction could be the basis for making the adjustment. This would lead to the use of market values of the common stock as the basis of recording the assets and stock equity of a firm.

In some situations, there is no market value for the common stock given in payment for the acquired firm. Since goodwill cannot be evaluated directly, the lack of market value would make the application of the purchase method highly subjective.

The use of pooling resulted in a gain of $5 million despite the fact that an asset costing $20 million is being sold for $15 million. The gain results because the assets of the acquired company were not adjusted to reflect the real cost to the stockholders of the acquiring company. Since the assets are recorded at $10 million, despite the fact that the real cost to the stockholders of P is equal to $20 million. Although the example illustrated an extreme situation, the immediate disposal of all the acquired assets, the same type of situation occurs if the assets are sold through time as a result of normal operations.

Conventional accounting, using historical costs, does create situations of distortion through time. However, the failings of conventional accounting are accentuated when a firm, by means of a merger, acquires assets whose market price exceeds this historical cost basis, and uses the pooling method of accounting. Pooling is an extreme form of cost-based accounting, since it ignores the economic implications of the most immediate transaction, the merger. We can expect that the FASB will modify the accounting rules that apply to mergers and acquisitions.

THE AMOUNT OF PREMIUM PAID AND TAXES

There are two sets of stockholders affected by a merger or acquisition, those of the firm being acquired and those of the firm doing the acquiring. We will primarily consider the effect of an acquisition on the well-being of the stockholders of the firm doing the acquiring.

What is the perception of a common stockholder of an acquiring firm when a large premium over market price is offered? Consider a stockholder of a company which offers $30 a share for a company which is currently selling at $25 per share. This is a 20% premium over market price and well within reasonable bounds established by other acquisitions. Assume the offer of $30 per share is rejected because of the possibility of a competitive offer and the new tender price shoots up to $41.67 per share. This is a 67% premium over market and the average investor of the acquiring firm may start wondering whether the acquisition is being made in the interests of the stockholders or for the interests of management.

Returning to the situation where the stock price is $25, let us consider the situation where the acquiring corporation has excess cash and the acquisition at a price of $41.67 per share will be accomplished by the use of this cash. Assume the firm's stockholders are in the 40% tax bracket and the choice to the corporation is an acquisition of the firm at a price of $41.67 per share or to give the funds to the shareholders in the form of a cash dividend. To keep the analysis simple, we will assume there is only one firm to be considered and the investors in the acquirer would buy the target firm stock if they had the cash.

Why can the firm pay $41.67 for a stock that has a market value of only $25? If the $41.67 is distributed as a dividend, the stockholders being taxed at a 40% rate would pay $16.67 of tax and would net out $25. If the stock could be purchased for less than $41.67, the stockholders would actually be better off with the acquisition than with a cash dividend.

The amount that the firm could afford to pay would be somewhat reduced by the fact that the tax basis is increased with the cash dividend and then reinvestment. It has been convenient to assume the tax basis change is worthless (and thus we obtain an offer price of $41.67). However, we can also compute an indifference price if there is assumed to be value to the tax basis change.

In justifying the offering price, we have assumed that the choice is between the acquisition of the firm and a cash dividend to be taxed at ordinary rates. Consideration of other alternatives will modify the maximum price that can logically be offered for the common stock. Also stockholders with different tax rates will have different perceptions as to the reasonableness of the price that is offered. If the stockholders have a zero tax rate, they will tend not to be in favor of paying a premium over market price. They would prefer to receive a cash dividend to paying an amount in excess of the current market price of the common stock since on the receipt of the cash dividend they could use the cash to acquire the stock without the premium.

LEVERAGED BUYOUTS

Leveraged buyouts became very popular in the late 1970s and the decade of the 1980s. While more or less the same process had been going on for many years, during the 1970s several new twists were utilized.

With a leveraged buyout, debt funds are obtained from insurance companies and banks (or other entities willing to accept a large amount of risk). The debt is layered with the degree of protection ranging from mortgage bonds to highly subordinated debt. Some of the debt will have equity kickers in the form of either warrants or conversion features. Preferred stock may also be used, but it is less widely used than debt.

The promoters get the common stock. It is not uncommon for 90% or more of the new capital to be in the form of debt. In the early years of the new firm essentially all the cash flow is committed to debt service.

One important aspect is that the managers of the corporation tend to be given a significant portion of the new equity at a reasonable price. Thus they are apt to be friendly to the takeover and have a financial incentive to make it work.

BE A MONOPOLY

One of the easiest bits of advice for a consultant to offer a corporation is "Be a legal monopoly." Preferably one wants to have a legal monopoly of a product where the demand is inelastic (that is, people cannot do without the product; if price is increased, there will be a very small decrease in the amount demanded). The organization of OPEC is an example of the formation of a monopoly. The world has not learned how to do without oil in the short run; thus the price of oil can be increased at a rapid rate to relatively large amounts without greatly decreasing the amount of oil consumed. The owners of the oil reap large profits.

The corporate management which can find a product similar to oil, where the supply side can be legally organized in a manner similar to OPEC, has tremendous profit opportunities. Unfortunately for corporate managers but fortunately for consumers, these "star" products are difficult to find, since legislation makes it illegal to form monopolies by combining the operations of competing firms or by colluding on price. Thus mergers that tend to reduce competition are likely to attract governmental attention and are apt to be declared not in the common interest and to be disallowed. It may be possible to merge in an attempt to round out a product line where it can be argued that there is an increase in competition.

DEFENSIVE MANEUVERS

A company will sometimes seek a merger or make an acquisition in order to move to a better defensive position relative to thwarting the advances of a firm which is trying to acquire it. This might be good strategy from the point of view of management, but is unnecessary from the stockholders' viewpoint. The stockholders can accept or reject the offers of raiders based on the merits of the offer. They do not need management to move the firm to a more defensible position. The move has no value to the stockholders as a collective group. They do not have to be saved from themselves.

TAX-FREE EXCHANGE

For an acquisition to be tax free to the seller, it is necessary for the stockholders of the acquired firm to receive stock. This is a strong incentive for the acquiring corporation to use common or preferred stock. It is not necessary that only stock be used, but only stock gives rise to a non-taxable transaction.

THE SPIN-OFF: SPLITTING THE CORPORATION

If it is desirable for some corporations to merge, it may be desirable for other firms to divest. There are several situations where divestment may logically be desirable. In the first place, the unit may be more valuable to another corporation because synergy of some type would result. In fact, all the reasons for mergers are, with slight adjustments, reasons for divestment.

There is another basic reason for divestment. Assume a corporation has a major unit that is not healthy. The financial difficulty of the major unit may overshadow the fact that other units of the corporation have excellent prospects. In such a situation bond covenants might prevent the spinning off of profitable units, since these units are a major part of the debt security. However, there is no reason why a suitable split of the debt cannot be arranged so that the debtholders are approximately as well off (or better off). Adding warrants or conversion features is one method of accomplishing the acceptance of a corporate spin-off.

A third reason for divestment exists when the central core of the corporation adds overhead costs but little or no value. In fact, it can be that the large size of the corporation reduces managerial flexibility as well as preventing identification by employees with the well-being of the corporation. Smaller organizational units standing on their own bottoms might collectively be more valuable than an entire set of units operating as one corporation.

There are several different ways of splitting a corporation. With a *spin-off* the shareholders of the parent receive shares in the unit being separated (this transaction tends to be tax free and inexpensive). With a *carve-out* the shares are issued to the public (cash is raised). With a *split-off* the shareholders choose to convert some or all of their shares into the shares of the diverted corporation (protects the parent's stock price).

The Coverage Incentive

Firms like to have their common stock be well received by the market and for the market price to fully reflect the value of its components. The stock of a complex firm may be undervalued and not adequately covered by analysts, because it does not fit neatly into an industry classification. The firm's components might be difficult to value as part of a large corporation and thus the firm's market value does not fully reflect the value of the sum of its parts. To gain a recognition of full value (and coverage by more analysts) firms have been known to spin off components. The extent of coverage by analysts is a major factor in the divestment decision process.

Low Growth and Divestment

Should a unit with low or zero growth be a leading candidate for divestment? Growth possibilities should dictate whether or not investments in capacity should be made, but growth should not affect the spin-off decision except indirectly. If you forecast zero growth and a firm bidding for the business forecasts growth and thus bids high, the growth forecast will affect the willingness of the selling firm to accept the offer to buy.

Assume there are no growth opportunities and the forecasted growth is zero. The book value of the unit is $20 million, and it is currently earning $2 million of cash flows per year. The parent requires a return of 0.20. Since the unit is not growing and is not earning the required return, should the unit be divested?

One important fact has not yet been revealed. The best price that has been offered for the unit is $8 million. The firm is earning $2 million/$8 million = 0.25 on the unit's opportunity cost; thus the firm is meeting the defined required return and the unit should not be divested.

The growth rate is not relevant except as an input into the cash flow forecast. The opportunity cost, the amount being earned, and the required return are relevant. A perpetuity (zero growth) may have large value, as may a decaying cash flow stream; the type of generalization that leads to divestment if there is no growth is not valid. Computations of values consistent with different strategies must be made to make the decision.

CONCLUSIONS

Members of the accounting profession have long argued that both the pooling and purchase methods should be allowed to record business combinations. The consequences of allowing the use of pooling have not always been welcomed, but there has been a willingness to accept them. Too frequently, the choice of the method of accounting has been made based on the consequences of the method on the income measure of the firm, rather than with an aim to presenting the most useful information to present and potential investors.

Mergers and acquisitions will always be with us as one way in which a firm may grow (while the investors of the acquired firm change the nature of their investment). We may see the government defining limitations on situations where firms may merge, but it would be surprising to see legislation that discouraged mergers and acquisitions from taking place.

Financial planners must consider the possibilities of mergers and acquisitions from two different prospectives. One is the opportunity to acquire new firms, and the other is that their firm is a possible candidate for someone else to acquire. It is extremely difficult for managers to view a merger completely objectively. If their firm is acquiring another firm, the process is looked at as being beneficial to all parties. If their firm is being acquired, the acquiring firm is a "raider."

A firm with under-utilized assets and little debt that is undertaking less-than-profitable investments and has outstanding large amounts of preferred stock is a likely merger candidate. The foregoing reasons may not all be valid, but these situations do tend to attract merger-oriented firms. The financial planner should keep this in mind. Hopefully, the decisions that are made will be aimed at maximizing the well being of the stockholders.

There are many motivations that lead to mergers and acquisitions. The payment of a large premium over market price does not necessarily indicate an unwise decision. Unfortunately, sometimes management might not be able to reveal all its reasons for offering the large premium. Thus stockholder unrest can arise where there would not be unrest if all the facts were known. But even worse, there can also be situations where management's analysis is faulty and the purchase price is excessive. Time will reveal which is the true situation. Looking back, any one of us can be wiser than the wisest manager trying to make decisions under conditions of uncertainty.

Chapter 13

Risk Management

Appraisal of risk management is easiest applying 20/20 hindsight. The United States government guaranteed a loan to the Lockheed Corporation. When the guarantee expired, the government had made over $30 million of profit. *Ex post* the guaranty turned out to be profitable for the government, but before the final results were in, there was considerable risk and doubt regarding the loan.

In trying to sell atomic energy equipment, Westinghouse salespersons found it useful to guarantee uranium to fuel the reactors it was selling. Westinghouse initially owned enough uranium to cover the guarantees, but business was so good it soon guaranteed more uranium than it owned. When the price of uranium went up significantly, Westinghouse found itself with a liability for supplying high cost uranium. Should the company have committed itself to supplying uranium at a fixed price when it did not have contracts at fixed prices to obtain the uranium? *Ex post*, it is clear the company should not have made the commitments to supply uranium unless it was willing to accept the large amount of risk or implemented ways to control the risk or to hedge the risk.

In a comparable situation the Rolls-Royce Corporation contracted to supply airplane engines by a specified date to Lockheed when the engine had not yet been designed. In fact, they did not know how to produce the metal necessary for the engine. As might be expected, both companies moved into financial difficulties when the engines were not available at the due date.

Risk management is sometimes equated with the purchase of conventional insurance. While this is one aspect of risk management, we will broaden the definition to include any actions taken that will affect the risk-return characteristics of the firm. A firm may be "buying insurance" when it makes an investment that does not have a positive net present value, but rather has a desirable set of risk characteristics.

THE RISKS OF BUSINESS

Corporations face many types of risk, not all of which can be managed. For example, there is risk that the firm's product will become obsolete because of a completely new product (horse drawn wagons replaced by trucks) or the economy becomes depressed for a prolonged period. But this chapter is concerned with risks when management has a considerable control over the extent of the risk. For example, they are:

Commodity price risk. DuPont, a chemical company, used a large amount of oil as a raw material. It bought an oil company (Conoco) to insure a supply of raw material. Many companies buy futures or forwards to achieve protection against undesirable price changes.

Capital structure risk. Financing long-term investment projects with long-term capital reduces the risk that the capital suppliers will change their willingness to supply the capital. Also, the use of equity rather than debt reduces the financial risk.

Foreign exchange risk. If components of production are purchased in one currency and the end product is sold in a second currency, there is a large amount of foreign exchange risk. Foreign currency swaps, currency futures, and forwards are used to reduce this risk.

Interest rate risk. A firm that has assets whose cash flows are sensitive to interest rate changes but the outstanding financing is fixed-rate debt is exposed to interest rate risk. An interest rate swap is one solution.

Risk of obsolescence. A corporation fearing that the capital assets being purchased might soon be obsolete, might prefer to lease the assets with a cancelable lease.

We are all familiar with fire insurance and car accident insurance. Corporations have the same desire to insure against catastrophic risks. There are also risks that affect earnings or cash flows less dramatically, but where management would like to reduce the consequences of unfavorable events. In addition to the use of conventional insurance, they use derivatives to control the outcomes of uncertain events.

DERIVATIVES

A *derivative* is an instrument whose payoff is defined by the value of an underlying basic security. For example, a call option on a stock is a derivative. An option on a stock gives the owner the right to take action (buy the stock), but the owner of the option does not have to buy the stock. Its value at maturity is defined by the price of the stock on which it is a call. If the stock price at maturity exceeds the exercise price of the call option then the call option has value.

The two basic uses of derivatives are to hedge (reduce risk) or to speculate. In this chapter we are concerned only with the use of derivatives to reduce risk, but one of the major managerial problems is to set-up controls so that the persons implementing the risk reduction strategy do not engage in unauthorized speculation. This is an agency problem. The agent, the "trader," may have different objectives than the person who authorized the purchase of derivatives to reduce risk. The manager must understand the risks of different derivatives so that the hedging activities actually reduce risk.

We will consider in this chapter only three basic types of derivatives: (1) forward contracts, (2) futures contracts, and (3) swaps. There are a large number of variations (including combinations of the above), but these three types capture the basic characteristics of many of the derivative contracts. By the end of the century the notional amount of derivatives issued exceeded the total outstanding amount of stocks and bonds.

Forward Contract

A forward contract gives the owner the obligation to buy an object at a specified forward price. The classic hedging model using forwards is directed at risk elimination. Assume that in June a wheat processor (a miller) wants to be able to sell flour to a bakery in November at a given price of $10 per unit. In order to do this, the miller must buy 100 bushels of wheat at $9 per bushel. The bakery wants a fixed commitment in June, because it is signing contracts to supply bread at a fixed price and it does not want the risk of a rising flour price to jeopardize its profits. The miller buys a forward contract to buy 100 bushels in November at $9 per bushel.

In June a farmer is afraid there will be a glut of wheat in November and wants to make sure that he obtains $9 per unit for November wheat. The farmer sells forwards to deliver 100 bushels of wheat in November at $9. In June the miller has bought forward contracts to buy the wheat for $9, with delivery to take place in November. The farmer selling forward contracts is insured the $9 selling price. The miller is insured against an increase in wheat prices, and the bakery can contract with the miller for a fixed price for flour.

The farmer, miller, and the bakery are hedged. They have simultaneously sold and bought wheat, flour, and bread.

Futures Contracts

Future contracts are very similar to forward contracts, but there are significant differences. Futures contracts are traded on an exchange, thus futures are normally more liquid and the contracts are standard. The buyers and sellers can sell and purchase their positions (net-out) before the delivery date.

Futures are marked-to-the-market price daily (payments are made or received) while a forward contract may or may not be marked to market. Returning to the above forward contract example, assume a futures contract is sold by the farmer to deliver 100 bushels at a price of $9 a bushel on November 1. The buyer of the futures (the miller) agrees to pay $9 a bushel at that time. If the next day after the contract is signed the price increases to $10 the seller (the farmer) must pay $1 per bushel ($100) to the broker who then pays the exchange. The buyer of the futures contract receives $1 per bushel ($100). The daily mark to market requirement limits the risk exposure (default risk or counterparty risk) of the market. For example, if the price falls so that the price is $4 per bushel on November 1 the buyer of the futures contract will prefer to buy the wheat in the market than execute the contract at a price of $9. But, because of the daily mark to market the buyer has already paid $5 to the exchange so that when the wheat is purchased at $4 the total cost is $9, consistent with the price defined by the futures contract. The mark to market feature and margin requirements protect the market exchange from the default risk of the losing party to the contract.

Basic Swaps

There are several basic types of swaps used to hedge and for other purposes. For example, there are interest rate swaps, currency swaps, and commodity swaps. There are several reasons for engaging in swaps. The arranger of the swaps (a principal or intermediary) seeks to earn a spread that can result in profits. The counterparties engage in swaps to:

1. Find arbitrage opportunities (market inefficiencies) that reduce the interest rate at which funds are borrowed.
2. Speculate (gamble).
3. Manage (reduce) risk.

The Structure and Risks of a Basic Swap

Any interest rate swap transaction has three parties of interest:

a. A counterparty who swaps an interest obligation.
b. A principal who is in the middle of the swap transaction and who has legal obligations to pay the counterparty. Instead of a principal there can be a second counterparty.
c. A lender to the counterparty.

We can have asset swaps or liability swaps. The following example will illustrate liability swaps but the same principles can be used for asset swaps. There are many different variations of the swaps that are illustrated. A "Principal" has a legal obligation to pay counterparties but an "Intermediary" does not.

The following example of an interest rate swap consists of a situation where both counterparties and Principal benefit from the swap. This example implies an inefficiency would exist in the world capital markets without the swap. If the facts are as given, then a swap may be profitable for all the parties.

The Situation:

Corporation AAA wants floating-rate debt.
Can borrow for five years at a 0.1015 fixed rate
Can borrow at LIBOR (a six month floating rate reset every six months).
Corporation BB wants fixed-rate debt.
Can borrow for five years at 0.1165 fixed in a second market.
Can borrow at LIBOR plus 50 bp (a six-month floating rate reset every six months in a second market). bp stands for basis points where 100 bp = 0.01. The reset period may be different than six months.

Assume:

> AAA borrows fixed rate at 0.1015.
>> Swaps: pays (LIBOR − 0.50 bp) floating to Principal
>> receives 0.1015 fixed from Principal
>
> BB borrows floating rate at LIBOR + 50 bp.
>> Swaps: pays 0.1125 fixed to Principal
>> receives LIBOR plus 50 bp from Principal
>
> Principal has the following spreads:

Fixed	0.1125 − 0.1015	=	0.0110
Floating	LIBOR − 50 bp − (LIBOR + 50 bp)	=	−0.0100
	Net Spread		0.0010

Principal makes 10 bp or $1 per $1,000 notional amount per year. The results for the counterparties are as follows:

AAA pays (LIBOR − 50 bp) rather than LIBOR	=	$0.0050
BB Pays 0.1125 rather than 0.1165	=	+0.0040
Benefit to AAA and BB		+0.0090

This swap is profitable for both counterparties. If there are no defaults it is profitable for the Principal. The "notional amount" defines the amount of swap amounts. At maturity no exchange of principal (face amount) takes place.

Interest Rate Swap Spread

Interest rate swaps are frequently quoted in spreads over a U.S. Treasury security with the same maturity as the term (life) of the swap. Assume the spread is 57-62 for two-year swaps. The 57 is the bid spread over the two-year Treasury and the 62 is the offered spread. Assume U.S. Treasuries maturing in two years are yielding 0.0806. With these facts one counterparty is paying a fixed rate of 0.0806 + 0.0062 = 0.0868 to the Principal and the second counterparty is receiving a fixed rate of 0.0806 + 0.0057 = 0.0863.

The Principal has a net spread of 0.0868 − 0.0863 or 0.0005. It receives 0.0868 from one counterparty and pays the other 0.0863. In addition, it receives LIBOR and pays LIBOR.

Equivalents to Interest Rate Swaps

Synthetic interest rate swaps can be constructed using combinations of other securities. Thus the swap can substitute for other securities, and other securities can substitute for swaps. The transaction costs may differ for the other securities and the swap.

A Currency Swap

Assume a currency swap where the price quotes are 8.65-8.75. This represents a 0.0865 bid and a 0.0875 offer in Dm. LIBOR would be received (or paid) in dollars. There is 0.0010 spread for the Principal. The Principal receives 0.0875 and pays

0.0865 in the foreign currency. There is not a swap of the principal payments in this situation, but in another currency swap the principal payments may also be swapped.

Currency swaps are quoted bid-offer in terms of the foreign currency fixed interest rates. The floating rate is paid (or received) in terms of dollars. To receive dollar LIBOR, firms pay the offered fixed foreign currency rate.

The Functions of the Principal

It is useful to remember that the Principal of a swap earns its spread by performing the following economic functions:

1. seeks a lower cost of money for the counterparty by using the world markets.
2. acts as a lender (when there is risk at settlement).
3. enhances the credit of less than AAA rated entities by guaranteeing payment of interest.
4. absorbs interest rate risk in unmatched swap transactions.

The Principal has several different types of risk with matched swaps. With matched swaps the primary risks are credit types of risks. Thus analysis of a swap from the viewpoint of a Principal is very close to the credit analysis performed by a lender. While the Principal does not match each swap with an opposite swap, to manage risk the Principal does not want the portfolio of swaps to be unbalanced in material amounts.

Why Use Swaps?

Swaps are an efficient method of exchanging one stream for a second stream. Thus an interest rate swap might lead a counterparty to convert a fixed-rate debt to a floating-rate debt. If the counterparty has floating-rate assets the swap reduces the risk (it is a type of hedge).

The swap can involve currencies or currencies and interest rates. A firm that has borrowed pounds in England but is earning Japanese yen might swap yen for pounds to insure protection against the yen decreasing in value compared to the British pound.

An oil company selling oil in Britain but pumping oil in Alaska might swap quantities of oil with another company selling oil in California and pumping oil in the North Sea.

There are many reasons for participating in a swap. The primary reasons are:

risk reduction (hedging)
efficiency (swapping of commodities)
speculation (swapping into floating-rate debt on the expectation (hope) that floating rates will decrease)
lower cost (swaps facilitate the ability to borrow at the lowest cost)

THE VALUE OF HEDGING

Hedging is one type of risk management. For example, using less debt and making less risky investments also manages risk but is not hedging. The objective of hedging is to use a derivative to reduce or eliminate the consequences of an unfavorable event. It is obvious that corporations extensively hedge both interest rate and foreign exchange rate risk. But why should they hedge? What are the pros and cons of hedging? To evaluate hedging activities we will start with two assumptions:

1. The expected value of hedging is negative because of transaction costs and hedging considered by itself will reduce the expected value of the firm's cash flows.
2. Effective hedging activities will tend to reduce the firm's variance of cash flows and earnings thus reduce the firm's non-systematic risk.

Does hedging increase shareholders' value?

The Expected Value of Hedging

The fact that the expected value of hedging is negative is hidden by the fact that the hedging activities, omitting transaction costs and the gain or loss on the hedged item, have approximately a 50% probability of having a gain. With transaction costs included, the expected value of the hedging process is negative if we do not consider profits from the operations that are facilitated.

The hedging firm's variance of outcomes will tend to be reduced by the hedging activities. Normally a hedging gain will tend to balance the loss on the hedged activity. While it is possible to construct examples where ineffective hedging actually increases the variance of outcomes, it is more likely that the hedge will dampen the spread of results compared to what would have happened without the hedge. A reduction in the firm's variance of outcomes, thus a reduction in the firm's risk, is assumed to result from hedging activities.

Why Should a Firm Hedge?

Hedging can be evaluated from several different perspectives, among them are:

1. the firm
2. managers
3. common stockholders
4. debtholders

If only systematic risk affects a firm's value, the random fluctuation of exchange rates should not affect the stock's value. However, reducing the gains and losses due to currency fluctuations can increase debt capacity. Shareholders do not need hedging of unsystematic risk if they are well diversified.

The Firm

The direct consequences of hedging to the firm is to reduce the expected value of the firm's cash flows because of the hedging transaction costs and to reduce the variance of expected outcomes. These consequences apply to all firms that hedge effectively.

The indirect consequences of hedging are more complex and will be heavily situation dependent. They include:

1. Reducing the expected costs of financial distress by decreasing the likelihood of financial distress occurring.
2. Increasing the expected value of the tax deductions by increasing the likelihood of having taxable incomes for each foreign subsidiary.
3. Increasing the firm's debt capacity and lowering the cost of debt.
4. Increasing the likelihood of executing the planned capital expenditures.
5. Facilitating an expansion of operations that would otherwise be too risky.

Thus, there is on one hand the cost of hedging, and on the other hand benefits to the corporate entity. The benefits of hedging will differ among firms and will not always outweigh the costs.

The Managers

The interests of the managers follow closely the above effects of the hedging on the firm, but they are also likely to be affected by the accounting measures of profitability. This introduces a new dimension. Prior to this point it was implicitly assumed that the function of hedging was to eliminate (or reduce) economic risk measured by the variance of the cash flows, but reducing the variance of the accounting incomes may also be relevant. Unfortunately, an effective economic hedge might not reduce the variance of the accounting earnings because of accounting conventions involving expected transactions (see *Financial Accounting Standard 133*).

Another complexity is that managers are very likely to be concerned with the performance of the common stock, and the effect of hedging on the value of the common stock.

The Common Stockholders

At a meeting of a firm's top executives, a company treasurer said "We hedge to decrease the risk to stockholders and increase the value of our common stock." Consider this statement if only the direct consequences of hedging are considered (a decrease in the firm's expected cash flows and a decrease in the variance of outcomes). A common stock is an option on the assets of the firm where the exercise price is the value of the debt. A decrease in the firm's expected cash flows and a decrease in the variance of outcomes will both result in a decrease in the value of the option (the value of a share of the stock). By making the firm's return less risky the value of the firm's debt is enhanced, but the value of the stock is decreased (the lower expected cash flows and decreased variance harm the stock value, all things equal).

If we remove the constraint of only considering the direct consequences, the effect of hedging on the stock value is less easily predicted. Any or all of the items listed in the discussion of the firm can also increase the value of the stock. However, it is also possible that the effect of these items on the stock value of a specific firm is very small or zero. The net effect of hedging on a stock value is far from obvious.

One conclusion is clear regarding the risk reducing value of hedging for the well-diversified investor. While the firm might have a well thought out hedging strategy to reduce the risk of investors who only own its stock, it cannot forecast the effect of its actions on the risk position of investors who own a portfolio of investments. Hedging reduces unsystematic risk, but unsystematic risk is reduced to zero by the well-diversified investor. This investor does not need the firm to hedge to reduce unsystematic risk. A widely owned firm should not justify hedging by claiming risk reduction for all its stockholders.

The Debtholders
Consider both the debtholders who currently own the corporation's outstanding debt and the investors who are considering buying part of a new debt issue. If a corporation does not hedge its foreign currency exchange risk, but the buyers of the debt thought hedging would take place, then the variance of the outcomes is increased compared to expectations, and the risk to the debtholders is increased compared to the forecast. The value of the debt will go down (this is a form of event risk). Since the stock's value can go up or down (with reduced variance and reduced expected cash flows), we cannot be sure of the direction of the change in the stock value, but the decrease in the debt value can result in a stock value increase.

If a new debt issue is being purchased the investors will require a higher expected return if there is no hedging than if hedging is expected to take place. The firm's outcomes have a larger variance and a larger expected value than with hedging. Forecasting the effect on the stock value of not hedging while adding to debt is difficult, and depends to a large extent on the costs of hedging.

The distinction between already issued and to be issued debt is significant. A change in the hedging strategy will affect the price of the outstanding debt and will change the required return of the debt to be issued.

The Special Case
Proponents of hedging can offer a special case to illustrate why hedging is desirable. Consider a business transaction where a very large amount of funds can be invested to earn 0.10 and the capital costs only 0.08. There is a 200 basis point spread and the transaction appears to be desirable, but there is interest rate risk that can be hedged. Without the hedge, the investment is too risky (a significant likelihood of causing financial distress). With the hedge the firm nets a certain 150 basis points after hedging costs. The hedging process enables the firm to expand its operations and increase its income by increasing the amount invested.

This is a different situation than where there is little or no risk of financial distress and management merely wants to reduce the variance of cash flows (or accounting earnings) resulting from interest rate, exchange rate, or price changes.

Corporate financial managers tend to act as if they believed that the expected value from hedging exceeds the expected cost. It is important to define whose value change we want to consider. But the effects of the decision to hedge are very difficult to measure, and even if it is decided that the firm should hedge, the amount of the hedge is not obvious.

Hedging is a form of insurance, and like all insurance it has a cost. As individuals we do not attempt to insure all risks, and we can conject that corporations also should not insure all risks. Partial hedges should be considered to be a reasonable strategy requiring evaluation as should no hedges. Each corporation should ask "What is the expected value to the shareholders from hedging?"

Utility Considerations for Decisions

It is common practice to write down a set of cash flows for an investment and make the decision using that one set of cash flows. The one set of flows is frequently implicitly assumed to have an expected monetary value, the result of summing the set of monetary outcomes each multiplied by its probability. That is, behind the one cash flow may be many possible outcomes, each outcome measured in dollars with each outcome having a probability. For simplicity this will be illustrated by the flipping of a fair coin (the probability of each outcome is 0.5), with the outcome being $100,000 if there is a head and $20,000 if there is a tail. It costs $35,000 to play the game.

There is a somewhat simplified version of the decision outcomes. The net cash flows for each path are $65,000 if the gross outcome is $100,000 and a $15,000 loss if the outcome is $20,000.

The gamble has an expected monetary value of $25,000 ($0.5 \times 65,000 - 0.5 \times 15,000$); thus on an expected monetary value basis the investment is acceptable. Would you be willing to try the gamble? Could you accept the 0.5 probability of losing $15,000?

Most large corporations would accept the investment. If three zeros were added to the monetary outcomes so that there was a 0.5 probability of losing $15,000,000, it would not be safe to predict what percentage of division managers would accept the investment. Even where the board of directors found the investment acceptable, a division manager who liked her job might find the investment excessively risky with the 0.5 probability of a $15,000,000 loss. Where a decision maker rejects the gamble with a positive expected monetary value, we have an illustration of risk aversion. The fact that people and organizations have risk aversion attitudes is generally summarized by the statement that they have utility functions.

A "utility function" represents the value an individual places on different amounts or changes in amounts of money or wealth. It reflects the wealth preferences and risk attitudes of a person. While we know how to determine the utility function of a person, we do not know to determine to the utility function of a group of individuals (e.g., a corporation) or how to compare the utility measures of one person with the utility measures of another person. Thus formal utility analysis has severe limitations as a decision-making tool for a complex organization such as a corporation. But utility theory can be an important way of evaluating and describing alternatives.

In the early 1960s a major theoretical breakthrough occurred which shifted the primary risk analysis from that of the individual investor's utility to a determination of the market's risk return preferences. The primary advantage of the theory is that actual returns may be observed and be used to determine the price the market is placing on risk. The model, called the *capital asset pricing model*, is an extension of the portfolio literature of the 1950s and early 1960s. The main change is that the capital asset pricing model makes use of the prices that the market is setting for return-risk trade-offs rather than using subjective measures of attitudes toward risk (such as the utility functions of investors). We first illustrate the importance of portfolio considerations and then very briefly describe the types of calculations that can be made to evaluate real investments, applying the capital asset pricing model.

Portfolio Considerations

Take a situation in which an investor can make a $2,000 outlay and undertake an investment that promises to pay either $5,000 one period from now or $0. Both the events have 0.5 probability.

Although the expected cash flows of the investments have an internal rate of return of 0.25, this is an extremely risky investment, and we might be reluctant to undertake an investment in which one of the outcomes is a loss of $2,000, and this outcome has a 0.5 probability.

Now let us consider a second investment that also costs $2,000 and promises to pay back $4,000 one period from now or $0, and again both events have a 0.5 probability. The expected cash flows of this second investment have a zero rate of return, and this second investment has very little to be said in its favor (its expected present value is negative using any positive rate of interest). Thus we have two investments, one of which has a large amount of risk, and the second of which has both large risk and a zero rate of return. Taken individually, neither investment is very desirable to a person wishing to avoid risk.

But now add the information that when the bad event occurs for the first investment, the good outcome occurs for the second investment and a comparable set of outcomes occurs with the other event. The outcomes of undertaking both investments are reasonably desirable for the two possible events. For an investment of $4,000, we either get back $5,000 or $4,000, and the rate of return of the expected cash flows is 0.125. The possibility of a large loss has been eliminated. Analyzing the portfolio of investments gives us information that was not available when we considered only the individual investments.

THE CAPITAL ASSET PRICING MODEL

The capital asset pricing model (CAPM) assumes investors have available a market basket of risky securities and the opportunity to invest in securities with no risk of default. Risk preferences of investors dictate a combination of the market basket of the risky securities and the riskless securities. In equilibrium, the return of any security must be such that the investor expects to earn a basic return equal to the return on a default-free security plus an adjustment that is heavily influenced by the "correlation" of the security's return and the market's return.

If the return from the investment is positively correlated with the market return, the equilibrium return will be greater than the default-free return. If the correlation is negative, the equilibrium return will be less than the default-free return. We can develop a capital budgeting technique that makes use of the correlation of the investment with the market returns. If the investment is positively correlated with the market returns, there will be a subtraction from value for the risk of the investment. If the investment is perfectly independent there will be no adjustment for risk. If the investment is negatively correlated, there will be an addition to the value of the investment, since the investment tends to reduce risk. The correlation with the market return is a measure of the "systematic" risk of an investment.

If we assume that an investor is extremely well diversified and if we believe that the CAPM applies, exact formulations for the risk adjustment of an investment can be obtained. This formulation will omit the so-called "nonsystematic" risk, the risk of the firm's common stock that is independent of the market fluctuations. It is assumed that the investor is adequately diversified; thus this nonsystematic risk does not give rise to the need for a risk adjustment.

The concept of splitting a firm's risk into two components is one important justification for studying the CAPM. While the CAPM assumes nonsystematic risk can be diversified away by investors this is not relevant, the manager would think the risk is relevant if it affects the firm's viability. A manager is not likely to rely exclusively on the CAPM to make decisions for the firm.

The Market Portfolio

The market portfolio includes some of all securities. While for empirical purposes the definition has tended to exclude investment opportunities that are not in the form of securities (e.g., real estate, art, gold), there is no reason why in theory these items should not be included. The amount of each security included in the market portfolio is based on the securities' current market prices. Securities are included in proportion to their market valuation. Thus if a specific common stock represented 0.001 of the total value of all investable assets, 0.001 of the market portfolio would be invested in this stock. In designing the market portfolio, no attention is paid to the prospects of the security or the risk preferences of the investor. The specific risk preferences of the investor come into play in splitting the investment fund between the market portfolio and the default-free securities.

The CAPM Formula

Define

$\bar{r}_i$ = the expected required rate of return of security i if the market is in equilibrium

r_f = default-free rate

$Cov(r_i, r_m)$ = the covariance of the return of security i and the market portfolio r_m

The covariance measures how the changes in the returns of the security i and the market portfolio are linked together. It is common practice to define the beta (β) of a security as:

$$\beta_i = \frac{Cov(r_i, r_m)}{\sigma_m^2} \tag{1}$$

The basic CAPM is:

$$\bar{r}_i = r_f + (\bar{r}_m - r_f)\beta_i \tag{2}$$

This is the conventional formulation for the expected return for a stock. The term $(\bar{r}_m - r_f)$ is the market's risk premium. Note that when the beta of a security is equal to 1, the security must have a return equal to $\bar{r}_m$, the expected return of the market.

Equation (2) gives the required return for different amounts of systematic risk, where systematic risk is defined in terms of the investment's beta. The required expected rate is not affected by the investment's unsystematic risk.

The required expected return for an investment is a function of how the investment's returns are correlated with the market's returns (that is, it depends on the beta of the investment). The use of a weighted average cost of capital for a firm with a beta of 1 is clearly not appropriate for a specific investment with a different beta.

Most importantly, equation (2) gives the required return only considering systematic risk. Most managers would also want to consider nonsystematic risk since managers are not perfectly diversified.

RISK AND CAPITAL BUDGETING

The objective of any corporate capital budgeting criterion is to select investments that will maximize the value of the common stock. With no uncertainty, we take only the time value of money into consideration. We accomplish this by application of the factor $(1+r)^{-n}$ to future dollars to transform them back to the present.

Consider a dollar to be received in two years and a 0.10 time value factor. The present equivalent of $1 to be received in two time periods is $0.8264 using a 0.10 time value factor. We can say that $0.8264 is the price that we would place on $1 to be received at time 2.

Now if we allow uncertainty about receiving the $1, we must take the uncertainty into consideration. Assume that the $1 is received if event e_1 takes place, and that there is a 0.8 probability of that event taking place and our receiving the $1. It is intuitively appealing to multiply the $0.8264 present value factor obtained above by 0.8 to obtain a probability adjusted time value factor of 0.6611.

Now time value and probability have been taken into consideration. However, there is a third factor to consider. Is there a risk preference? Is a dollar to be received at time 2, with the given event e_1 occurring worth more or less than $1? For example, event e_1 may be a very prosperous year and $1 is worth somewhat less than $1, because we already have many dollars. Or the event giving rise to the $1 may be a disaster (for example, the death of the bread-winner of a family) and $1, given that event e_1 has occurred, is very valuable. Thus the risk preference factor must be applied to the 0.6611 obtained above. Assume the event e_1 is a good year, and the risk preference factor is 0.95. We would then obtain a risk-adjusted present value factor of 0.6291 that would then be applied to the number of dollars to be received at time 2 with the given event for the specific investment being considered.

The 0.6291 is the product of 0.8264 and 0.8 and 0.95, which are, respectively, the time value factor, the probability of the event, and risk preference of the investor. If desired, the risk preference factor may be obtained using the capital asset pricing model, rather than subjectively as illustrated in the previous example. At a minimum the manager must realize that merely applying the present value factor $(1+r)^{-n}$ to future cash flows might not be an adequate way of taking both time value and risk into consideration.

The objective of this section is to describe an approach to capital budgeting under uncertainty that is consistent with maximizing the value of the stockholders' position. A procedure can be developed that is very much similar to the net present value procedure except that the "present value" factors for each time period take both time value and risk into consideration.

The particular model used either makes use of the capital asset pricing model or subjective evaluations. The computations of the former model take into consideration how the cash flows of the investment vary with the overall market conditions. A difficulty with the capital asset pricing model is that a nondiversified investor may also be interested in "nonsystematic" risk, that is, the risk that the investment has independent of the market fluctuations. In a situation in which the investors of a firm are well diversified, or alternatively, the investors are willing to make investment decisions as if they were perfectly diversified, the CAPM solution techniques are useful.

Implications for Financial Strategy

In evaluating investments, many firms tend to use a weighted average cost of capital to implement the discounted cash flow capital budgeting techniques. This measure reflects average risks and average time value conditions and cannot be accurately applied to unique "marginal" situations, that is, to specific investments. There is no reason to think that the weighted average cost of capital of a firm can be inserted in a compound interest formula and then be applied to future cash flows to obtain a useful measure of net present value that takes both the time value and risk of a unique investment into consideration in an effective manner.

The capital asset pricing model offers hope for accomplishing a systematic calculation of risk-adjusted present value. The required return measure reflects the opportunities for investments with alternative return-risk trade-offs available to investors. This is analogous to the rate of interest on a government bond reflecting investment opportunities when there is no default risk. Unfortunately the model presently formulated is a one-period model, and the extension into a useful multiperiod tool requires further theoretical developments. Nevertheless, the model offers many useful insights that are presently applicable to financial decision making.

For example, an investment with a low or event negative expected return but desirable risk characteristics (e.g., the investment's return is independent or negatively correlated to the market's return) may become acceptable, and investments with high returns but more than average risk (e.g., their returns are highly correlated with the market returns) will find it more difficult to be accepted.

We find that since the CAPM is based on the viewpoint of a well diversified investor it is not necessary to consider the spread in outcomes of the investment, nor even the risk of all the firm's assets joined together in one portfolio, but rather it is necessary to consider the relationship of the investment's return with the market's return. At a minimum we can expect the CAPM to affect investment decisions in a qualitative manner. That is, after the internal rate of return or net present value is computed, arguments will be made that will attack or advance the investment based on its risk, where risk is defined in terms of market risk. In the long run, we can expect the calculations of the CAPM to be accepted because despite their limitations and complexity, they are better than many measures that are currently available.

One important limitation of the CAPM should be kept in mind. The model assumes that the investors are very widely diversified, and even more important, it assumes that the managers of the firm are willing to make investment decisions with the objective of maximizing the well-being of this type of investor. This means that certain types of risk (for which the investor is well diversified) may be ignored in the evaluation of investments. These risks that are assumed not to affect risk premium of an investment are called "nonsystematic risks." By spreading the funds to be invested over a wide range of available opportunities, the nonsystematic risks are driven to zero for the investor's portfolio. This assumes that the investor is widely diversified and that any specific investment is a very small proportion of the market portfolio.

It is well known that objectives of firms and managers are complex and there will be a reluctance of managers to ignore types of risk just because they do not affect the well-diversified investor. The major asset many managers possess is their career in the specific firm for which they are working. The argument will not be persuasive to them that a major risk that jeopardizes the existence of the firm can be ignored since the investors in the firm are well diversified and the risk is unsystematic. Thus even if the importance of the CAPM is acknowledged, the financial manager will still want to consider risk factors that the formal model considers not to be relevant. The "nonsystematic" risk is not something that is likely to be ignored by a management, which includes among its objectives the continuity of existence of the firm.

VALUE AT RISK

Value at risk is a popular risk management tool widely used by financial institutions. The objective is to determine the level of risk for a given financial strategy. There are several different methods but the general approach is to use the recent past history to determine the probabilities of different levels of loss. Thus a $100 million dollar portfolio of 100% very short-term debt securities would have close to zero probability of losing $10 million (10%) in the coming year. On the other hand, a portfolio of 100% common stock would have a probability of the magnitude of 8% of losing 10% of its value in the period of a year.

Obviously, constructing the model to incorporate changing conditions that affect the probability of the loss is highly desirable. But even acknowledging the limitations of current practices, the attempt of management to estimate the amount of risk exposure is to be praised.

A variation to the conventional value at risk process is to determine the sensitivity of the firm to the change in a specific variable such as the level of interest rates, the price of oil, or the Dow-Jones Index. The probability of the change could then be estimated.

It is important that the significance of low probability but very significant events be considered. An event might not have occurred for 30 years, but if its occurrence would cause bankruptcy, it should be considered. An event might not have occurred in the recent past, but if the event is feasible, the consequences might be so important that management wants to consider explicitly this contingency.

CONCLUSIONS

Risk can be studied at several different levels. The first and by far the most important error is to ignore risk completely. To have the type of tunnel vision that only allows the possibility of one event occurring in the future is likely to lead to bad decisions. One must allow for contingencies and buy insurance.

Management has a responsibility to consider the risk implications of specific decisions, but more importantly it is suggested in this chapter that the risk of a specific decision cannot be considered in isolation. It is necessary to consider, not the risk of the specific project, but rather its effect on the entire portfolio of the firm's assets if we are approaching the decision from the point of view of the corporation as an entity.

If we switch our focus from the legal fiction that is called a corporation to the individual investor and apply the logic of the capital asset pricing model, we find that we are not concerned with the diversification effects of the new investment on the firm. The statistical relationship of the investment's return and the market's return is of crucial importance.

It follows that for a widely diversified investor an investment should not be undertaken just because it reduces the risk of the firm. It is necessary to know how the investment's risk-return characteristics compare to those of the market. The individual investor can achieve diversification by the use of the market portfolio, and the individual firm does not have to seek risk diversification for the investor. The justification for risk diversification at the firm level must be found either in the investor who is not well diversified or in the interests of the managers and workers, who have a major interest in the continuity of existence of the firm.

Chapter 14

Corporate Capital and the Put-Call Parity

T he put-call parity is one of the most useful financial relationships. Given the ready markets for derivatives, the use of derivatives to raise capital has increased, and it is necessary for people working with financial investments and raising of capital to understand the underlying relationships. The put-call parity formula is the foundation for many of the relationships.

THE BASIC FORMULA

We will use the following notation:

T = time till expiration of options and bond maturity
P_0 = the initial common stock price
Put = the value of a put with exercise price E
Call = the value of a call option with exercise price E
r = the risk-free interest rate

Then

$$P_0 + \text{Put} = E(1 + r)^{-T} + \text{Call}$$

This equation requires explanation. The maturity value of the debt is E and the debt's present value is $E(1 + r)^{-T}$.

The left-hand side of the parity says the investor buys a share of stock with a price of P_0 and to eliminate a loss in excess of $P_0 - E$ buys a put option with an exercise price of E. This strategy gives upside potential with no downside loss beyond $P_0 - E$ given that E is the put's exercise price. The right-hand side of the equation gives the present value of a debt with a value of E at maturity plus the upside potential of the call option with an exercise price of E. The outcomes of the left- and right-hand sides of the equations are identical.

Stock Price at Maturity is Less Than the Exercise Price

Let the common stock price at maturity be P_T. Assume the price at maturity is less than the exercise price. For the left-hand side of the equations where a share and a put option with an exercise price of E have been bought, we have:

This chapter has more new ideas, is more complex, thus more difficult to understand than previous chapters. It is included because of the importance of the concepts.

Value of stock: P_T
Value of put (gain): $E - P_T$
Total: $\overline{E}$

For the right-hand side of the equation where debt and a call option have been bought, we have:

Value of debt: E
Value of call option: 0
Total: $\overline{E}$

The outcomes of both strategies are equal.

Stock Price at Maturity is Greater Than Exercise Price

Assume the price at expiration is larger than the exercise price. For the left-hand side of the equation we have:

Value of stock: P_T
Value of put option: 0
Total: $\overline{P_T}$

For the right-hand side of the equation we have:

Value of debt: E
Value of call option: $P_T - E$
Total: $\overline{P_T}$

The outcomes of both strategies are equal.

Since the outcomes are equal for any value of P_T the costs must also be equal to insure there are no arbitrage opportunities.

Put-Call Parity Example

To illustrate the put-call parity relationship, assume:

$r = 0.10$, $P_0 = \$80$, Value of call $= \$11.56$, $T = 1$, E $= \$85$

Therefore

$\$85(1.10)^{-1} = \$77.27$

Value of put $= \$8.83$

Then

$P_0 + \text{Put} = \$80 + \$8.33 = \$88.83$

$E(1 + r)^{-T} + \text{Call} = \$77.27 + \$11.56 = \$88.83$

Payoffs at Maturity

Let's look at the payoffs at expiration. Assume $P_1 = \$100$, then

Stock	$100	Debt	$85
Put	0	Call	15
Total	$100		$100

Assume $P_1 = \$20$, then

Stock	$20	Debt	$85
Put	65	Call	0
Total	$85		$85

The outcomes of both strategies are equal for any value of P_T.

APPLYING THE RELATIONSHIP: CONSTRUCTING A SYNTHETIC COMMON STOCK

Many interesting results can be obtained by rearranging the put-call parity relationship. For example, subtracting the value of the put from both sides we obtain:

$$P_0 = E(1 + r)^{-T} + \text{Call} - \text{Put}$$

Thus, a strategy involving buying debt and a call and selling a put is equivalent to buying a share of stock. For example:

$$P_0 = \$85(1.1)^{-1} + \$11.56 - \$8.83 = \$80.00$$

For the issuer:		For the investor:
Selling debt of	$77.27	Buying debt
Selling call of	11.56	Buying call
Buying a put	− 8.83	Selling a put
Equivalent to	$80.00	Equivalent to buying a
issuing a share		share of common
of common		

From the viewpoint of a corporation raising capital, issuing a debt and a call option and buying a put is equivalent to issuing a share of stock. The amount of debt and exercise prices of the put and the call must be consistent.

Another interpretation of the right-hand side of the put-call parity relationship is that it is a convertible debt where the bond must be converted at maturity (a bottomless convertible).

Given the different tax treatments of debt and common stock distributions, these relationships are of practical significance.

Constructing a Synthetic Debt

It is not clear why anyone would want to construct debt from the issuance of common stock, a put option, and the purchase of a call option, but the following is the equivalent to borrowing:

$$E(1 + r)^{-T} = P_0 - \text{Call} + \text{Put}$$

The firm can either borrow or:

1. issue common
2. buy a call with exercise price E
3. sell (issue) a put with exercise price E

Buying the call eliminates the upside associated with the issue of stock for the investor. Selling the put eliminates the downside (the issue of the stock results in a gain on the stock price decline, but there is a loss with the stock price decrease on the put that was sold).

Does any of the above have any real world significance? First consider the type of security that is called a PERCS, DECS, etc.

The PERCS Type of Security

To simplify the analysis we will only consider the payoffs at maturity. At maturity the holder of the PERCS receives common stock but there is a cap on the gain. Assume the cap is $50. Then if the common stock price is above $50 at time T the investor receives $50/P_T$ shares. For example, if $P_T = \$100$, the investor receives in exchange for the PERCS one-half a common stock share with a value of $\frac{1}{2}(100) = \$50$.

A PERCS is equivalent to:

Buying a share of common and selling a call
or
Buying a debt and selling a put.

Put-Call Parity

We know that

$$P_0 + \text{Put} = E(1 + r)^{-T} + \text{Call}$$

Rearranging the terms to obtain a PERCS:

$$P_0 - \text{Call} = E(1 + r)^{-T} - \text{Put}$$

A PERCS is equivalent to buying the stock and selling a call. It is also equivalent to buying a debt and selling a put (there is a possibility of loss with the put).

A company issuing a PERCS is issuing a common stock and buying a call or equivalently issuing debt and buying a put.

The different variations of PERCS that one sees in the financial community involve the buying and selling of additional calls and puts. There is no limit to the amount of slicing and dicing that one can do once one understands put-call parity.

FORWARD STOCK UNITS

The use of forwards expands the amount of financial engineering that can be accomplished based on put-call parity. To simplify the presentation we will only assume forwards on the issuer's stock, but in practice the forward may be on any firm's stock.

First, we must recognize that a synthetic forward can be constructed by buying a call and selling a put all with the same exercise price of E. Buying the synthetic forward will give the same payoff as buying the basic forward.

A forward contract for a common stock gives the holder the obligation to buy the stock for a price of E. If P_T is larger than E the investor has a gain of $P_T - E$. If is smaller than E the investor has a loss of $E - P_T$.

Now consider a synthetic forward. If P_T is larger than E, the put has zero value and the call that was purchased has a value of $P_T - E$. This is the same gain as the holder of the forward earned.

If P_T is smaller than E the call option has zero value. The put that is sold has a loss of $E - P_T$. This is the same loss as that of the forward when P_T is smaller than E.

Example

Suppose $P_0 = \$40$, $P_T = \$41$, and $E = \$44$ where P_0 is the initial stock price and E is the forward price and the exercise prices of the put and call. For the forward we have the following. With the stock price (P_T) of $41 and the $44 forward price, the loss is $41 − $44 = $3. The investor pays $44 for a share when the value of a share is $41.

For the synthetic forward we have the following. The call with an exercise price of $44 has zero value with $P_T = \$41$. The put has a loss of $3. The stock can be bought for $41 (the total cost is $44 including the $3 loss on the put).

The outcomes of the forward and the synthetic forward are identical. Both suffered a loss of $3.

Now assume $P_T = \$50$ (P_T is larger than E). For the forward we have the following. The gain on the forward is $50 − $44 = $6. The investor buys the stock at a cost of $44 when the value is $50.

For the synthetic forward, the call that was purchased has a gain of $50 − $44 = $6. The put that was sold has zero value. The stock can be bought for $50 (the net cost including the gain on the call is $50 − $6 = $44).

Returning to the Put-Call Parity

The put-call parity is:

$$\text{Debt} + \text{Call} = P_0 + \text{Put}$$

Rearranging terms the synthetic forward's value is:

$$\text{Call} - \text{Put} = P_0 - \text{Debt}$$

Assume at time 0 the value of the forward is \$0, we then have:

$$P_0 - \text{Debt} = 0$$

$$P_0 = \text{Debt}$$

Define $\text{Debt} = (1 + r)^{-T}E$, then

$$P_0 = (1 + r)^{-T}E$$

and

$$E = P_0(1 + r)^T$$

This establishes the necessary value of E for the forward to have zero value.

If a corporation issues

$$\text{Debt} + \text{Forward}$$

and since the Forward = Call − Put, we have:

$$\text{Debt} + \text{Forward} = \text{Debt} + \text{Call} - \text{Put}$$

which by put-call parity is equal to P_0; thus issuing debt and a forward is equivalent to issuing stock.

The implications of the relationship are large. With a strategy of issuing (selling) debt and a call option and buying a put, a corporation is essentially issuing a stock. More simply, by issuing debt and a forward stock unit, the corporation is essentially issuing stock.

Example

Let's use our earlier example to illustrate the above. Assume at maturity $P_T = \$41$. If the corporation issues a share of stock at time zero, there is a \$41 payment (an opportunity cost or the cost of retiring the stock) at time T. Now assume that the firm issues debt (maturity value $E = \$44$) and a call and buys a put. Then

Debt payment at time *T:*   −$44
Call pays at time *T:*   0
Put receives (a put has been bought):   + 3
Net: −$41

The two outcomes are identical. Since with the debt issuance there is not a share of common stock outstanding, the common stock issued at time zero must be repurchased.

Now assume $P_T = \$50$. If the company issues a share of stock at time zero, there is a $50 payment (an opportunity cost or the cost of retiring the stock) at time *T.* Now assume that the firm issues debt and a call and buys a put. Then:

Debt payment at time *T:*   −$44
Call payment: −6
Put receipt: 0
Net: −$50 Payment

The two outcomes are identical.

The issuance of debt and a forward stock unit (with the amount of debt and the forward price being consistent with the stock price) is equivalent to the firm issuing a share of common stock.

While it appears the firm is issuing debt (with tax shields), since there are also stock forwards being issued, the firm is actually issuing common stock.

CONCLUSIONS

Wall Street investment banks are developing a flood of exotic securities. It is difficult to understand these securities unless you understand the put-call parity relationship and the fact that buying a forward contract is equivalent to buying a call option and selling a put.

The securities being developed start with debt and forwards and then build on top of these two fundamental securities additional calls and puts.

The important message is that common stock and debt can be constructed each from the other by using forwards, puts, and calls. Both the prices and the outcomes of these securities are all linked.

Chapter 15

Performance Measurement

This chapter will consider and evaluate different quantitative financial measures of performance including return on investment and economic income. One of the underlying issues is whether performance measurement and decision making of a firm should be on a decentralized or centralized basis. Any multidivisional firm can be turned into a completely self-contained unit by doing away with profit centers, and by considering the entire corporation as an operating entity. The arguments of this chapter are applicable to entire firms, self-contained operating components of a firm, or components that are not self-contained but in which there is a reasonable transfer pricing procedure. Although the desirability of profit centers is to a large extent separate from the quantitative performance measurement, in one sense the issues merge. To compute any quantitative performance measurement of an operating unit, it is necessary to arrive at reasonable income and investment measures for the unit.

PERFORMANCE MEASUREMENT AND MANAGERIAL COMPENSATION

Measuring managerial performance for praise or compensation determination is a difficult task. Any measure used is subject to valid objections. It is desirable that there be congruence between the firm's goals and the measures that are used. One cannot expect managers knowingly to take actions that are desirable for the firm if those actions will adversely affect their career path or compensation.

The recommendation is to use several measures. Since all measures will be subject to some sort of gaming, the use of several good measures reduces the likelihood that managers will knowingly make undesirable decisions for the firm.

Performance Measurement

There are four basic measures that can be used:

1. Accounting measures (e.g., income, return on investment, economic income, etc.).
2. Market measures (the return earned on an investment in the company's common stock).
3. Non-accounting but quantitative measures (e.g., customer and employee satisfaction).
4. Qualitative measures (subjective evaluations).

Accounting Measures

The accounting measures we will consider are:

1. sales revenue
2. operating margins: percentages or dollar amounts
3. income
4. return on investment or return on equity or return on assets
5. economic income (residual income or economic value added)
6. earnings per share (for a period of years)

Sales revenue is an attractive accounting measure since there are relatively few arguments as to the magnitude. Add the share of market and growth in sales and one can become enthusiastic about the usefulness of the sales measures. But obviously something is missing, profitability.

The operating margin is a popular profitability measure: subtract from sales revenue the direct costs of generating the revenue. For example, the operating margin of a retail store is sales minus the cost of the merchandise sold. With a manufacturer the definition of the expenses to be subtracted to compute the margin is not as exact as for a retailer.

If sales are $100 and the cost of goods sold is $60, the operating margin can be expressed as a dollar amount, $40, or as a percentage, 40%. Operating margins as a control mechanism are very useful. If operating margins are maintained, it is likely that a positive bottom line (income) will result. On the other hand, many expenses (including capital costs) are omitted from the calculation, thus the operating margin can only be one of several measures that are used.

Income is revenue minus expenses as defined by generally accepted accounting principles. Unlike the operating margin it includes the fixed expenses as well as the variable expenses.

The primary area where the income measure is deficient is the expense of the equity capital used. There is deducted a depreciation expense, but the measurement of expense is likely to be deficient since the implicit cost of the equity capital used is normally not deducted in computing the income.

It is essential that the costs of the capital used affect the performance measures. The two common measures are return on investment in some form and economic income. Economic income deserves to be used more extensively (its use is growing rapidly).

Return on Investment (ROI)

Advocating the use of *return on investment* (ROI) implies that it is a better measure of performance than is obtained from using just the income of the operating unit. While this is normally the situation, not all subsidiary operating units should be judged using ROI, and ROI should always be only one of several measures. For many operating units, marketing efforts are not autonomous, and it is more appropriate to use cost minimization rather than profit maximization (or its near equivalent, maximization of ROI, subject to constraints).

Some managers tend to place excessive faith in a ROI measure, neglecting the fact that the measurement of performance (so that the measure actually reflects performance) is much more difficult than using one measure. It should be realized that ROI is not necessarily the best measure of performance, but that ROI can be a useful measure. Consider what a good ROI measure can accomplish. We have first a measure of income; but before concluding that the income level is satisfactory, we relate the income to the amount of assets used to earn the income. While $1 million of earnings may be termed to be very good, if you are told that the operating unit used $100 million of capital to earn the $1 million, your conclusion might well shift from good to bad. To evaluate performance it is necessary to consider the amount of assets used in earning the income. Thus the use of ROI has advantages over the use of income, but may not be the best performance measure.

Instead of ROI some firms use the *return on equity* (ROE). While the two measures have comparable uses, the ROE measure has several limitations.

a. It is affected by capital structure (which may not be controllable by the management being measured).
b. It adversely affects certain types of decisions (investment and divestment) because it is a percentage.
c. Equity investment creates biases unless the analyst distinguishes between investments in the equity of a subsidiary and investments in real assets.

The second limitation (b) applies equally to ROI as it does to ROE. Other terms commonly used instead of ROI are *return on net assets employed* (RONAE), *return on funds employed* (ROFE), *return on capital applied* (ROCA), and *return on assets* (ROA).

Components of ROI For some purposes it is useful to break ROI into two components (this is sometimes referred to as the Dupont formulation):

$$ROI = \frac{Income}{Assets}$$

$$ROI = \frac{Income}{Sales} \times \frac{Sales}{Assets}$$

where income is measured after interest and taxes.

The term sales/assets measures the degree of asset utilization. The term income/sales measures profitability. The product of the two terms gives the return on investment.

The primary contribution of ROI (or ROE) is that management is held responsible for the capital used. However, it does this in a somewhat flawed manner (may adversely affect certain types of investment or asset retention decisions).

ROI and Investment Decision Making The use of ROI to evaluate perfor-mance can affect investment decisions because the manager knows that after accepting an investment its operations will affect the performance measurement. This leads to an incentive for the divisional (or other subcomponent) manager to reject investments that yield a lower return on investment than is being earned on the currently owned assets even though the investments are attractive for the firm.

Not only should top management be concerned with the return on invest-ment of the assets being used, but also the growth in assets and income. *Growth* as well as return on investment is important. A static division earning a 30% ROI may well be evaluated as being badly managed, whereas it may be concluded that a division that is growing and earning 15% is well managed.

The investment decision problem resulting from a desire to maintain a high ROI highlights the necessity of not relying on one performance measure (ROI or something else) but rather bringing in sufficient measures to restrain the impulse of persons trying to circumvent the control-evaluation system. Any defense of ROI should be based on a desire to use it as one method of evaluating the performance of investments, not so that it may be used to evaluate the desir-ability of undertaking investments. ROI is not an acceptable method of evaluating perspective investments.

The Case of the Resource Benefiting the Future Measures of performance used in an incorrect manner will tend to lead to incorrect conclusions. There is a necessity to improve the measures and to use them intelligently. Consider the case of a division manager of a timber company who has the opportunity to invest in 500,000 acres of prime timber land. The catch is that the trees on the land are all seedlings and they will not mature for 30 years. It is agreed by the planning group that the land is a good investment. However, the manager's performance is mea-sured using return on investment. The manager knows that the land will increase the denominator (investment) now, but it will be 30 years before the numerator (income) is also increased. Since the division manager only has five years to go before retirement, the investment in land is rejected.

This case has a reasonable solution. The land should be excluded from the investment base in measuring performance unless the value increment is allowed to affect the income. Unless something like this is done, there will be a distortion in the investment performance analysis, and thus distortion in the investment decision-making criteria applied.

Now consider a plant being built with excess capacity to service the expected demand of year 2020. Is the normal performance measurement scheme capable of taking this situation into consideration? Probably it is not. Generally accepted accounting principles do not do a good job of assigning expenses through time.

The Computation of Income and ROI It is widely known that straight-line depreciation or accelerated depreciation, except in very well-defined and specific situations, will distort measures of ROI. Also, the ROI that results for each year will differ from the internal rate of return computed at the time of acquisition, even when the expected results are realized.

Define depreciation to be *the decrease in value of the investment during the time period*. Although the definition becomes more complex if there are additional investments made during the period, the theory can be used to compute the income that is used in the ROI calculations. The following example is used as a vehicle to show that return on investment, when properly calculated, gives useful performance measurement information.

Assume the net cash flows (and net revenues) associated with an investment costing $3,000 at time zero are:

Time	Cash Flow
1	$1,300
2	1,200
3	1,100

The firm uses straight-line depreciation and has a time value of money of 10%. This investment has a yield (internal rate of return) of 10%. There are zero taxes.

Exhibit 1 shows the income and investments for each of the three years of use. The fact that each year has identical returns on investment equal to the internal rate of return of the investment seems to be a coincidence. However, if we inspect Exhibit 2, which shows the present value of the investment at four moments in time (V_i is the value at time i), we see that in each period the decrease in value is $1,000 (the value of V_3 is zero), and that in this very special situation the use of straight-line depreciation is correct (if the cash flows are different, the depreciation schedule would be different). The present value at time 0 is $3,000, at time 1 $2,000, and at time 2 $1,000.

Exhibit 1: Equal ROIs

Year	Cash flows or net revenues	Depreciation	Income	Investment at the beginning of the Period	ROI (Income divided by investment)
1	1,300	1,000	300	3,000	0.10
2	1,200	1,000	200	2,000	0.10
3	1,100	1,000	100	1,000	0.10

Exhibit 2: The Values

Time	Flows	Period 1 present value factors	\Time 0 present values	Period 2 present value factors	Time 1 present values	Period 3 present value factors	Time 2 present values
1	1,300	0.9091	1,182				
2	1,200	0.8264	992	0.9091	1,091		
3	1,100	0.7513	826	0.8264	909	0.9091	1,000
			$V_0 = 3,000$		$V_1 = 2,000$		$V_2 = 1,000$

Define depreciation expense to be the change in economic value. The procedure works with any set of cash flows. There need not be distortion in ROI because of the method of depreciation. In this simplified example, the internal rate of return of the investment is equal to the firm's time value of money, and the cash flows of each period equal the net revenues. Different assumptions would add to the complexity of the calculations, but these complications can be solved.

The Economic Income Method

Some managers call the method to be described the *residual income method* and others call it *economic value added* or EVA. The main characteristic of the method is that interest on equity is deducted from income to obtain the net income. This procedure is very useful if we properly define income and investment, the correct interest rate is used, and interest is appropriately assigned to time periods. Unfortunately, the above requirements may not be fulfilled in a manner that will give theoretically sound (and useful) results if one uses conventional accounting in a situation where the benefits are increasing through time. Using the previous example, we illustrate an application of the economic income method.

Define economic income as net revenue less a capital consumption expense (depreciation) and the interest cost of the investment. Continuing the ROI example, the expected economic incomes for the three years are:

	Year 1	Year 2	Year 3
Revenues	1,300	1,200	1,100
Depreciation	1,000	1,000	1,000
Interest Cost	300	200	100
Economic Income	0	0	0

Note that if the internal rate of return is used as the interest rate (the basis of computing the interest cost), the economic incomes are equal to zero. Zero economic income is not a bad result since investors earn the asset's internal rate of return which is above the firm's required return.

When the actual revenue of year 1 is $1,500 (beating the $1,300 expected revenues), there will be $200 of economic income.

Now assume the internal rate of return is 0.20 but the firm uses a 0.10 capital cost to compute the economic incomes. The revenues are now $1,600, $1,400, and $1,200 for years 1, 2, and 3 respectively. The asset again costs $3,000. The expected economic incomes are now:

	Year 1	Year 2	Year 3
Revenues	1,600	1,400	1,200
Depreciation	1,000	1,000	1,000
Interest Cost	300	200	100
Economic Income	300	200	100

The net present value (NPV) of the economic incomes is:

$$NPV = \frac{300}{1.1^1} + \frac{200}{1.1^2} + \frac{100}{1.1^3} = \$513.15$$

This \$513.15 is also equal to the NPV of the cash flows:

$$NPV = \frac{1,600}{1.1^1} + \frac{1,400}{1.1^2} + \frac{1,200}{1.1^3} - 3,000 = \$513.15$$

The present value of the economic income measures is tied to (and consistent with) the NPV measures used to evaluate the investment.

Some consultants call this "economic income" calculation "economic value added." This is unfortunate since the economic value added by the investment is \$513.15 at time zero. The operations in the first year (with revenues of \$1,600) result in the following value:

$$\text{Value at time one} = \frac{1,400}{1.1^1} + \frac{1,200}{1.1^2} + 1,600 = \$3,864.46$$

Since the initial value of the investment was \$3,513.15, the economic value added for year one was \$351.31, not the \$300 of economic income. The measure that is being computed is an income measure not a value or a value change measure.

Comparing ROI and Economic Income Economic income offers several significant advantages over ROI as a performance measure. First, and most importantly, the use of ROI might discourage division managers from accepting investments that offer returns that are larger than the firm's required risk-adjusted returns, but that are less than the ROI the division is currently earning. If the new investment is accepted, the division's ROI will be decreased.

For example, suppose a division is now earning \$30 million (a perpetuity) on an investment of \$100 million. Then,

$$ROI = \frac{\$30,000,000}{\$100,000,000} = 0.30$$

The division can invest an additional \$50 million and earn 0.15 ROI or \$7.5 million per year (a perpetuity) on this new investment. The firm's required return for this investment is 0.10, thus the investment is economically desirable. Should the division accept the new investment? If it is accepted the division's ROI is reduced from 0.30 to:

$$ROI = \frac{\$37,500,000}{\$150,000,000} = 0.25$$

Based on the adverse effect on the division's ROI, a manager might reject this economically desirable investment. This problem does not arise if economic income is used. The economic income before the new investment is:

Initial Economic Income = $30,000,000 − $10,000,000 = $20,000,000

Note that the interest cost is computed on the $50 million of new investment, not just the portion financed by debt. After the investment:

New Economic Income = $37,500,000 − $15,000,000 = $22,500,000

Based on economic income there is an incentive for the division manager to accept the desirable investment and increase the economic income by $2,500,000.

The second problem with ROI is related to the first. ROI gives faulty evaluations of relative division performance. Consider two divisions, one with a ROI of 0.30 and the second with a ROI of 0.25. Which of the two division managers is doing the better job? Above, we showed that accepting the economically desirable investment reduces the division's ROI from 0.30 to 0.25. The division earning 0.25 is being managed better than the division that earns 0.30 and that rejects good investments. Using economic income to measure performance solves this problem that exists with ROI.

The third advantage of economic income is that it allows more flexibility. For example, if short-term interest rates are 0.20 and long-term rates are 0.12 (the pattern of 1980), the 0.20 interest rate could be used for working capital items in computing economic income. The ability to use different interest rates for different assets introduces a flexibility that ROI lacks.

Summary of Complexities The complexities of applying economic income to performance measures or compensation are:

1. the method of calculating depreciation expense
2. the choice of the capital cost (interest rate)
3. the changing value of assets (e.g. inflation or technological change)
4. risk
5. non-controllable factors affecting the measure.

Summary of Economic Income Advantages Economic income offers three primary advantages.

1. Any investment with a positive net present value or an internal rate of return larger than the firm's required return will have positive economic incomes.
2. The use of economic income will tend to not affect adversely investment or divestment decisions.
3. With the use of economic income, management is charged for the capital it uses, thus has a direct incentive to use capital economically.

Economic income is a very sensible measure.

Market Measures

The stockholders are the firm's residual owners and they are interested in the stock's total return. How well did the CEO perform? What was the stockholders' total return?

Unfortunately, the stock's return does not always track the CEO's performance, especially in the short run. A company may do well but the stock might go down (e.g., with an interest rate increase). Nevertheless, tying a CEO's compensation to the stock's market performance is sensible (as long as it is not the only basis of compensation calculation).

There are several comparisons that can be made. The firm's performance can be compared to a defined target return, the return earned by the market, or the returns earned by a set of comparable firms.

In addition to relating compensation to the current year's performance, it is reasonable to reward today's managers in the future for performance for the next 10 years. It is desirable to give today's managers an incentive to make decisions with a concern for the future.

Non-Accounting Quantitative Measures

Given the generally accepted criticisms of accounting (e.g., it is cost based) most analysts of business affairs search for other quantitative measures to complement (or replace) the accounting measures. These measures include:

1. market penetration
2. customer satisfaction
3. employee satisfaction and turnover
4. units sold
5. diversity measures
6. quality control measures (percentage of defectives)

If reliable useful measures can be obtained, then the non-accounting quantitative measures can take their place with the accounting measures. In many situations they will be more important than the accounting measures since they give a hint of the level of future incomes.

Qualitative Measures

There are many qualitative aspects that enter into an evaluation. For example, a manager might be reliable and easy to work with. A manager might have laid the foundation for future growth by hiring the future mangers and researchers. Does the manager generate enthusiasm and creativity? There are many ways that a manager can enhance the firm's future profitability and value by actions that do not lead to current profitability. Has the manager enhanced the firm's reputation among customers and suppliers? To evaluate a manager's performance it is necessary to consider these factors.

In addition, firms can have goals other than a measurable effect on profitability. This might involve the local society or society in a broader sense (e.g., protecting the environment beyond the legal requirements).

Intangibles are factors not easily measured, but they can be important to the long-run success of a corporation.

MANAGERIAL COMPENSATION

The basis of compensation should be both the operating results of the manager's specific unit and the results of the firm. The manager should have joint loyalties.

The basis of compensation should include quantitative objective measures, but not to the exclusion of qualitative measures. The existence of the qualitative considerations reduces the tendency of managers to game the system.

To some extent some of the compensation should be deferred and be tied to the firm's future performance. We want managers to make decisions from a long-run perspective. The basis of compensation should be both accounting measures and market measures. The return earned by the shareholders should affect the compensation of the managers.

Agency Theory Applied to Corporate Management and Performance Measurement

Problems of agency arise when a principal employs an agent to perform a task, and the interests of the principal and the agent are not identical. The corporate form is fertile soil for agency problems to take root. Consider the relationships between shareholders (the principal) and management (the agent). For many reasons including the increase in power, management might want the firm to grow while the shareholders would be better off with a small firm and a large cash distribution. It is necessary for the compensation method to be efficient in terms of eliminating the possibility of a management to undertake knowingly undesirable investments from the viewpoint of shareholders.

There can also be agency problems with different levels of employees. Consider the CEO and traders of a bank. They are all employees. They all want to increase the bank's profits. But the traders might have bonus arrangements that encourage them to take excessive risks from the CEO's perspective in order to earn a large bonus. This strategy might be good for the traders but bad for the expected profits of the bank. A trader who wins becomes rich. A trader who loses gets an identical job with the bank across the street.

Another type of agency problem arises when one group is in a position to take advantage of a second group. Let us consider a firm financed by $9 million of 0.08 debt and $500,000 of common stock. There are zero taxes. Without any new investments there is certainty of the firm earning $800,000 (before interest) and being able to pay the $720,000 interest on the debt. The stockholders would earn

$80,000 per year. The firm is considering a $1 million investment financed by 0.08 debt. With this investment there is 0.5 probability that no debt interest will be paid. The initial debtholders do not want the $1 million of new debt to be issued.

Obviously, the initial debtholders will attempt to structure their indentures so that they limit the ability of the stockholders to change the nature of the business in a manner that adversely affects the position of the debtholders. This is a variation of an agency problem.

Agency costs consist of several types. One is the transaction cost. Buyers of debt have to hire a lawyer that protects the debt buyers interests. Corporations hire consultants to establish systems so that the traders of derivatives cannot bankrupt the firm. These are transaction costs or agency costs. Another type of agency cost arises because of the necessity to reward the agent in a manner that makes the agent's interests congruent with the principal's interests.

Non-Controllable Factors

An oil company executive's firm is losing $500 million per year. The CEO is in danger of being fired. Then oil prices double and the firm makes $800 million. It is the same manager managing in the same way but the work environment has changed. Obviously some attempt could be made to separate out the factors that are and are not controllable by the manager. But this is difficult, and is apt to introduce subjective measures into the evaluation.

This problem is an example of the qualitative aspects of performance evaluation.

A Non Zero Net Present Value

The basic example used in this chapter sets the net present value of the investment equal to zero, that is, the internal rate of return of the investment is equal to the time value factor for the firm. Obviously this will only rarely be the case. We expect most investments to have expected returns in excess of their required return. For example, let us assume that the three-year investment costs $2,760 instead of $3,000. The net present value of the investment at the time of acquisition is $240, and its internal rate of return is 0.15. There are several possible paths we can take. Two methods will be described. The most straightforward would be to use 0.15 as the rate of discount to compute the depreciation expenses and returns on investment.

Using 0.15 as the rate of discount we obtain:

Period	Revenue	Depreciation	Income	Investment	ROI
1	1,300	844	416	2,760	0.15
2	1,200	919	281	1,876	0.15
3	1,100	957	143	957	0.15

The primary difficulty with this solution is that the time value of money is defined to be 0.10 not 0.15. Thus the values of the investment at each time period are greater than those shown above. A second solution is to adjust immediately the value of the investment to $3,000, the present value of the benefits, despite the fact that the investment cost is only $2,760. This procedure would not be acceptable for conventional financial accounting purposes because of the implicit threat of manipulation, but it would be acceptable for internal managerial purposes. It is a very appealing procedure because it is relatively simple and yet is correct from the standpoint of accounts reflecting values.

Incentive Consideration

The use of book value based on cost to measure the investment (the denominator in the ROI calculation and the basis of the interest cost in the economic income calculation) or even the use of estimates of price level adjusted cost is subject to severe criticism. There is no reason why a system based on values estimated by management cannot be used for internal purposes instead of cost based conventional accounting. Here we have an opportunity to apply ingenuity to bypass a valid objection by managers to cost based accounting.

Rather than asking an accountant or another staff person to supply the number on which the managers are to be judged, let us ask the managers to supply the value estimate. The procedure would be simple. Take a set of eligible managers and ask them to "bid" periodically for the assets they want to manage and for which a change in management is appropriate. The manager whose bid is accepted takes the asset, and the bid becomes the accounting base for performance evaluation. If the manager bids too high, that manager gets the asset but will find it hard to meet the return on investment and economic income requirements. If the manager bids too low, a competing manager will win, or alternatively the "board" may reject the bid and ask for revised bids. There is one major difficulty with this procedure. Managers can rig the time shape of projected earnings so that early targets can be easily attainable. This tendency would have to be controlled by the top managers awarding the bid. Large deferred benefits would have to be discounted.

The proposed procedure would have many advantages. It would establish an investment base whose measure is acceptable to both the operating manager and to the top level of management (the former sets the value, the latter must accept it). The accountant serves the very important and proper function of supplying relevant information that is used by the managers in making their respective judgments and bids. The ROI and economic income measures are improved because the investment base is appropriate to the specific investment and manager being evaluated rather than being the result of a series of historical accidents (such as the year of purchase and the method of depreciation). Most important, it requires managers to set, describe, and quantify their plans for the utilization of the assets. It would tie together planning, decision making, and control.

Deferred Benefits

Conventional depreciation accounting combined with the uses of ROI is at its worst when the benefits produced by the asset are expected to increase through time or when the benefits are deferred. The early years are greatly penalized by conventional accounting, with the managers having an incentive to avoid such investments so that their performance evaluations do not suffer.

For example, assume an investment costing $3,000 is expected to have the following benefit stream:

Period	Benefits
1	$1,100
2	1,210
3	1,331

The firm's cost of money is 0.10 and is equal to the investment's discounted cash flow internal rate of return. The results using conventional accounting and straight-line depreciation will be (assuming the actual benefits are equal to the expected):

Period	Revenues	Depreciation	Income	Book Investment	ROI
1	1,100	1,000	100	3,000	0.03
2	1,210	1,000	210	2,000	0.105
3	1,331	1,000	331	1,000	0.331

The first year's operations are not acceptable.

Defining depreciation expense to be the decrease in value of the asset, the results would be:

Period	Revenues	Depreciation	Income	Book and Value Investment	ROI
1	1,100	800	300	3,000	0.10
2	1,210	990	220	2,200	0.10
3	1,331	1,210	121	1,210	0.10

The depreciation calculations are:

$V_0 = 3,000$ value at time 0 $d_1 = 3,000 - 2,200 = 800$ depreciation of period 1
$V_1 = 2,200$ value at time 1 $d_2 = 2,200 - 1,210 = 990$ depreciation of period 2
$V_2 = 1,210$ value at time 2 $d_3 = 1,210 - 0 = 1,210$ depreciation of period 3

The distortion caused by conventional accounting can be increased by assuming no (or very low) benefits until period 3. The operating results of the early years would appear to be even worse than in the example.

Cash Flow Return on Investment

Recognizing the inadequacies of conventional depreciation accounting, some managers have attempted to solve the problems by using cash flow return on investment. Since cash flows are used to evaluate the investment, why not use them to evaluate the investment's performance?

Define the cash flow return on investment to be:

$$\frac{\text{Cash flow}}{\text{Investment}}$$

The computation seems to be appealing because depreciation is not computed, but unfortunately, the computation merely makes a bad analysis worse. Using the previous example where the investment has a 0.10 internal rate of return, we would obtain:

Period	Cash Flow	Investment	Cash Flow ROI Cash Flow/Investment
1	1,300	3,000	0.433
2	1,200	2,000	0.600
3	1,100	1,000	1.100

Some firms have actually tried to use the historical measures as required returns for additional investments. You should note that for an investment yielding 0.10 over its life, the cash flow ROIs for the three years are 0.43, 0.60, and 1.00. The measure greatly overstates the ROI the asset is actually earning.

Another difficulty of the measure is that it will tend to bias management in favor of capital intensive methods of production, because capital cost is omitted from the numerator of the performance measure.

It is better to use the conventional ROI with income (after depreciation) in the numerator than to use the cash flow ROI, which is extremely difficult to interpret and has no theoretical foundation. The use of the measure illustrated above will get management into one or more interpretive difficulties. There are alternative methods of using cash flow return on investment that are improvements over the method illustrated.

PLANNING IMPLICATIONS

The fact that there may be a conflict between the investment criteria used and the performance measures means that corporate planning must take into consideration the fact that all desirable investments (from the corporate standpoint) may not be submitted upward. It would be naive to expect a division manager to recommend a plant with 60% excess capacity where the analysis of mutually exclusive investments indicates that this is the best alternative, if the performance measures for a period of five years will be adversely affected by the choice. Rather the division manager is likely to bury this type of alternative so the board of directors is not confused by the number of alternatives and this "undesirable" alternative specifically.

The board of directors has a similar type of conflict when it evaluates major investments that satisfy normal investment criteria, but have adverse effects on the ROIs and earnings per share of the next few years because of conventional accounting.

The planner rejecting investments with positive net present values may gain short-run benefits (nondepressed earnings) but will have a long-run cost in that future earnings will be depressed compared to what they could have been.

One alternative is to use the recommended investment criteria and hope to modify the accounting conventions that cause the distortions. Alternatively, failing that, management can attempt to explain the characteristics of the investment (and the deferred benefits) to the investing community.

The best solution would be for the accounting profession to encourage a wide range of depreciation methods, if these methods are justified by the economic characteristics of the investment. Currently too rapid write-off (R&D, training, plant & equipment) leads to (1) bad measures of performance and (2) non-optimal decisions.

CONCLUSIONS

Annual or quarterly accounting profits can be a poor measure of what has been accomplished during any relatively short period of time. Also, it is often difficult to assign responsibility for a deviation from the profit objective. Many economic events with long-run implications are not recorded by the accountant. One should not use any performance measure without considering factors, including those factors not normally appearing in the management information system.

In some cases the ROI or economic income should not be used for operating units because it is too difficult to measure either the income or the investment. Normally, the measure of ROI can be used to gain an impression of managerial performance, but the use of ROI should always be supplemented by economic income. This is necessary if the top management of a firm is to attempt to measure the effectiveness of the utilization of assets controlled by persons at different levels of the firm. The economic income is a very useful means of accomplishing this, if efforts are made to measure income and investment in a useful way. Economic income combined with economic depreciation is very good. It can be made as complex or simplified as you wish.

In conclusion, to measure performance you *can* use ROI (never by itself), but economic income is strongly recommended. To make investment decisions you *cannot* use ROI.

Although performance measurement is a difficult task when exact reliable measures of income and investment are not feasible, it is necessary that all managers evaluate persons for whom they are responsible. As guides and indicators, ROI and economic income have their uses.

Chapter 16

Financial Strategy and Policy

It is somewhat pretentious to talk about financial strategy rather than financial decisions, but there were several reasons for making the major thrust of this book financial strategy. First, there was a desire to avoid becoming bogged down with excessive details. But even more importantly, there was a desire to establish a perspective, or, a state of mind. Let each corporation map out a financial strategy. This implies that financial officers gain a realization that they have a wide range of choices and these choices can influence the value of the firm's securities to different groups of investors.

SETTING THE OBJECTIVES

The primary objective of a business corporation is to "make money." Defining the objective more exactly, we can say that the objective is to maximize the present value of the stockholders' position. If the shareholder maximization is consistent with maximizing the "well-being" of managers, other employees, society in general, etc., there is no problem. For simplicity it is sometimes convenient to assume the objective to be to make decisions in the interests of the stockholders.

The importance of setting this objective can be readily seen by considering other possible objectives. For example, one can define sales growth or percentage of market share as the objective. In themselves these are not valid objectives. Only if they have a desirable effect on the profits of the firm (properly measured) or more exactly the shareholder value can we say that growth and increasing market share are desirable.

Consider the seemingly innocent procedure of awarding top management bonuses based on earnings per share and growth in earnings per share. It is assumed that, if earnings per share go up, the stockholders are better off. Well, that is not quite correct. If all things are equal and if earnings per share are increased, the stockholders are better off. But if the increase in the earnings per share results from increased investments and if the increased investments are not economically sound, the economic position of the stockholders is not improved even though the earnings per share have increased. Two factors should be noted.

First, the accountant does not record the opportunity cost of stock equity capital in computing earnings per share. In fact, unless the capital is in the form of debt, no entry is made for capital costs. This means that a management being measured on the basis of earnings per share can profitably accept any investment earning a positive return as long as common stock capital is used. The second factor is that earnings per share can be increased by accounting changes or real decisions that increase the reported earnings even though the real earnings may not have changed for the better. For example, a decrease in research and development expenditures will increase the reported earnings, but the expected real earnings of the period are not affected by such a change. The future earnings may be adversely affected.

Conflicts in Goals

To describe the primary goal of a corporation in terms of the stockholders' well-being is convenient but it is excessively simplified. There are other "clienteles" who have vital interests in the affairs of the corporation. One very important such group is management. Not only is management an important factor but normally the in-house management has a large amount of power. The stockholders may be diffuse and their powers small if they are not organized. With a widely spread ownership it is not surprising that management has stepped into the power vacuum. Another factor is that many investors have thought it inappropriate for common stock investors to exercise control. Thus in the past universities and pension funds tended to vote their proxies consistent with the wishes of management.

It has implicitly been assumed that the objectives of management and the objectives of the stockholders are completely consistent with each other. Frequently managers are also shareholders; thus it would not be surprising if there were considerable overlaps in their objectives. On the other hand, it would also be surprising if management, not controlled, always managed a firm considering the well-being of the managers.

The chairman of one of America's largest corporations was asked to rationalize and justify his firm's latest and largest acquisition. He spoke of the necessity of keeping management's interest at a high level. This justification can be interpreted in either of two ways. One interpretation would be that if the company did not grow, good managers would be lost and the firm would suffer. A second interpretation is that business is a game and the managers want to have fun playing the game. In this case the former is probably the fairest interpretation. But it is a mistake to act as if the corporation exists solely for its managers.

Other important clienteles of a corporation are its workers, its customers, the locality where the firm does its business, and the various governmental jurisdictions in which the firm operates. Obviously, corporate goal setting can be complex.

SUCCESS AND FINANCIAL STRATEGY

Financial strategy cannot turn an operating disaster into a dramatic success. It can enhance the value of an operating success and increase the likelihood that the firm will survive long enough to attain that success. At the other extreme a large amount of debt can increase the probability of financial disaster, and a small amount of debt can decrease the probability.

If a person shops for a suit, the type of suits to be found at Brooks Brothers is no surprise. If one shops for a common stock, it is much more difficult to know the type of financial strategy that one is obtaining. In the marketing of products there is a realization that there are wide ranges of different customers and that it makes sense to go after a segment of the market. The marketing of a product should have a focus. Let us define the issuance of securities as a type of marketing. In the marketing of the common stock of a firm, there is frequently not the same focus as is found in the marketing of the firm's products. The marketing of securities other than common stock is generally well focused, but common stock is an exception.

Frequently a company with zero long-term debt will start adding debt. A company not paying a cash dividend will suddenly think it is a good idea to pay a dividend. There is some consistency through time in financial strategy but generally no attempt to target the company's common stock for a segment of the market.

From the point of view of investors trying to plan an investment strategy, it would be useful for firms to describe their financial strategies. This would make known the planned capital structure decisions but even more importantly the intended dividend policies. While it would be indicated that events might necessitate a change in strategy, at least management's intentions would be revealed.

In many situations firms follow strategies that please few and annoy few. Pay some dividends (say 0.4 of earnings) but not too much and do some share repurchasing. Have some debt (say 0.35 of common stock) but not too much. The financial managers look at other firms and follow their lead. But since most managers are looking at each other, there are few leaders — we have a circle where each firm is looking at each other firm and is seeing itself.

Corporations should have well-defined financial personalities so that stockholders can knowingly invest in those firms which best suit their interests. Today there is apt to be a blurring of policies, and differences are not well defined. Corporations tend to try to please broad spectrums of investors, or even all conceivable investors, with their financial decisions. It is not possible to achieve this objective, and at some stage in the future we can expect either stockholder revolts, or an evolution in procedure whereby stockholders' preferences receive more consideration.

In the past, the interests of the managers and the investors have been assumed to coincide. In the future, natural differences in the objectives of the two groups can be expected to become more well defined. For example, although managers have tended to perform well in growth situations, there is evidence that they are less likely to recognize the need for contraction (giving cash back to the investors) until financial disaster strikes, and then it is likely to be too late. When a firm's common stock is selling at one times its cash flows, and the value of its plant as scrap is greater than the market value of its stock, the market is indicating a lack of faith in the ability of the management of that firm to justify its current or future investments. Combining this situation with an announcement by the firm of a massive investment project doubly compounds an unhealthy situation from the point of view of common stock investors. Although it can be argued that management knows things that the market does not know, and thus the firm should go ahead with its investment plans, it is also possible that management is excessively optimistic or serving its own interests. Market valuation of common stock of the type described indicates that a lot of people are placing bets (and money) on their judgment that the investments being made by the corporation are not justified.

There is a time in the life of all firms when investment opportunities are not bright, and the funds should be returned to investors, just as there are times when a zero dividend is justified because of the growth possibilities arising from internal investments. There is a necessity to identify the stage of life that the firm is currently in, and execute the financial plan that is consistent with the economic realities and in the best interests of the management and investors.

SEVEN MYTHS

There follows a list of seven generalizations that may be classified as "myths". These myths tend to reappear in practical finance literature and business practice. The list is followed by a few comments on each myth to explain why we describe them as myths. See if you can identify the fallacy in each statement before reading the explanations.

1. The use of the net present value method to evaluate investments and setting a "minimum required return" discourages growth.
2. Even without taxes, the use of debt enables a firm to accept investments with a lower internal rate of return than the use of stock equity would allow.
3. If a lower dividend payout leads to a higher growth rate, the lower dividend is desirable.
4. A portion of a firm with low or zero growth should be divested by a "growth" firm.
5. A firm earning 0.10 per year on new investments can grow at 0.20 per year using only retained earnings.
6. The cash flows of an investment whose returns are uncertain should be discounted at a higher rate of discount than an investment with less uncertainty.
7. A firm earning higher returns should use a higher investment discount rate (cut-off or hurdle rate) than a less profitable firm (or division).

Let us consider briefly each of the above.

1. Compared to less theoretically sound investment evaluation procedures and criteria (such as the payback method and short required payback periods), a properly applied risk-adjusted present value calculation may actually encourage investment and growth. Also, growth without earning the properly determined required return is not desirable.

2. It is true that the incorporation of the debt cash flows in the present value calculations will increase the internal rate of return of the net of debt cash flows (the internal rate of return will be a return to stock equity capital), but the required return would increase accordingly. Thus the use of debt does not make acceptable an investment that would otherwise be unacceptable. Without taxes, debt and common stock have the same effect on the firm's weighted average cost of capital.

3. The low dividend may increase the expectation of future growth, but if the return on investment is relatively low, the stockholders might be better off with a return of capital to them and a lower corporate growth rate.

4. A perpetuity (zero growth) may have large value, as may a decaying cash flow stream; the type of generalization offered is not valid. Compare the proceeds from selling with the present value from retaining the asset.

5. Only using retained earnings, if a firm earns 0.10 on new investments and reinvests b portion of its earnings, it can expect to grow at $0.10b$. If $b = 1$, and all earnings are retained, the growth rate will be 0.10, not 0.20. It is true that, in the short run, a firm can grow by being more efficient, by using resources more intensively, or by being lucky (e.g., receive a windfall price increase), but in the long run growth comes as a result of profitable investments. New equity capital can result in an increase in the growth rate.

6. The choice of a rate of discount and the incorporation of uncertainty into investment analysis are much more complex than is implied by a recommendation to use a higher rate of discount for more uncertainty. Generally, the compound interest formulations $(1+r)^n$ cannot be used effectively with a risk-adjusted discount rate to evaluate real investments involving more than one time period.

7. Past profitability should not affect the investment criteria used to evaluate future alternatives. For example, a firm earning a zero return should not use a zero rate of discount to evaluate investments. The opportunity cost of the new capital is relevant as is the risk of the project being considered.

These statements are meant to be illustrative of the types of misconceptions that currently affect business decision-making. There are many more that could be listed.

While the explanations offered are somewhat incomplete, they should suggest that further study and thought are needed before generalizations such as these are applied. In business finance, relationships are frequently linked together by firm mathematical relationships, and these relationships should not be ignored.

For example, in discussing myth 5 it was claimed that a firm earning 0.10 on new investments cannot grow at 0.20 using only retained earnings. Let us consider a firm of size $1 million currently earning $100,000 per year. If the entire $100,000 is reinvested, the firm will be of size $1,100,000 and will still earn 0.10

or now $110,000, which is a growth rate of 0.10. Although a 0.10 growth rate is feasible with zero dividends, assume that the president of the firm announces a cash dividend of $50,000 and a growth rate of 0.10. What is the president assuming will happen? For the prediction to be accurate, the firm must do something different in the future than it has in the past, such as earning more than 0.10 on new investments or raising additional capital in the market.

SOME GENERALIZATIONS ABOUT FINANCIAL PLANNING

Having argued against a set of generalizations, we will offer several generalizations about financial planning for your consideration. First and most important, the financial planning process must be integrated with the overall planning of the firm, and the planning taking place in other components of the firm. Financial decisions (such as the decision whether to relax or tighten credit terms) should not be made independent of the marketing strategy and the production plans for the company.

Other major economic events such as the lapsing of contracts and leases should also be noted. The full financial implications of signing any contract should be realized and such contracts carefully scrutinized. Many firms have gone bankrupt after an executive committed the firm to executing a contract when there was a small probability of a large loss, and the bad event actually occurred. The uncertainty may be in design (an exotic material is needed for an engine) or because of price changes (a contract to supply energy long term at a fixed price can lead to financial difficulties).

Second, the financial plans must chart the course of the firm through time. It is not unusual to find firms that know their current debt position and the debt coming due in the next 12 months, but have failed to compute the debt payments coming due over the next five years as well as the predictable major cash expenditures for that time period. One major objective of good financial planning is to have a very small probability of management being unpleasantly surprised. Surprises should be very rare and difficulties well anticipated. The classic "joke" that banks do not lend money to firms that need it ("Come back when you do not need the funds") has enough truth so that management should act so that future cash needs are anticipated.

Finally, to have successful financial planning, it is necessary to interrelate all financial decisions. All decisions are linked to all other decisions. Consider the capital structure decision. With zero taxes and transaction costs, it can be shown that the capital structure decision is not a very important decision (investors can delever and lever firms using suitable strategies), but when we add taxes and costs of financial distress, the capital structure decision is more complex and more important. The tax deductibility of interest dictates the use of a large amount of debt. However, the fact that retained earnings are not taxed to individual investors means that common stock has an advantage compared to debt, since the investors' income tax can be deferred (assuming that investors are subject to taxation of personal income). Thus there are good tax reasons for issuing debt and good tax reasons for issuing common stock. The optimum solution will depend on the corporate and personal tax rates and provisions of the tax code as of the moment when you read this book, the availability of capital, as well as the nature of the firm's business.

Arriving at a solution to the capital structure decision will involve an assumption about the dividend policy that the firm will follow in the future. Dividend policy and capital structure decisions cannot be solved in isolation, but rather are decisions that interact with each other. But, in addition, the investment decisions depend on the availability of cash (investible funds) and this depends on the dividend policy that is being executed. The other side of the coin is the fact that the willingness of a firm to pay dividends (or other forms of cash distributions) should depend on the availability of good investments (the presence of good investments suggests that a deferral of dividend and reinvestment of earnings is desirable). Thus the dividend, the capital structure, and the investment decisions are all linked.

Crucially important to an understanding that the financial decisions are linked is a realization that a corporation and the interests of its investors cannot be separated. The decisions being made involving dividend policy, investments, and capital structure can only be made after considering the interests and preferences (not always expressed or listened to) of the investors.

In the future we can expect several significant changes to take place in the management of public corporations. For one thing, labor can be expected to want to have a larger say in the type of policy decisions that are made by the board of directors. Concurrent with this event, stockholders can be expected to take a more active interest in the choice of the board of directors of a firm and the decisions made by the board. Although at present the boards are chosen by the stockholders, there are seldom any efforts to organize stockholders and influence how they vote, or to offer stockholders interesting choices. In the future we can expect to have the stockholders offer choices of candidates to the board of directors with platforms that indicate commitments to different strategies.

CONCLUSIONS

Perhaps an appropriate closing on strategy is:

> Strategy: Confidence
> Sapience
> Watch expense
> Diligence
> Excellence
> Intelligence
> Common sense
> And Providence!
>   FMK

A strategy approach to financial decisions is necessary, since exact normative financial decision recommendations are frequently based on simplified assumptions. Financial strategy implies that the interconnection between specific decisions should be recognized.

If the financial managers of a firm deviate from the norm, the financial investing community will exert pressure via bond rating agencies and investment banking advisers which will tend to cause the firm to conform. Unusual financial strategies are difficult to implement. There are many pressures toward conformity.

A QUESTION TO CONSIDER

Assume preferred stock can be issued to yield 0.10 and common stock currently requires a yield of 0.14. Debt cannot be issued. Choose one of the following:

1. Preferred is cheaper than common stock and should be issued.
2. Preferred costs the same as common stock and there is indifference.
3. We cannot tell from the information.

You receive a passing trade if you did not choose statement 1. We cannot tell from the above information if preferred stock is cheaper than the common stock. An issuance of preferred stock creates prior claims to earning streams and thus results in higher costs to common stock. With the issuance of the preferred stock the common stockholders will require a higher yield than 0.14. If 0.14 is required without the preferred stock, with the issuance of preferred stock a higher return than 0.14 will be required. The amount of preferred stock issued will also affect the cost of the next issue of preferred stock (the number of dollars of earnings committed to investors will affect the required return since the risk changes). Even though 0.10 is less than 0.14, we cannot be sure preferred stock is cheaper than common stock, since we do not yet know the effect on the weighted average cost of capital. We can also say that we do not know the marginal costs of the preferred stock and common stock where the marginal cost includes the effect on the cost of the other security.

Neither common stock nor preferred stock has any advantages at the corporate level where the basic cash flows are earned. There are good reasons for assuming that the two securities must have exactly the same cost (that is the weighted average cost is not affected by the choice) if there are zero taxes. Investors can follow a strategy that forces the two securities to have the same cost. A difficulty arises if there are taxes and we consider the consequences to investors in the securities and define the cost or return from the investors' perspective. Since common stock returns and preferred stock returns are likely to be taxed differently, there could be a preference at the investor level where there is indifference at the firm level. Equilibrium analysis would require that the final yields of the two securities reflect not only the corporate tax structure but also the personal taxes that are imposed on investors.

If you answered that statement 1 was the correct statement, do not despair. The way the question is worded, it is easy to conclude (incorrectly) that the 0.10 and the 0.14 are fully descriptive measures of cost to the firm. Unfortunately, as is frequently the case, we must consider the dynamic elements of the decision. In this situation it is necessary to consider the consequences of the stock issuance on the costs of all other securities. The question must always be asked, What else is affected by the decision? What are the real effects of the choice?

Chapter 17

Ten Ways to Increase Shareholder Value with Financial Decisions

It is no exaggeration to state that good financial decision making can double the shareholder value of the average publicly owned firm. There follows a list and brief description of ten of the best ways to increase value with finance. Your financial consultant might prefer the substitution of one or two contenders, or prefer a less extreme strategy, but it is unlikely that there would not be agreement with the inclusion of all items to follow on a list of ways to increase value.

Obviously each item listed requires a theoretical proof and examples. Space and limitations prevent their inclusion, but they do exist for most of the items.

NUMBER 1: CAPITAL STRUCTURE AND TAXES

The chief financial officer and corporate staff people must understand how the tax laws affect the desirability of different types of capital, and use this information in their decision-making. Since the laws and regulations keep changing, the optimum capital structure decisions keep changing.

The relevant laws are both the corporate and the individual tax provisions. The relevant laws are both domestic and international. For example, when Japan did not tax capital gains and defined original issue discount accumulations to be capital gains, this led firms in the United States to issue zero-coupon bonds.

The U.S. tax laws tend to favor the issuance of debt. Thus U.S. corporations and their investment bankers try to issue securities that are defined to be debt for tax purposes, but are equity from financial and accounting viewpoints.

NUMBER 2: DISTRIBUTION POLICY

How and when should cash be distributed from the corporation to its investors?

Retaining earnings is a sensible policy during the period when the corporation is growing rapidly and needs all the capital it can find or obtain. Cash dividends compare unfavorably to the use of retained earnings as long as the corporation can earn more after corporate taxes than the investor can earn after investor taxes.

When the firm decides that cash should be distributed to its investors, a share repurchase policy offers many advantages compared to the payment of cash dividends. If cash dividends are paid then a dividend reinvestment plan (a DRIP) should be considered if the conservation of cash by the corporation is desired.

With the tax rate on ordinary income as high as 0.396, while the tax rate of capital gains is only 0.20, dividends are not welcome by the well-informed, high tax investor.

Corporations should have well-defined financial personalities (policies) so that investors can choose the firms that are best for them. When all the firms in an industry follow the practices of the industry leader it may become impossible for the investor to be well diversified and also hold a tax efficient portfolio.

NUMBER 3: PENSION PAYMENT TIMING

The timing of payments by the corporation into the firm's pension plans has important tax arbitrage opportunities. Assume a firm can borrow funds at a cost of 0.08 (a 0.052 after-tax cost) and contribute to a pension fund which can earn 0.08 tax-free and in addition the $100 payment results in an immediate $35 tax saving.

The tax laws limit the amount a firm can pay into its pension or health benefit funds, but all firms should investigate how much they can legally transfer to their funds, thus reducing or eliminating the amount of future obligations, and enjoying the benefits of tax free accumulations. The desirability of different strategies should be evaluated.

NUMBER 4: "CORRECT" CAPITAL BUDGETING DECISION RULES

We know a great deal as to how to make better capital budgeting decisions. We also know that when there are large elements of uncertainty the evaluation process moves from giving exactly correct answers to the application of business judgments. The following steps will greatly improve the capital budgeting decisions of many corporations.

1. Use the net present value (or the equivalent) method to evaluate mutually exclusive investments.
2. Do not use return on investment (ROI) to evaluate investment alternatives.
3. Do not use one risk adjusted discount rate to evaluate all investment opportunities.
4. The cost of retained earnings is lower than the cost of new capital (there is a discontinuity of costs).
5. Make an attempt to value the "options" associated with the investment opportunity.
6. Be willing to supplement the quantitative calculations with business judgment.

NUMBER 5: PERFORMANCE MEASUREMENT AND INCENTIVES

Have a sensible performance measurement system using both quantitative and qualitative inputs. While ROI (or ROE) can make an important contribution to performance measurement, it should be subordinate to the dollar measures of absolute gains or losses. Economic income (sometimes inaccurately referred to as economic value added) is an extremely important and useful measure.

If the managerial incentive system is not consistent with the corporate goals, the firm might be paying to increase shareholder value but only succeed in increasing risk or decreasing growth.

NUMBER 6: BUY VERSUS LEASE ANALYSIS

The buy versus lease analysis should not introduce a bias for either alternative.

The calculation of the leasing cost that uses a risk-adjusted discount rate to compute the present value of the after-tax leasing cash flow is fatally flawed unless the buy analysis is adjusted so that it is comparable to the lease present value (this is not the conventional calculation).

NUMBER 7: CREDIT GRANTING DECISIONS

Credit granting decisions are important marginal decisions and they deserve correct economic analysis.

Assume a bank is considering a $1 million loan that will (if successful) earn 0.08 interest. The bank can earn a 0.05 return risk-free. What probability of collection is needed? If p is the probability of collection, then at least a 0.97 probability of collection is required:

$1,050,000 = $1,080,000 p

$p = 0.97$ (assuming either 100% or 0% of the loan is collected)

Next we assume a bus company is considering a sale of $1 million when the incremental costs of manufacturing for the $1 million sale are $400,000. It is expected that a reclaimed bus would be worth 0.3 of its sale price.

The break-even for the bus company occurs with a 0.17 probability of collection:

$$\$400,000 = p\frac{\$1,000,000}{1.05} + (1-p)\frac{\$300,000}{1.05}$$

$p = 0.17$

The required probability of collection for this customer went down from the 0.97 required by the bank to 0.17 required by the bus company.

NUMBER 8: MERGERS AND ACQUISITIONS

The one crucial point that must be recognized by a firm or an individual doing acquisitions is that the objective is not to accomplish the purchase, but rather the goal must be to acquire the target firm at a price that will lead to a large probability of success after acquisition.

It is also important that the sources of possible gains be identified and quantified realistically.

NUMBER 9: CONTROL SPECULATION AND HEDGING

It is natural for a firm to want to manage its risk. One risk management technique is the use of derivatives to hedge risk. When derivatives are used to hedge there is a tendency for the hedging operation to shift into a speculation mode since there is a natural tendency for the managers involved to want to report a gain from the buying and selling of derivatives rather than merely reporting a break-even of gains and losses from dealing with the hedging derivatives and the hedged item.

It is important to realize that hedging, even if perfectly effective, has a cost. Is the risk being hedged small enough so that stockholders can bear the risk more efficiently than the firm can hedge it? The possibility of not paying for the cost of risk reduction should always be considered. For example, it is costly to reduce the foreign currency risk and if the consequences of currency value changes are not material, perhaps the risk should not be hedged.

NUMBER 10: FINANCING LONG-TERM INVESTMENTS WITH SHORT TERM CAPITAL

The problem with financing long-term investments with short-term capital is that the lenders' willingness to lend might disappear. A more desirable strategy is for the borrowing firm to borrow on a long-term basis at a fixed rate of interest and if it wants to pay a short-term rate of interest to engage in an interest rate swap (swapping from fixed to floating rate).

CONCLUSIONS

Good financial decisions are important if the firm wants to maximize shareholder value. Unfortunately, financial decisions do depend on the institutional factors that apply, thus the financial decisions depend on where the firm is operating on the globe. While the decisions depend on location, the method of analysis and factors that must be considered are universal.

Index